CHADWICK *Yankee Composer*

VICTOR FELL YELLIN

CHADWICK
Yankee Composer

SMITHSONIAN INSTITUTION PRESS   WASHINGTON AND LONDON

© 1990 by the Smithsonian Institution Press

Editor: Gretchen Smith Mui
Production Editor: Duke Johns
Designer: Alan Carter

Library of Congress Cataloging-in-Publication Data
Yellin, Victor Fell.
  Chadwick, Yankee composer / by Victor Fell Yellin.
    p. cm.
  Includes bibliographical references.
  ISBN 0-87474-988-3 (alk. paper)
    1. Chadwick, G. W. (George Whitefield), 1854–1931. 2. Composers—
United States—Biography. 3. Chadwick, G. W. (George Whitefield),
1854–1931—Criticism and interpretation. I. Title.
ML410.C395Y4 1990
780'.92—dc20
[B]   89-39869

British Library Cataloguing-in-Publication Data is available
Manufactured in the United States of America
97 96 95 94 93 92 91 90   5 4 3 2 1

⊚The paper used in this publication meets the minimum requirements of the American
National Standard for Permanence of Paper for Printed Library Materials Z39.48-1984

Contents

Contents

Preface

My interest in George Whitefield Chadwick began when I was a musically minded youngster growing up in Boston during the 1930s. Chadwick's textbook, *Harmony,* had been brought into the apartment by my older brother, who had preceded me in a promising musical career. Later as a freshman at the New England Conservatory, I heard the Chadwick name often, for many of the faculty had begun their association with the conservatory during his administration. After World War II Harvard's legendary Archibald T. ("Doc") Davison opened my eyes to the necessity of obtaining a doctoral degree if I intended to teach on a university level and asked me to consider an area of research I might be interested in specializing. Following through on my undergraduate thesis on Virgil Thomson and Marc Blitzstein as dramatic composers as well as on my recently produced one-act opera *Prescription for Judy,* I decided on the history of American opera. Very soon it became clear that such a large area was not an appropriate subject for a thesis. I then concentrated my focus on Chadwick and his stage works.

The choice was cause for surprise in some quarters, for Chadwick, if known at all, was considered strictly an orchestral composer. I well remember the questioning look of his son Theodore, sitting at his desk in an executive office at the brokerage firm of Paine, Webber, Jackson, and Curtis on Federal Street, when I announced my intentions and asked for whatever assistance he could give. His father, of course, was a symphonic composer, he informed me. He dismissed the importance of the theatrical adventures and, in so doing, seemed to betray traditional local attitudes of the relative aesthetic or moral values of concert as opposed to stage music. But I could not be dissuaded, especially after I had discovered the beautiful orchestral score of *The*

Padrone, with its socially conscious theme of the exploitation of Italian immigrants. I was also fascinated by the contradiction between Chadwick's image as a patrician from Boston's Back Bay and this sensitive, emotionally expressive document of American realism.

A review of the composer's biography as handed down in dictionary entries, articles, and textbooks together with other documentary and archival evidence soon began to paint a somewhat different picture of the man's life. It was obvious that when answering all manner of questionnaires, Chadwick spun a story particularly about his beginnings that avoided certain details he preferred to keep private. Theodore Chadwick was governed by this same inbred aversion to publicity in his cooperation with me. I would submit to him specific questions, and he would then consult personal papers to see what answers he was willing to give. My doctoral dissertation, "The Life and Operatic Works of George Whitefield Chadwick" (Harvard College, 1957), may seem to have overemphasized these details as well as the significance of the theater as a driving force in the composer's career. Yet it led me to an understanding of the man behind the image and of how his long concern for musical theater, American diction, and popular melody informed his more abstract compositions.

This book, then, is the culmination of a long and many-sided interest in the man and all his music. Guiding and helping me along the way was Virgil Thomson, who patiently listened to me on many occasions and made valuable suggestions about the ways of American music. Above all, if any merit may be found in my verbal descriptions of the music, it is owed to the man who first wrote about music in plain English and created a systematic and artistic recitative for it.

Isabel Satenig Joseph (whom I first met underneath the Thomas Crawford statue of Beethoven in the lobby of the New England Conservatory and whom I later married) read, edited, and corrected almost every word I ever wrote. It is impossible to say how much I am indebted to her powerful intellectual skills and emotional support. That she never lived to see the fruit of her concern diminishes whatever satisfaction I may feel.

To Martin Williams I owe a debt of gratitude for reviving my interest in writing a Chadwick book and encouraging me to complete it by his constructive criticism and gentle prodding. Thanks also go to my friend and Edward MacDowell scholar Margery Morgan Lowens for reviewing the typescript, making many practical suggestions, and giving me access to the Irving and Margery Lowens Correspondence Collection.

Nowhere is the efficacy of the biblical advice to cast one's bread upon the waters better confirmed than in the cooperation and assistance given me by my erstwhile student and present colleague Steven Ledbetter. His research on the Boston school and his efforts in getting its music performed and recorded are in part responsible for the noticeable changes in opinion toward this large repertory. Especially helpful was his "George W. Chadwick: A Sourcebook" (1983), where are gathered for the first time reviews of Chadwick's music and bibliographical and performance information. Unless otherwise indicated, most of the quotations from contemporary critics were derived from Ledbetter's "Sourcebook."

Special mention for her tireless and stylish production of the various drafts of the manuscript is due to Paula Tofil. Last, thanks, Garo!

Acknowledgments

I wish to express my thanks to the heirs of George Whitefield Chadwick for giving me permission to use photographs from their collection and musical examples. I am especially grateful for their cooperation in allowing me to photograph the Joseph Rodefer De Camp portrait. All musical examples that are edited condensations from orchestral scores have been specially prepared for this book by the author.

Introduction

A century after the start of a successful career would seem to be enough time for a first book to be published about a great artist. Had Chadwick been a painter, a builder, a poet, or a sculptor, one whose achievements are easily visible, a study of his life and works would exist by now. But for a composer, working with the creative stuff of invisible sound and dependent on the whims of succeeding generations for its materialization, the decline of performance, especially in the last golden age of live music, was a great impediment to interest. In time his works seemed to evaporate, their essence preserved only as markings on paper. In place of their sounds arose opinions based not so much on audition as on generalized estimations and assumptions.

Without a tradition of performance, passing commentators understandably tried to cram Chadwick into neat pigeonholes of their design. But their theological dualism—American v. European, vernacular v. cultivated, all perhaps useful textbook categories—simply do not fit the man.

Today, a hundred years after his debut, as more of his music is heard, such one-dimensional characterizations of the Yankee composer as an "academic" or "classicist" who aped his German betters to satisfy the taste of pretentious Bostonians lose authority. George Chadwick is noteworthy precisely because he rises above the commonality of American composers of his era as a craftsman, while at the same time cherishing the tonalities of his tribe and the rhythms of its speech.

Just as the growing availability of his works in performance gives us the chance to revise received opinions of their merit, so basic biographical investigation permits us a better understanding of the man. Although there are no startling revelations to be made, a more objective portrait discloses one who was destined by background and personality to write the kind of music he wrote. Here the fresh and native sonorities from his imagination and the unvarnished facts of his life conjoin.

PART ONE ❧ CHADWICK *The Man*

One clue to the essential nature of Chadwick the extraordinary composer is that he was really an ordinary man. We look in vain for those early portents of self-destructive genius sometimes found in romantic biographies. If he indeed had problems with weaknesses of the mind or flesh, he seems always to have been smart enough to keep things under his belt. The intimate details of his life cannot be exploited, as were Stephen Foster's alcoholism, Louis Moreau Gottschalk's womanizing, and Ethelbert Nevin's pathological depressions. There is no startling mystery waiting to be revealed as an explanation of the artist's work. There were no guardian angels. He had no eccentric father, as did Charles Ives; no famous, wealthy opera-star wife, as did Sidney Homer; no doting mother or devoted widow to nurture and protect a lasting image, as did Edward MacDowell.

Chadwick was a common man. In appearance, he might just as well have been a bookkeeper or a merchant. When other artists cultivated a persona of either monastic spirituality or fleshly decadence, Chadwick was content with a clean shave, short hair, and a flannel wool suit. It was not until he arrived at his mature years that the moustache he first grew to make himself look older added a distinctive feature to his face. A colleague who remembered him after the New England Conservatory moved into the new classical building on Huntington Avenue remarked that his most vivid impression of this giant among American musicians was of Chadwick eating a plate of beans on a tray at the local Hayes-Bickford cafeteria across the street. He must have looked like one of those anonymous figures in an Edward Hopper painting, so well did he blend in with the typical American cityscape.

This appearance of anonymity should not obscure the fact that Chadwick had a unique and even commanding personality. Like a face in the crowd when singled out, enlarged, and scrutinized, his commonness portrays the archetypal qualities of ruggedness and individuality that characterized Americans of his day. As a callow youth of twenty-one trying to hide his upper lip under a just visible, wispy ribbon of hair, he took on publicly such a grand establishment figure as George Frederick Root for composing meretricious songs. An older, avuncular Chadwick was once reported to have smashed with the gold knob of his walking stick the glass window of the locked door of the conservatory music store in order to get some manuscript paper after closing hours.

He was a short man. But somehow he early knew he could rely on his towering music for him to be noticed. He needed none of the external stigmata of genius that so many of his artistic contemporaries felt called upon to display. While he was not shy about promoting his works, he abjured self-aggrandizing publicity. He loved to explicate the works of the masters but said little about his own music. When William Lynes Hubbard asked him to write a history of American music, he agreed only on the condition that he might omit mention of his own role, so secure was he in his estimate of his artistic worth. He refused to blow his own horn, for, he must have felt, if he had to, of what satisfaction would it be?

He was not a performer. No one ever paid a nickel just to see Chadwick. Not that he never desired or received applause for his music. But given the number of performances, he could hardly have nourished his ego on such demonstrations alone. Unlike the performing artist, he was satisfied to live in the expectation of the immortality of his sonorities long after he passed from the scene.

Commonness is not without great price, however. We may never know the answers to the questions about American music in general and Chadwick's in particular. Why was it so inhibited during the heyday of romantic expression? Why did it always stop short of the leap into the abyss of imagination? Why did it pull back from the ultimate freedoms of the sublime? It may be that, common or not, Chadwick simply did not have the inner vision of his more justly famous European colleagues. It may well be that it was impossible for him in one fell swoop to assimilate attitudes that Europeans seemed to have inherited genetically. It may very well have been that objective conditions for art in America denied the visionary craftsman a fertile environment.

If he was destined not to realize the sounds of a fantastic imagination or a tortured mind, the music he heard as a common man with a splendid ear and special skills made him an extraordinary American composer. His commonness kept him from going down aesthetic blind alleys better left to those with more savoir-faire. It guided him, unlike his fellow Lowellian James Abbott McNeill Whistler, to remain true to his ethnic roots. It ultimately led to his one great contribution—an American symphonic style.

CHAPTER I

The Family Chadwick

Chadwick was born in 1854 in Lowell, Massachusetts.[1] His mother and father, a millwright, were from New Hampshire. Actually, Chadwick was not born in Lowell proper, by then a textile center crowded with Irish immigrants, but across the Merrimack River in a tiny district with the self-contradictory name of Centralville. The town itself, originally a planned industrial community, was laid out as an experiment in harnessing the productive energy of water and enlightened capitalism to the labor of young, unmarried farm girls. They would thereby amass dowries to attract husbands and this, so the idea ran, would stay the westward flow of New England men seeking their fortunes in the rich alluvial soil of upstate New York and Ohio.

While these maidens, under the strict moral supervision reminiscent of later finishing schools, tended water-driven looms, wrote poetry, and developed domestic skills, the mills demanded maintenance. It was inevitable, therefore, that someone like Chadwick's father, trained from his earliest years as a jack-of-all-trades and facing the prospects of a hard-scrabble existence in New Hampshire, would gravitate toward the mills to fill the need. In so doing, he returned to the commonwealth to which his English ancestors had come almost two centuries before during the first years of the Puritan emigration.

The same forces that in the mid-eighteenth century sent Chadwick's father south on a quest had in 1631 driven one line of Chadwicks from a Watertown farm on the Charles River north to Bradford (a village now gone), coincidentally near the site of Lowell. Under the notion that as long as they were on the south bank of the Merrimack they were protected by Massachusetts, settlers like the Chadwicks inched up the river despite the fact that it turned abruptly north. As they later found out, they had crossed inadvertently into New Hampshire.

Edmund Chadwick of Boscawen, New Hampshire, great-grandfather of George, may be considered the Abraham of the clan. A patriot, he signed a petition against the Boston Port Bill in 1772 and fought at Bunker Hill. "Who can measure the influence of the courage [the refusal of Boscawen's founders to retreat under Indian attack] upon those who came after them?" asked the town historian. "If they had been pusillanimous then, would Lieut. Samuel Atkinson, David Burbank, Edmund Chadwick, Asa Corder, David Flanders, and their comrades have stood like a wall of adamant at Bunker Hill?"[2] When he returned home after the fighting in Massachusetts, Edmund was elected constable and became collector of taxes in 1790. Two years before his death, in 1818, he was made a deacon of the church.

Edmund's son, James, George's grandfather, is mentioned as a schoolteacher. A visitor to his classroom reported "the Master very easy in instruction and government," a characterization that may be construed either as a negative comment on his teaching skills or as an indication of James's liberality. In any case, he seems to have figured in a church controversy later in 1832. In the attempt to maintain uniformity of thought, the Reverend Ebenezer Price excommunicated one Nathaniel C. Couch. According to a local pamphleteer, Couch had confirmed "in their sins, Maj. Abbot, Rice Corser, Bitfield Plummer, and ——— Chadwick who were without and destitute of religion. . . ." Whatever his sin may have been (it seems to have involved the demon rum), James's character as a free spirit may also be inferred from the name he gave to his son, George's father: Alonzo Calvin. The first name must have derived either from his reading of novels or perhaps from trips to the Boston theater, where London-style melodramas with exotically named heroes and picaresque scenarios were presented. The second name may have represented a curious balancing of the romantic with the religious. Alonzo Calvin was thus at least nominally prepared for all the contradictions of the new century.

A tiny hamlet of 1,400 souls, Boscawen had already made its place in history not only because of the valor of its Revolutionary War soldiers but also as a key locale of Daniel Webster's early career. It was Boscawen's sage,

Dr. Samuel Ward, who prepared the young Webster's early career. Later, Webster would remember the impact of reading *Don Quixote* at the Boscawen library, a book James might have also read. And when the future senator and secretary of state became a lawyer, he chose Boscawen as the venue of his first legal exercises.

Musical history in the town seems to have begun with Deacon Enoch Little, whose namesake son later became a member of Lowell Mason's Boston Academy of Music. The deacon was the town's first music teacher and, with Yankee shrewdness, offered students a free term of instruction to study the gamut. He set his rules in rhyme and believed that triple meter was best suited to pensive music.

A musical organization, the Boscawen Musical Society, was in existence before 1801. Singing books were ordered and a school established. Webster, a member of the society during his stay as a lawyer, was paid for a purchase he made on its behalf:

ORDER

Lieut J Gerrish treas of the Musical
Society Boscawen please to pay Mr. Daniel
Webster Esq. thirty-four Dollars a compensation
for a Bazoon by order.

Somersby Pearson
Joshua Morse Com.
Benjamin Clark[3]

In 1821 several singers and musicians of the town met to form a new musical organization, the Martin Luther Musical Society, for the purpose of raising the standards of performance and repertory. In the group's library were works by Handel, Haydn, Mozart, and Beethoven. According to the local chronicler Charles C. Coffin,

> The Society made great progress, and soon brought about a revolution in the style of music used on the Sabbath. The fugues, that for a third of a century had been the delight of a people, gave place to compositions richer in harmony,—the production of the masters whose compositions still have the power to charm the human ear.[4]

Along with the desire to absorb the new cosmopolitan culture that was sweeping up from Boston and other coastal cities, the society seems to have taken with equal seriousness the new morality in which art was joined to religion for the social good. On the occasion of the Reverend Price's bull against the unfortunate Couch, the society became involved in a town temperance rally:

> On the 14th of July 1832 a temperance meeting was held at the meeting house on Corser hill. The light infantry military company paraded, marched to Dea. James Kilburn's, and escorted the Martin Luther Musical Society to the meetinghouse, where addresses upon temperance were made and songs were sung. The churches and the leading men in the community having been engaged in the reform, public drinking soon became disreputable.[5]

The arrival of the last of the itinerant Yankee, singing-school teachers, Nathaniel D. Gould, signalled an important visitation for the village. He provided a middle way between the wholesale discard of the native and populist musical styles of the Yankee tunesmiths and the uncritical adoption of sophisticated European repertory. Of William Billings, the Boston tanner-tunesmith, Gould wrote, "As Billings is the father and pioneer of American compositions, so was he of choirs, public singing-schools, and concerts."[6] But his many imitators and followers produced musical publications in which a lack of the knowledge of "scientific" music was not balanced by Billings's genius. This, according to Gould, left the door open for a new generation of church musicians who were strongly influenced by the music of the European masters. "As the American music had been discarded *en masse,* it seemed no more than justice that those who had pronounced it worthless should give their reasons."[7] Thus, while accepting the "advance of science" or the introduction of the great masterworks from across the sea, Gould nonetheless appreciated and reminded his pupils of their own musical heritage. By his own count, Gould, whose own career spanned the years 1790 to 1840, taught more than 50,000 students from New Hampshire to New Jersey. In Salem, Massachusetts, a few years before his journey up the Merrimack to Boscawen, he typically advertised that he would "give lessons in Plain and Ornamental Writing" and "the rudiments and practise of Sacred Music." Although his appeals for community support were made on the promise of enhancing congregational singing, the popularity of his singing schools may be traced to their usual location, a tavern, and to their hidden dividend, meeting members of the opposite sex.

One important result of Gould's musical evangelism in Boscawen probably was the reorganization of the Martin Luther Musical Society. In 1837, at a meeting in his own house, Alonzo Calvin was elected president. But the society did not last much longer; according to Coffin's *History*

> emigration was telling upon the society, and the members, after a while, ceased to meet. During the two decades,—1820 to 1840—, the choirs in town were accompanied by a variety of stringed and wind instruments— bass and double-bass viols, violins, flutes, clarionettes, bugles and French horns. At the east end John Jackman, Dr. John Rogers, Alonzo C. Chadwick and Charles J. Chadwick played the viols, Jacob Gerrish the flute, J. Coffin the trombone, which Rev. Mr. Price, not for the moment remembering the name, once appropriately called a 'shoveration.'[8]

The emigration responsible for breaking up the Martin Luther Musical Society was nowhere better illustrated than by the romance that must have been sparked by Gould's 1833 singing school and brought to flame in the society itself. In 1837 the following notice appeared in the *Town Records:*

> The Intention of marriage between Mr. Alonzo C. Chadwick of Boscawen and Miss Hannah G. Fitts of North Candia was published July 3rd 1837.
>
> Hezh Fellows
Town Clerk.[9]

Coincidence follows upon coincidence. It appears that not only did Daniel Webster lend a certain significance to Boscawen by his early association with the town, but he comes into the Chadwick family picture as well since his grandmother, Jerusha, was a Fitts or Fitz.

The Fitts family pedigree was similar to the Chadwick clan's. The American branch was started by Robert Fitts, who settled in Ipswich, Massachusetts, in 1635. Like the Chadwicks, the family remained in that area until the mid-eighteenth century, when Abraham Fitts moved to Chester and then Candia, New Hampshire. Also, like Edmund Chadwick, he was a soldier during the Revolutionary War and fought as an officer at the Battle of Saratoga. "Lieut. Fitts and the most of his descendants were musicians, and Asa [an eccentric who published a tune book in 1847] believed that his grandsire, on his visits from the Celestial regions, performed various tunes upon the fife, his favorite instrument." [10] Louis C. Elson, who knew George Chadwick as a colleague and friend (and so he is reporting what he must have learned from the composer himself), summed up his New Hampshire family musical background: "Both of his parents were musical; his father taught in an academy and singing-school near Concord, New Hampshire, and his mother sang in the church choir. All of his uncles and aunts were more or less active in the old style of psalmody." [11]

In the seventeen years between the announcement of their intention to marry and George's birth, the young couple, together with their son Fitts Henry, followed the pattern of emigration from their Yankee Arcadia. Some, lured by advertisements of land companies, went west. The Chadwicks went south, down the River Merrimack to Lowell, close to where a great-grandfather had settled a century earlier in Bradford. As already mentioned, its new textile mills, whose looms were operated by maidens, required men skilled as carpenters or mechanics, and Alonzo Calvin, who had probably worked for his uncle Joseph, the celebrated manufacturer of clocks with wooden works, was a logical job seeker. The 1845 Lowell directory lists "Chadwick, A.C., carpenter, house Lowell Street." [12] In 1847 he was working for the Merrimack Mills. In 1851 he worked in the Merrimack Print Works; the family lived in the company boardinghouse. He was paid, as all the workers were, on "the Saturday before the 16th of every month." The "average wage of males, clear of board, was per day $.80." [13] In 1853, the year before George's birth, Alonzo worked for the Massachusetts Mills and moved across the river to Centralville. There, George Whitefield, [14] named after the silver-tongued eighteenth-century evangelist, was born the following year.

CHAPTER 2

Childhood and Youth

By 1854 Lowell had been transformed from an idyllic experiment in welfare capitalism to a grim mill town. Contemporary reports detailed the effects of cheap labor and depression on an economy already ruled by the cruel laws of supply and demand. Hoards of immigrants, particularly those fleeing famine in Ireland, provided a source of millhands, whose scarcity had originally motivated Boston entrepreneurs to provide such extraordinary benefits for Yankee farm girls. The airy, well-appointed, and chaperoned dormitories became crowded, filthy warrens, now rented to foreigners who spoke a strange dialect and worshiped even stranger saints. Wage rates were lowered with the oversupply. And when the mills eventually produced more than could be sold profitably, thousands were fired and put out on the streets. A particularly hard time was during the Panic of 1857, when almost half of the 12,000 workers—male, female, and children—were thrown out of work and left to beg on the streets. Those fortunate enough to remain employed were forced to take up to a one-third reduction in their wages. Such were the conditions of life in Lowell about the time George was born. If the general grimness was not enough of a gloomy beginning, however, more personal shocks came in quick succession.[15]

The joy of his birth on November 13, 1854, was soon tempered by his mother's death of puerperal fever little over a week later. Then an aftershock occurred. No sooner was Hannah buried, so it seemed, than Alonzo Calvin, listing himself as a carpenter, married a twenty-nine-year-old neighbor, Susan Collins, on February 3, 1855.[16] The generous accounts and interpretations of the circumstances surrounding Chadwick's sad beginnings are themselves fascinating. Since they all ultimately stemmed from the composer himself—it is doubtful that any original research was done—these varied reports of his birth indicate the depth of the composer's feelings and his sensitivity to publication of the facts, especially after he had achieved a success in his art and in society far beyond his wildest dreams. How it must have pained him when replying to enquiries that his mother had never known of his conquest of musical Boston and musical America or that he lived in a townhouse in Boston's fashionable Back Bay. How such questions must have reminded him of his father's hasty remarriage and his own exile for the first three years of his life.

When in 1924 Carl Engel wrote the first biography and appreciation of the composer, then considered the dean of American musicians, he significantly created a different chronology. Although he correctly mentions Hannah's death at George's birth, he then has "the motherless infant placed in the care of relatives in Boscawen," remaining there for three years. "Then," continues Engel (doubtless informed by Chadwick himself), "the father married a second time and took his little son back to Lowell." In this narrative, events happen in a logical and respectable, if not sensitive, manner. Father Chadwick, despite his grief, bereft of his life's helpmate and already saddled with one fourteen-year-old son, does the decent and sensible thing: He keeps the older, self-reliant sibling and puts the infant in the care of his experienced parents. But the actual facts of the matter could not have eluded George Chadwick, for his brother, Fitts Henry, was old enough to know what was going on. Thus, even if Chadwick had had no other source of information, he certainly must have been told by his older brother the real sequence of events. Besides, Engel's statement that he was sent to Boscawen (i.e., Chadwick's assumption that he had been sent there) may itself be wrong since the baby's paternal grandmother had died in 1851. On the other hand, Hannah Chadwick's mother, in Candia, New Hampshire, who lived until 1865, would have been a more likely choice to raise the infant rather than the aging, free-spirit grandfather James. Since the baby was returned to Lowell in 1857 (when, coincidentally, James died), he may very well have been shipped to Boscawen immediately after his birth.[17]

John Tasker Howard, writing six years after Engel, in 1930, seems to echo and embellish the story by emphasizing Chadwick's parents' morality:

"He was of New England stock on both sides of his family tree, Orthodox, devout Congregationalists. His mother died when she gave him birth, and he was placed in the care of relatives until he was three. Then his father married again, and had a wife who could take care of little George." Here Alonzo Calvin ostensibly sends the baby to New Hampshire because he had no wife to care for the infant. After a decent interval of three years, the period of mourning over, the father remarries for the purpose of having someone who can raise the three-year-old baby. A melancholy story, indeed, but the father acts in a respectable way. Such phrases as "placed in the care of relatives" and the adjective "little," as in "little son" or "little George," all imitate Engel's spelling out of Chadwick's refusal, even at the end of his illustrious career, to admit the truth of his father's remarriage and rejection.[18]

In place of Howard's stereotype portrait of the composer's father as a sturdy, devout Yankee Puritan perhaps may be substituted a picture of Alonzo Calvin as a man of passion spurred on by the romantic promise of his first name. Insensitive to his public image, he marries the much younger woman next door. Instead of himself nurturing and caring for his infant, he sends him away in the middle of winter.

Before the age of Eugene O'Neill and *Desire Under the Elms* (the play was produced in 1924, the same year that the Engel article was published), George Chadwick responded to biographical inquiries with just enough detail to satisfy his questioners but not enough to reveal the dark side of his origins and the real source of the later friction with his father that may have launched his improbable musical career.

In 1858 Alonzo Calvin Chadwick had himself listed as an insurance agent. Obviously a significant change had occurred in his financial and social position. He may have been motivated by the sharp downturn in mill employment. Perhaps he was aided in his decision to change his line of work by an inheritance he received when his father died in December 1857. At any rate, that year also marked George's return to the family after a three-year exile. Later the entire family—Alonzo Calvin, his new wife, Susan Collins, the eighteen-year-old Fitts Henry, and baby George—removed eleven miles downriver from Lowell to a house on Newbury Street in Lawrence, a similar but newer town founded only about a decade before, in 1847.[19]

With a new identity, Alonzo Calvin's "Mutual Insurance Association . . . enrolled in it half of the inhabitants of Lawrence." Although he may be charged with exaggeration, Engel's report is accurate in demonstrating the marked improvement in the Chadwick's family finances and status from blue- to white-collar professional. But even though George was now growing up as the son of a reputable father, it was his daily contact with his brother that transmitted the musical nature of the mother he had never known. Elson says it was Fitts Henry who taught him "enough about organ playing . . . to substitute for him at church in Lawrence. . . . With helpful counsel he had guided the first steps in the musical career of George."

The musical instruction that young Chadwick received from his brother could have been of only short duration. When George was but eight years old, Fitts Henry left for military service in the Civil War. In 1863 he joined the Massachusetts Fourth Infantry,[20] and he never returned home to live with the family after his year's enlistment was over, despite the fact that there was by then an apparently flourishing insurance agency in Lawrence to which he could apply his business acumen. Instead, he took a job as an accountant with the A. J. Wilkinson Company, the hardware emporium of Boston, and as an organist in the suburbs. Without excessive speculation, Fitts Henry's actions may be interpreted as a rebuff to his father, if indeed Alonzo Calvin had hoped that his elder son would now validate his success as an entrepreneur and citizen by rejoining both family and firm. The fact that Fitts Henry chose to serve in the infantry (he or his father could have purchased a substitute) and did not return home seems to support an interpretation of filial rejection. Evidently even a fourteen-year-old's memory and imagination of his mother's death were not easily distracted or dulled by the experience of war and the passage of time.

Nevertheless, the gloomier aspects of George's childhood were balanced by "following hand-organs all over town," Sunday church music, and family get-togethers "when uncles, aunts and cousins some of whom were the possessors of excellent voices sang praises to the Lord in rich and vibrant harmony."[21]

George's regular education was entrusted to the new Massachusetts public school system, which had been inaugurated only a few years before, in

1852, by Horace Mann, many of whose ideas had been foreshadowed in Lowell Mason's musical textbooks and teaching methods. Besides instruction in regular subjects, the Lawrence public schools offered "declamation and vocal music," given by its first teacher, Rueben Merrill, who received the not inconsiderable salary of four hundred dollars per annum.[22] So the young boy was influenced not only by the Yankee tunesmith's musical wares supplied by his extended family but also by the newer disciplined and "scientific" music distilled from the great works of European masters. Soon he was composing little songs and dances for the piano; according to Elson, "some of these he preserved and used a quarter of a century later, in his successful comic opera 'Tabasco.'"[23]

The elder Chadwick, busy as he was with his insurance career, had not entirely given up his interest in music; he was a member of the Lawrence Musical Association. In the account of the great 1869 Peace Jubilee in Boston, conceived and organized by the musical Barnum Patrick S. Gilmore, Alonzo Calvin is listed among the chorus of ten thousand that was recruited from a wide arc outside the city.[24] Fitts Henry, as a member of the Boston Oratorio Class, also took part in this monster chorus.[25] Considering their participation and the notoriety of the occasion, it is probable that the fifteen-year-old George was present too.

The impact that the Peace Jubilee might have had on the impressionable teenager cannot be overestimated. It commemorated the successful end of a bloody war in which his brother had fought, true, but it also presented the rare phenomenon of mass music sonorities produced by a chorus of ten thousand and an orchestra of a thousand to an even larger, mesmerized audience. In Gilmore's own words:

> The first piece upon the program was Luther's grand choral GOD IS A CASTLE AND DEFENCE for full chorus, organ, orchestra and military bands. The first peal of the organ was the signal to the chorus and the orchestra to prepare; the ten thousand singers arose, and the thousand musicians placed their instruments in position. All eyes were now directed to the uplifted baton; chorus, organ, and orchestra were to come in fortissimo at its very first move. For a moment all seemed hushed into breathless silence. Then—"In the name of God"—the wand came down, and grandest volume of song that ever filled human ear rolled like a sea

of sound through the immense building; grander and grander came wave after wave, now loud as the roar of the ocean, now soft as a murmuring stream. O how beautiful, how pure, how heavenly; what sublime chords, what ravishing harmonies! Not a jarring note from the first to the last, but like the mingling of many waters, organ, voices, instruments, all blended together in one noble flood of music, sweeping away forever in its mighty and majestic flow every vestige of doubt and fear, and carrying upon its swelling tide a joy to all hearts, and bearing the fact to the world abroad of a glorious triumph for art and for the musical people of America.[26]

Was this the boy Chadwick's epiphany? Was this the occasion when the answer to his questions about what he was to become was made manifest? Although he had not shown any of the usual signs of exceptional musical talents, we can imagine that it was then that he decided to make music his life.

All his other endeavors, especially those that would have been approved by his father, seem to have been relegated to secondary status. His public school education, begun at the age of eight, was prematurely terminated in his sixteenth year; he had two more years to go to complete the requirements for a high school diploma. Later, even after it mattered little, Chadwick was so concerned with his lack of educational pedigree that he must have in some way misled Engel, who reported erroneously: "Graduated from high school, George was allowed to study the piano with Carlyle Petersilea. . . ."[27] Gilbert Chase, writing a generation later, echoed Engel when he claimed: "Chadwick went to work after finishing high school."[28] The simple truth was that having entered the Oliver High School as of February 1868, Chadwick did not graduate with his class. He left in June 1871, in his sophomore year, according to the surviving school records.[29] At this time he entered his father's insurance business.

Alonzo Calvin may have been reconciled to George's quitting school by his active participation in the business; it seems that, for his part, George had longer-range plans. Going on business errands to Boston, the insurance clerk could also take musical instruction from some of the best teachers. In 1872 he began to study piano with Carlyle Petersilea and entered the New England Conservatory as a special student in organ with George E. Whiting and harmony with Stephen A. Emery. According to Chadwick's son Theodore, Alonzo Calvin Chadwick planned to open an office in the capital city with George as its representative. Since his brother Fitts Henry was living in Boston, they probably saw each other often. And the future composer's lifelong friend, Theodore Presser (1848–1925), who was to found a leading music publishing enterprise, also afforded young Chadwick a pied-à-terre at times. Chadwick remembered these early days: "I was at the time clerk in my father's insurance office in Lawrence, and I found Presser's lodgings very convenient whenever I stayed in Boston for an evening's concert." [30]

In a humorous and anecdotal reminiscence Chadwick wrote for the 1907 New England Conservatory yearbook, he recalled those years with great nostalgia through an imaginary conversation with Thomas Crawford's massive statue of Beethoven (originally presiding over the old Music Hall), which had been placed in the entrance hall of the new conservatory building. Chadwick, then director, had been locked in the building after working late and was waiting for the night watchman to make his rounds when suddenly he heard the statue speak:

> You were a little fellow, and were deposited in a seat in the middle of the hall by a gentleman who looked very much as you do now. He went away and came for you at the end of the concert. You stared about in wonder, especially at me and at Apollo in the second balcony, whom some of the old ladies thought was the president of the Handel and Haydn Society, and others disapproved of because he had no clothes on, and it was easy to see that you had never been there before.
>
> Pretty soon, Thomas began with my Eroica, and how you did perk up your ears when the trumpets came in at the first fortissimo, Thomas seemed to get ten feet high and his eyes glowed like fiery coals. *Donnerwetter, noch a' mal,* but that Thomas knew my music all right. . . .
>
> After that I saw you many times. Once you sat in the chorus of the Handel and Haydn and sang alto, and when you sat down your back came up against the nose of one of the female giants on the side of the organ. And how you did watch the organist reading his newspaper between the choruses! Then later I used to see you at the Quarterly Concert of the Conservatory, and at Dudley Buck's organ recitals, when I believe you climbed in over the second balcony fence, you rascal! I got to know your face pretty well by this time, but shortly afterward you disappeared for four or five years. . . . [31]

Considering the lack of any signs of genius or prodigy, something else must have impelled the now not-so-young man to undergo the disciplines of practicing at the keyboard and writing harmony exercises while earning his keep as an insurance clerk. Proof that Chadwick was well aware of his rather tardy beginnings of the study of music comes from his eulogy of Edward Mac-Dowell (1861–1908). He recalled to conservatory students later that "Mac-Dowell enjoyed one great advantage which was denied to most of the other American composers. He had acquired technical training early in life." At a time when Chadwick was playing baseball in Lawrence, MacDowell "was in Paris, delving at counterpoint and fugues, and that, too, at 6 o'clock in the morning."[32]

Moreover, his family musical background, fascinating though it might seem today, was neither unique in an America that was musical to begin with. On the contrary, his father must have started pressuring him at an early age for George to think seriously of insurance as a career. He could always, like his father and brother, make his living "working" and still have time to write dance tunes or play the organ Sundays. His musical cultural roots, reinforced by his public school music education, alone cannot account for Chadwick's choice of life's career. And the momentary rapture of an overwhelming musical experience such as the Peace Jubilee would have required continued reinforcement in order to have a lasting impact. Perhaps he was influenced by something more practical. Music schools and teachers were not subtle in their advertising. Using Barnum and Bailey typography, they made the kind of exaggerated claims calculated to impress young people pursuing independence from family while developing their talents. From every page of popular music journals and newspapers the message of easy success was proclaimed:

PETERSILEA'S
CARLYLE   MUSIC SCHOOL
This institution offers to those wishing to acquire a
MUSICAL EDUCATION
advantages unequalled by any Conservatory or Music School
in the world.
It is conducted on an entirely new and
ORIGINAL METHOD

which will advance pupils to a higher degree of perfection, with
LESS TIME AND LABOR
than any plan of instruction heretofore employed.
✶✶✶✶✶✶✶✶✶✶✶✶✶✶
very moderate terms
Carlyle Petersilea, Director.
238 Washington Street, Boston.[33]

Eugene Thayer, another of Chadwick's teachers, was no less interested in gaining students. Although his notices were more discreet, they nevertheless conveyed similar promises of success and jobs: "Mr. Eugene Thayer will devote his time exclusively to students desiring to become church organists or teachers of music. He has always been able to secure positions for all competent students. Address at Mason and Hamlin's, 154 Tremont St." And further down the same page this notice appeared: "CARD to organ students. As I have every year more applications from churches desiring organists, than I have been able to fill, organ students would consult their present and prospective interests by communicating with me. Eugene Thayer 'Care Mason and Hamlin, Tremont St., Boston.' "[34]

Small doubt that someone such as George Chadwick, convinced by such publicity of the soundness of his dreams, could, despite his initial late start, begin to believe so fiercely in his ultimate victory over all obstacles. All the rational arguments of his father notwithstanding—the reality of hard times for even well-qualified and proven musicians and the assurance of financial security and parental approbation if only he would stay in insurance—fell on deaf ears. The events of 1854–55, as witnessed by his older brother, evidently left too much emotional scar tissue for him to hear what Alonzo Calvin had to say. After three years serving as a clerk in the Lawrence insurance office and taking lessons in Boston, Chadwick made his move. His character had been formed. His manner had been set. He was independent, truthful, brusque.[35]

The four years from 1876 to 1880, from Chadwick's twenty-first to his twenty-fifth birthday (roughly during the years of Rutherford B. Hayes's presidency), were the most eventful for the young man from Lawrence, Massachusetts. During this brief period, the metamorphosis from a provincial high-school dropout and insurance clerk to the conquering musical hero of Boston would take place. Casting off successively the shells of mediocrity and filial conflict, he would suddenly find within himself the ability to impress people and gain their support to help develop his latent talents. In rapid succession he would become the director of music at Olivet College, in Olivet, Michigan; go to Germany, where he would be practically adopted as a son by one of its leading professors of theory and composition; form musical friendships that would last a lifetime and materially aid his career; and, finally, in a burst of creative energy, capture the first prize in composition at the annual conservatory concerts and win enthusiastic notices for his initial essays in the capital of the music world, Leipzig.

CHAPTER 3

Independence

The precipitating external factor in Chadwick's decision to leave home in 1876 was an illness in the family of George Howard, a Bostonian teaching music at Olivet College in Olivet, Michigan. When Howard requested a leave of absence, a search for a temporary replacement was begun.[36] Chadwick well remembered the circumstances. Theodore Presser, six years his senior, who had only recently been so hospitable to him on his visits to Boston, aided him again. In a reminiscence published in the January 1926 *Etude,* the musical magazine Presser had established, Chadwick recounted:

> In 1876, he [Theodore Presser] was at Greenwich, Rhode Island, in Dr. Tourjee's Summer School, a branch of the New England Conservatory. To this place came Dr. Butterfield, the President of Olivet College, Michigan, looking about for a director for his musical department. He offered the place to Presser who was already engaged for another place, but on the strength of Presser's warm recommendation of me, Dr. Butterfield came to Boston and engaged me for the position.
>
> He was rather aghast when he first saw me, as my face was innocent of any hirsute decorations; and I probably looked younger than my real age which was twenty-one. But Presser's enthusiastic endorsement got me the position through which I was able to save enough money to go to Europe the next year, which was the principal inducement in accepting it.[37]

Although the position was only a temporary one in a new school begun in 1874, this opportunity could be the springboard for his plan for independence through music. Chadwick leaped at the chance. With unbounded energy, he taught subjects only recently acquired: harmony, counterpoint, musical form, and composition. He gave recitals on the organ, an instrument only recently mastered, on which he played one of his early compositions, the Canon in

E♭, op. 16, no. 1. He taught instruments and voice, which he had not, as far as it is known, studied himself. He even delivered public lectures on various musical subjects. His academic titles more than matched his duties. He was "Professor of Music" in the general faculty, "Instructor of Music" in the preparatory department, and "Professor of Vocal and Instrumental Music" in the ladies' department of the Michigan Conservatory of Music, where he was also listed as its "Director." [38] All in all, not bad for someone who just a few months earlier was selling insurance. Away from home for the first time, his self-confidence obviously was growing. In the plains of south-central Michigan, half a continent away from a Boston crowded with musical talent, he could appear authoritative or at least far more authoritative than his gifts or experience might logically justify. Then, too, he must have been a bit of a show-off with Yankee hustle.

Having helped him get the job, Presser, who must have had a talent for organization as well as perspicacity, now invited his newly appointed academic colleague to become one of the founding members of the Music Teachers National Association (MTNA), whose first meeting was to be held that December in Delaware, Ohio, where Presser was then teaching. For this meeting Chadwick prepared a paper entitled "Popular Music—Wherein Reform is Necessary." "I was perhaps rather too much in earnest," Chadwick later admitted, "although there was nothing in the address which does not apply with even greater force, at the present time." [39]

The twenty-two-year-old professor from Olivet College was clearly no diplomatist. He must have known before he made his remarks that present among the founding members was to be none other than George Frederick Root, the established popular song writer who had just received an honorary doctorate of music from the University of Chicago. Every true but tactless observation must have cut the older man to the quick. [40] What was wrong with popular music, Chadwick asked his audience rhetorically? "Everything," was his answer. To begin with, it lacked truth. "The second [thing wrong with it] is its utter lack of originality. Why do we have it? Why does all this weakness, this trash, this dishonest, inartistic, miserable stuff . . . why does this flood our homes and choir galleries, and fill the whole land with its senselessness?"

Continuing with his Old Testament–inspired prose, the young man demanded to know:

> Why will, and do the people bow down to these brazen images instead of the true God? Because nothing better has been given them. . . . Those who furnish the popular music have not paid, either in money or in mental discipline, the price of true and first-class musicians. Therefore they furnish to the people their wares manufactured from the slender stock of knowledge they *have* acquired, at so cheap a rate that it floods the market to the exclusion of the true music.

As if he had committed himself to a crusade in which there was no turning back, Chadwick, with the naivete that only youth and inexperience may excuse, dug deeper into the reasons why

> music has been and still continues to be dragged through the mire. Our own business-like, avaricious, Yankee natures have caused us to forget, in this headlong race after money, that music as an art is a very different thing from music as a business. We want to get money. We want to get rich. Perfectly laudable desire, but have we any right to forget in our eagerness that we work for *art* first,—not money. Have we the right to debase our music simply to earn bread and butter?

He sounded the alarm "to make war most energetically upon *all* frauds, *all* shams, *all* false teachers and teaching perpetuated in her name, *and upon all false prophets.* . . ." Then, with a peroration worthy of his distant relative, Daniel Webster, he roused the audience of his betters to their duty: "Let the people's music be the popular music, but let us give the people music which will achieve a true popularity,—that is the popularity of *years,* not days. . . . I hope I shall not be misunderstood as deprecating simplicity in popular music." Chadwick's last sentence deserves to be quoted separately because it anticipated the theme of the would-be composer's future career as an American musician: "I do not ask you to make popular music classical—I ask you to make classical music popular."

Unfortunately, the complete reaction to this jeremiad is not known because, as a footnote to the meeting's proceedings indicates, part of the discussion following Chadwick's paper was not recorded because of the tardiness of the reporter, but he did arrive in time to catch Dr. Root's second comment. Clearly, the mild-mannered Root felt that he had been singled out by the young reformer, since he was the only "successful" composer of popular music at this first meeting of the MTNA. Root's "Rosalie, the Prairie Flower" was said to have earned the considerable sum of three thousand dollars, and his "Tramp, Tramp, Tramp, the Boys Are Marching" and "The Battle Cry of Freedom" certainly qualified him as a popular composer. Before the seventy-five members and honorary members, Root stood up and confessed:

> I never could say anything plainly, and am convinced of it more than ever. Now that I am up I must just add one word. Nathan Richardson started a large music store; stacked the shelves with only the highest order of music. His relatives who were furnishing the money to keep up the store soon found that they were in a money-losing enterprise. Something must be done, as the music published lay full of dust on the shelves. He came to me in this sorrowful time and wanted me to write him six songs. I did, so,—"Rosalie the Prairie Flower" among the rest. My efforts were commended by some musicians of eminence. I was ashamed of having written songs in that measure at all. I was ashamed to put my name to them; I am ashamed of that now. I put the German of my name, "Wurzel." I will only say that it shows what changes may come to any man. No matter if they are simple in character, I have no reason to be ashamed of them.[41]

The stuff of history is not usually recorded in such a dramatic scene between youth and age, puritanical truth and worldly compromise. Coincidentally, Root, like Chadwick, was a Yankee native of Essex County, Massachusetts. But where truth was concerned, Chadwick gave no quarter. Lest this confrontation be interpreted as the impetuous tirade of an angry man, it should be remembered that this bluntness was a fundamental trait of Chadwick's character throughout his life. Many of his colleagues and students recollected the mature composer and administrator as brusque and even obstinate when he thought he was in the right.

Before the 1876–77 academic year was over, Chadwick had already decided to seek his musical fortune in Germany. But for all his success in his chosen field and even his new national reputation as gadfly for a true people's music, he apparently failed to impress his father. Adamantly opposed to any musical career for his son, Alonzo Calvin made irrevocable the break that began with George's decision to take the Olivet job. He refused to support his son and, for all practical purposes, disinherited him. William Dana Orcutt in the *Christian Science Monitor* later recounted the situation:

> 'Chad,' as his friends affectionately called him, often joked about what a 'disappointment' he was to his father. 'Just another case of the modern generation,' he explained. 'The old man never had any idea except that I would join him in the insurance business. He strangled a bit when I accepted a position as teacher of music in Olivet College, in Michigan, but when I announced a year later that I was going abroad to study music in Germany, there was real trouble. Music as a pasttime appealed to him, but not music as a profession. But I had saved the money from my own earnings, and I went.'[42]

How much money Chadwick could have saved for an extended stay in Europe is not known. But considering the fact that salaries for ranking professors at Olivet were then about five hundred dollars per annum and that he, a tyro, was in no position to demand such a level of compensation, it is most likely that the young musician left for Europe on a shoestring. Carl Engel's reference to Chadwick's "riches thus accumulated" after Olivet must have been said with tongue in cheek. His own son Theodore (named after his friend) perhaps gives a more accurate picture of Chadwick's finances as a foreign student, for he remarked that his father often went hungry in Germany. Other facts confirm that Chadwick had only the minimum funds necessary for passage and tuition.

CHAPTER 4

A Yankee in Germany;
or, The Conquest of Leipzig

Chadwick did not immediately go to Leipzig upon his arrival in Germany in 1877. First he went to Berlin, where he sought out Karl August Haupt, with whom his organ teacher, Eugene Thayer, and Harvard's John Knowles Paine had studied. But discovering that Haupt was not prepared to instruct him in composition and orchestration, Chadwick left, even ignoring Haupt's suggestion to go to the Lebert School in Stuttgart, and headed for Leipzig and Salomon Jadassohn, a teacher at the conservatory who had been highly praised by a shipmate from Philadelphia, Samuel L. Hermann.[43]

In searching for clues to Chadwick's sudden transformation from clerk to America's best hope as a serious composer, the name of Salomon Jadassohn (1831–1907) stands out. Forty-six years old and an instructor at the Leipzig Conservatory for only six years when Chadwick arrived, he had not yet achieved the eminence and respect that his later published texts on all aspects of music theory and composition later brought him. A pupil of the great Liszt, he nevertheless lacked the artistry or showmanship necessary to sustain a career as a virtuoso. Although he had written and brought to public performance many works in the neoclassical style, he had the misfortune to compete with his better-known colleague Carl Reinecke, conductor of the Gewandhaus concerts, and especially with Brahms, whose genius cast a shadow over the whole Leipzig musical scene. Nevertheless, in addition to his pedagogical gifts he exhibited two important qualities that affected Chadwick greatly—humor and benevolence.

Chadwick was lucky. The official classes held in the conservatory did little to inspire students. As he recalled in an article written for New England

Conservatory students in May 1903, perhaps to indicate how fortunate they were, German music teaching left much to be desired.

> As illustrating the pedantry of the instruction of that time, mention may be made of a new pupil who came to our piano class in Leipsic and was asked what he had studied. He replied that he had played ten or twelve studies by Cramer. The teacher said, "very well, take number *thirteen,* but did not ask him to play anything. A student in the organ class was asked to play the scale of Á major on the pedals. He did so with entire accuracy, but by putting his right toe on G-sharp and his right heel on A. The teacher remarked, "My son, that is incorrect. All pedal scales should be played with alternate feet," which he proceeded to illustrate in the most painful and clumsy manner.
>
> Another illustration: a certain class in instrumentation was required to spend almost the whole forenoon copying a table of impossible trills for the flute, after which they were informed that all trills for the flute were now possible, according to the Boehm system, but that it was useful for them to know the trills on the flute *as it used to be.*
>
> It is such methods as these that make the average American student impatient of the grinding-out-process to which he is usually subjected in the German school.[44]

Chadwick's opinions were echoed by another observer, the nineteen-year-old Ethel Smyth (later Dame Ethel), who arrived almost simultaneously for the 1877–78 academic year. Reinecke's lessons in composition, she recalled, were "rather a farce" with "crowds of children prowling about the corridors of his flat." Jadassohn's classes "in the Conservatorium, were at least amusing. . . . when he arrived, always a quarter of an hour late, it was to stand with his back to the stove for another ten minutes telling us exceedingly funny stories with the Jewish lisp I came to know so well in Germany."[45]

Smyth's nasty racial innuendo found no sympathetic vibration in her American classmate. On the contrary, in his first biographical notice submitted shortly after his return to Boston, Chadwick characterized his Jewish teacher as "almost a father to him" who "gave him more than the usual encouragement,"[46] a significant disclosure in light of the frigid relationship with his natural parent. Engel adds the information that even though Jadassohn was not in very good health during the 1877–78 academic year, he

> took greatest pains in correcting everything that Chadwick brought him, and sometimes grumbled when his pupil shied a little at the exercises in counterpoint. If the next student rang the bell before the work

of the lesson was done, Jadassohn would put Chadwick aside and then take up the lesson with him after he had finished with the other.[47]

Evidently, Jadassohn's "Jewish lisp" did not bother the Massachusetts Yankee, or, if it did, he did not consider it important enough to record. Also, Chadwick was most likely thinking of those private lessons Jadassohn gave him in the months just after his arrival in Leipzig and before his matriculation in the conservatory in January 1878, whose records fortunately survived World War II:

> No. 2781 Mr. George Whitefield Chadwich of Boston, born in Lowell 13 November 1854, matriculated on 3 January 1878. His father Mr. Arlanso Chadwich is an insurance agent in Lawrence not far from Boston. Mr. Ch. had instruction for 3 years, with interruptions, in music theory and composition as well as in organ with his uncle and for 3 months with Mr. Petersilea, also in addition 3 months in composition with Herr Musikdirektor Jadassohn. Residence: Nordstrasse No. 25, 5th floor. Left at Easter in 1879.[48]

The last entry concerning Chadwick's quarters in Leipzig shed more light on the hand-to-mouth existence he is thought to have led. In the 1882 edition of the Leipzig *Adressbuch,* the house Chadwick gave as his residence was listed as a vacant building lot. So it is reasonable to assume that two or three years earlier, this property was in the same undeveloped state. Where the young composer actually lived is unknown.

His friend and benefactor, Theodore Presser, "turned up" unexpectedly in Leipzig in 1878.

> The students in the Leipzig Conservatory of those days were given a schedule of classes which they were supposed to attend; but very little fault was found with them if they did not do so, and the result was that they did very nearly as they pleased. He [Presser] immediately became a great favorite with the American and English boys, and was a ringleader in all sorts of practical jokes, some of which recoiled on his own head. We went to many concerts and rehearsals together, and as I seldom practiced if I could go to a rehearsal or a concert, he often said to me, 'Chadwick, you cannot pick up music on the fly," in which of course he was entirely mistaken.
>
> In the summer we made a walking trip of a week in the company of some other students, through the romantic region of the upper Elbe, known as Saxon Switzerland. Presser was the life of the party. He was

so irrepressible that on one occasion, the landlord of a little inn threatened to eject us.

When I was working on my Overture to Rip Van Winkle, which was to be played at the Annual Conservatory Concert, he was full of interest and enthusiasm, even predicting great success for me. He heard a private rehearsal with a local orchestra whom I induced to try the piece over, and at the Conservatory rehearsals he was equally enthusiastic; but when it came to the performance, he disappeared, and I did not see him for several days afterwards.

I was very much hurt by this, because the competition was very keen, and I wanted his moral support as my principal backer. When I finally saw him, and demanded an explanation, he shrugged his shoulders and said, "You have enough friends without me."[49]

In the course of his imaginary colloquy with the statue of Beethoven, cited earlier, Chadwick related that he was called "Hedwig" by his "brothers of the Concordia [a musical organization of students in Leipzig] because they could not pronounce my name." And Harry Newton Redman, a pupil and later a colleague of Chadwick at the New England Conservatory, related the following anecdote told him by Chadwick:

When Chad was a student in Leipzig he befriended a violinist in the Gewandhaus orchestra. On the day that Brahms was to rehearse for the first time in Leipzig his C minor symphony, Chad asked his friend if there was any chance of sneaking into the auditorium. His friend told him to carry his violin case through the door and leave it at the foot of the staircase leading to the auditorium. This Chad did and witnessed the whole rehearsal. Things were not going well and both Brahms and the orchestra were becoming increasingly aware of an impending impasse. Finally after one of Brahms' remarks to the orchestra, the oldest member of the group who was a timpany player stood up and respectfully addressed Brahms in the following manner: "We have played in our time symphonies by Mozart, symphonies by Haydn, symphonies by Beethoven, symphonies by Mendelssohn and Schumann and with your cooperation we shall play this symphony by Brahms." After which everything went well.[50]

Whatever he may have failed to gain in general from his official courses of study Chadwick seemed to have acquired from Jadassohn's private lessons and fatherly concern, so liberally dispensed from his Georgenstrasse residence. Then, too, there was the chance to hear "the music," particularly at the Gewandhaus concerts, and enjoy the camaraderie of a student life, which confirmed his feelings of self worth. All had a magical effect on Chadwick. By the end of the first term at the conservatory, his work in composition was so well considered that his Quartet in G Major for strings was chosen as the first piece for performance at the Gewandhaus public examination concerts. The correspondent for the *Monthly Musical Record* was delighted, as evidenced in his June 1878 report:

> During the course of the last few weeks the Royal Conservatoire has given seven more public examination concerts at the Gewandhaus, with satisfactory results. . . .
> Amongst the production of young composers we hold the best to be a string quartet by Mr. George Chadwick, from Boston, of which two movements, allegro and adagio only, were given. In style, form and contents it contains the best work produced by the pupils of the establishment during the present year.[51]

Demonstrating not only his new talent in composition but also a flair for publicity, Chadwick made the good news available for home consumption in *Folio,* a local Boston publication:

> MR. GEO. W. CHADWICK. It will gratify the many friends of this gentleman, the former Professor of Music at Olivet—now in Europe—to learn that his abilities are thoroughly appreciated even in Musical Germany. We quote from the Leipsic correspondent of the London *Musical Record.* . . .
> Mr. Chadwick writes that he will bring home with him ten finished works of his own, most of which have been or are to be publicly performed in Leipsic.[52]

The *Neue Zeitschrift für Musik,* one of the more influential German music journals, founded by Robert Schumann, took notice of the American's debut with less enthusiasm, although it should be mentioned that the critic admitted missing half the performance. While the composer may not exhibit special originality in invention, he reported, "still, in his favor may be mentioned the personal, clear, and free flow of ideas which spring forth from his work."[53]

If Chadwick's first year at Leipzig may be considered a success, his second, the 1878–79 academic year, was spectacular. Both in the fields of chamber and concert music, he won the competition for performance as well as for critical acclaim. It becomes difficult at this juncture to consider that just a few years before he was a clerk in a business office, contemplating a career as an insurance agent. In his diploma, or final report, Reinecke and Jadassohn heaped praise on the now self-styled Bostonian. The language indicates that it was probably Jadassohn who actually wrote the words:

> Mr. Chadwick possesses a quite unusual talent for composition, as is indicated by his thoroughly professional sounding works such as two string quartets, overtures for orchestra, etc. The hours spent with him were always a pleasure for me.
> Carl Reinecke   S. Jadassohn[54]

That Jadassohn's report on Chadwick's gifts as a composer was objective seems to be confirmed by his negative opinion on the American's promise as a pianist. Clearly, the magic of Leipzig and Jadassohn was not enough to make much of an improvement on Chadwick's limited keyboard abilities:

> Mr. Chadwick unfortunately has only very little inclination for the piano. He takes great pains, plays quite musically based on his generally splendid talent, but without any real keyboard technique.
> S. Jadassohn[55]

Johannes Weidenbach, another piano instructor, felt that Chadwick would have benefitted by more frequent attendance at his classes, and Henry Schradieck, the violinist who later became the head of the National Conservatory in New York, dismissed his ensemble playing with the complaint that he attended only occasionally.

Obviously, Chadwick had found his métier as a composer. He was not going to jeopardize his chances for success by wasting precious moments in piano practice or chamber music rehearsals. Preoccupied with composing, making fair copies and parts, he could not possibly have had time for keyboard exercises. The result of this feverish activity and stretching of his creative imagination was soon obvious. At the seventh *Hauptprüfung*, or graduation concert, on May 30, 1879, and at the ninth and last, on June 20, contests that had the excitement of Olympic meets, Chadwick was clearly the runaway winner.

The success of two works—Chadwick's String Quartet No. 2 in C Major and his concert overture *Rip Van Winkle*—confirmed Jadassohn and Reinecke's enthusiastic praise and went a long way to assure his future career.

German music critics heaped accolades on both works. According to Engel, the quartet, played at the seventh concert, on May 30, was cited by *Signale* for its "natural and healthy invention," while "the reviewer for the *Musikalisches Wochenblatt* detected in it 'interested traits which reflect an emotional life of personal cast.' "[56] The notice in the *Neue Zeitschrift für Musik* coincidentally appeared on June 20, the very day of the triumphant performance of *Rip Van Winkle,* which must have filled Chadwick's cup to overflowing. The notice summed up the chamber music recital:

> Of the three compositions from the pens of students given a hearing, one, the expressive and touching String Quartet in C major by George Chadwick of Boston, played by Winderstein, Muck, Oelsner and Rothlisberger, made a truly good impression by virtue of the considerable inventive power, uninhibited feeling and good sense of structure, especially of the first movement.[57]

At the ninth and final orchestral concert, the public evaluation of the best piece of the year was traditional. On the program were no less than four overtures. One was *Julius Caesar* by the English prodigy Algernon Ashton (1859–1937), who had been studying in Leipzig for seventeen years, since 1863, when he was but four years old. Another, *Hamlet,* was the effort of Paul Umlauft (1853–1934), who was designated the Mozart Scholar (1879–83). A third was by Richard Franck (1858–1938), later widely known as a pianist and teacher. But it was the Yankee's *Rip Van Winkle* that carried the day. An unidentified clipping pasted on the back of the manuscript score now in the library of the New England Conservatory (probably from *Signale*) and dated in Chadwick's own hand, "Mittwoch 25ten Juni," says of the overture: "Unstreitig ist dies beste Composition welche die diesjahrigen Compositionen bracht" ["Uncontestably this is the best of this year's compositions"]. Other critics were impressed by the fact that Chadwick "had his own poetic intentions" and that his music "had both color and a physiognomy."

CHAPTER 5

The Summer of '79

If there was any doubt of Chadwick's having made the wiser choice—exchanging parental approval and a certain future in his father's insurance business for the vague promise of a career as a composer and the final fracture of his relationship with his only parent—it must have been dissolved in the joy of praise that only youth may fully drink without any bitter aftertaste. After all, although he had worked long hours to attain success, he had been at the business of composition for only a short while. So his satisfaction was not diluted by long years of struggle and neglect, a sacrifice required of many of the greatest of creative artists. The one supreme emotion that his conquest of Leipzig could have afforded, however—reconciliation through his father's approval and demonstration of reflected glory—was denied to him forever. On December 5, 1878, Alonzo Calvin had died at the age of sixty-eight, never knowing that his son had indeed fulfilled what may have well been his own secret dream.[58]

The circumstances of the elder Chadwick's demise were somewhat irregular. In 1873, for reasons unknown, he had sold the house and land at 30 Tremont Street in Lawrence to Fitts Henry, George's older brother.[59] Thus, the fact that he died intestate was perhaps a moot point, if, in fact, the estate had been largely real property.[60] Nevertheless, it meant no legal provision for his second wife, Susan, or her heirs and nothing for George Whitefield. In any case, the latter did not return home either to attend the funeral or to clear up matters of inheritance. (Certainly, his father must have amassed some capital in two decades as an insurance man.) When George ultimately did return, a year and a half later, his activities did not indicate that he had recently come into any money.

That summer of 1879 began in a routine way with Chadwick scouting out the possibility of study with Gustave Merkel in Dresden, a suggestion made by Salomon Jadassohn. Chadwick, always sure of himself, decided instead to go to the center of German cultural life, Munich, and study with the younger, more charismatic composer Joseph Rheinberger. But he did not leave the Saxon capital before arranging for a performance of his prize overture, *Rip Van Winkle,* at the summer concerts of the Königliche Belvedere der Brühl'schen Terrasse.[61]

Then, a chance meeting with a wandering group of American painters transformed routine preparations for another academic year into one of the most formative experiences of his life. Even if he had gone to Munich lured by reports of the free and easy ways of the Bavarian city, second only to Paris as an artist's Mecca, he certainly found what he was looking for there. In associating himself with these Duveneck Boys, as they were later called, Chadwick was himself, especially at the inception of his career as a creative personality, not so much an isolated musician as a fellow artist. Frank Duveneck (1848–1919), mentor of the "boys," was himself only thirty. His good looks, independence, and fluency with the brush had attracted dozens of youthful Americans who preferred his dash to the academism of the Munich art professors. By 1878 the group about Duveneck had grown to more than one hundred, and the "old man," as he was affectionately called, moved out to Polling, a Munich suburb where he rented a deserted monastery for his "school." "They used the monk's cells for their studies and sleeping quarters . . . the walls of the monastery, offering large, white-washed surfaces, were soon covered with decorations from the brushes of the young foreigners."[62]

How did Chadwick encounter these carefree, exuberant painters, an experience that made a lifelong impact on the way he perceived reality and approached musical composition? It is difficult at this time to piece together the story with certainty, but in 1875 Duveneck had swept the Boston cultural scene with a bravura exhibition of five virtuoso portraits. Even the doubting Henry James, then writing as an art critic, admitted that Duveneck's reputation as the American Velasquez was well deserved. Perhaps James's opinion influenced his friend Elizabeth (Lizzie) Boott, an art student of William Morris Hunt, to purchase Duveneck's portrait of William Adams and later to study with him. Lizzie Boott was the daughter of Francis Boott, an indifferent mill owner and Harvard's first composer, donor of the still-awarded Boott Music Prize. Ironically the woman Alonzo Calvin married after George's mother died was employed as a mill hand at the Boott Mills in grimy Lowell while its musically gifted proprietor was living in the ethereal atmosphere of Rome with his nine-year-old daughter. At the Palazzo Barberini, home of the American artist William Wetmore Story, Lizzie Boott played one of Titania's fairies in a private performance of *A Midsummer Night's Dream,* with James Russell Lowell cast as Bottom. There, also, the absentee capitalist's first string quartet was played. Later, in Florence, the expatriate Bootts, father and daughter, lived in the Villa Castellani, to be immortalized as the models for the leading characters in Henry James's masterpiece *Portrait of a Lady.*

Had Chadwick, as a young music student, met the older Lizzie in Boston? Had he heard of Duveneck's Boston exhibit of 1875, or was it just by luck in Munich in the summer of 1879 that he was invited to join the liberated band of Duveneck Boys (and Girls)?

The summer itself proved to be just as significant for Lizzie. As Duveneck's student, she began a relationship that in seven years' time would blossom into marriage. In 1923 a nostalgic Chadwick remembered those halcyon days forty years earlier when, after his return to Boston, his best friends were "poets and painters . . . and the jovial brood of William Hunt, now organized as the Paint and Clay Club" who found it agreeable to drop in "to his lodgings in a little room in the historic Park Street Church," where he held his first job as organist.

According to his son Theodore, Chadwick accompanied the Duveneck Boys on a visit to France, where they spent time at Giverny, the town that was to become famous as the home of Claude Monet. Among the boys were William Merritt Chase, John Henry Twachtman, Joseph Rodefer De Camp, John White Alexander, and Charles E. Mills, all of whom became well-known artists. In his 101st year, Mills remembered the young American musician living and traveling with the troupe in Germany and France. While the others painted, Chadwick composed. At the end of the idyll, he even considered studying with César Franck in Paris. Ultimately, however, he decided to follow through on his original plans and return to Munich.

To wonder what this change would have meant for Chadwick and to the direction of American music, given his subsequent strategic position as an educator and composer, is idle speculation. Considering the French and Italian orientation of his mature style, however, it may not be too extreme to suggest that the seeds of this taste were formed by the fleeting exposure to French culture during these magic months of creative growth. The Duveneck Boys and the trip to Giverny expanded his aesthetic horizons to include the visual sensations of genre painting, the bold brush stroke, and the creation of form through dabs of color, all of which confirmed his inborn feeling for the aesthetic value of musical metaphor and commonplaces that could support an American veristic style in music. Trying to understand Chadwick's music by referring solely to the official list of courses with his German teachers can lead only to misconceptions. Only in a limited way can their precepts be related to the subject matter and style of those works for which he is best remembered. Luckily for Chadwick, his German teachers forged what might have been merely an undisciplined and chaotic energy into habits proper to a professional and so prepared him for the myriad tasks that could earn him a living and overcome obstacles to success. Once so organized, Chadwick's creative powers were directed from the start by his ethnic roots, his appreciation of things cosmopolitan, and by the fellowship of painters and literary people.

The summer was over. Chadwick returned to reality and Munich, while Duveneck and his band followed Lizzie Boott's suggestion. They headed south for Florence, where they were "photographed" by the words of William Dean Howells in his realistic novel *Indian Summer*, in which they were called the "Inglehart Boys." A few years later, Chadwick would be collaborating on a theatrical piece, *A Quiet Lodging*, for the Boston Tavern Club, of which Howells was first president.

CHAPTER 6

Reality and Rheinberger

From that time with the Duveneck Boys to the end of his life, Chadwick maintained close ties with painters and an active interest in painting. He bought the first work that Childe Hassam, the American impressionist, ever sold.[63] When Chadwick was married in 1885, he and his wife spent their honeymoon at Giverny, by then Monet's home. He also encouraged the eccentric painter-composer Harry Newton Redman. But possibly the most lasting memento of Chadwick's artistic summer is his portrait by Joseph De Camp, one of the Duveneck Boys, who in 1898 together with nine other artists, including Hassam, John Henry Twachtman, John Ferguson Weir, and Edmund C. Tarbell, formed the Society of Ten American Painters.

In the autumn of 1879 Chadwick enrolled at the Hochschule für Musik in Munich. He studied organ and composition with Joseph Rheinberger, whose romantic opera, *Die Sieben Raben,* and comic opera, *Des Thürmers Töchterlein,* had been produced in 1869 and 1873, respectively. Although he was considered anti-Wagnerian, Rheinberger's connection with dramatic music must have appealed to Chadwick. In addition, he worked with Ludwig Abel, concertmaster for the Wagnerian conductor Hermann Levi, in conducting and score reading. Thus Chadwick was not entirely isolated from the "music of the future."

Chadwick's choices were not without wider significance for American musicians. They were the beginning of a trend away from Leipzig and what was then called the German neoclassical school, and many American composition and organ students were to follow in his footsteps. Unlike the lax atmosphere in Leipzig, Rheinberger in Munich provided the challenge and training of a severe disciplinarian. According to J. Weston Nicholl (1875–1925), an English composer:

> All Rheinberger's pupils . . . stood in profound awe of him; respect mingled with admiration was the prevailing sentiment he inspired. Perfectly simple, honest, and straightforward, sparing not himself, he expected everyone to be the same, and any lack of effort on the part of the student called forth his severest censure. This was most noticeable in his organ class, which was very select, containing only four students. He expected, and in fact demanded, that a student should be technically perfect in an organ piece, before playing it for him. Rheinberger's four organ students—two Germans, an American and an Englishman . . . had to work very hard and conscientiously to satisfy the doctor. At a technical blunder the doctor would frown, and if later in the lesson the same mistake occurred he would expostulate. Punctually at eight a.m. every morning (summer and winter) Rheinberger's counterpoint class assembled at the Conservatorium. There they would chatter away at the tops of their voices, half a dozen languages going at once; suddenly the door would open, and the doctor would enter the room. Instantly, the conversation ceased, and the students would remain quietly and respectfully standing until he had taken his place at the head of the long table; then, in turn, each pupil would take to him his prepared lesson—generally a *canto fermo* worked in the soprano, alto, tenor, or bass with the various species of counterpoint. This over, Rheinberger would generally go to the piano and play a *canto fermo* which would at the same time be written upon the ruled blackboard by one of the students in any clef the doctor selected. Then various members in turn would add the necessary counterpoint. The exercise finished, Rheinberger called up one of the class to play it upon the piano; and, if this was not faultlessly done, the doctor would generally pass unpleasant remarks, which had sometimes the effect of making an individual look rather crestfallen.[64]

Some may dismiss Chadwick's academic German musical training as a handicap rather than a help in the development of a national school of American composition. No doubt things would have turned out differently had Chadwick indeed sat at the feet of Franck or even if he had absorbed more modern tendencies from Wagner's operas. But for a composer, the teacher is no guarantee of a student's success. In teaching those fundamentals of form that exist irrespective of personal style or current fashion, conservative pedagogues such as Jadassohn, Reinecke, and Rheinberger gave Chadwick the tools with which he could craft his own kind of music. His melodies, harmonies, and sonorities were not only as different as Lawrence and Lowell are from Leipzig but also, according to any aesthetic scale, far more interesting than anything his mentors wrote. If American composers of lesser talent who went through German conservatory mills produced correct but dull works, it was their fault. The German system, in any case, educated them beyond the elements of music as taught at home by Lowell Mason and exposed them to expressive possibilities wider than the church choir or brass band.

Critic Louis Elson summed up the case for study with the conservative composers of that day:

> While I consider Wagner's opera the highest point reached in this great school of music, I still deem that it is a very good thing that such men as Reinecke and Rheinberger, at the head of great schools, have not yielded to the Wagnerian influence. For Wagner wrote in a language which no other composer can speak. . . . all others who have tried to imitate, have found the path too thorny for success. Wagner swam in a 'sea of tone'—and his disciples only drown themselves in it and the conservative music schools mentioned above do a good work in forming themselves into a species of life-saving stations.[65]

As it happened, it was far better for Chadwick to have received a restrained but thorough musical training than to have tried to assimilate a musical ideology that would have made him more beholden to a more alien musical style. Without losing any of his native spirit and gusto, Chadwick had gained the sophistication of a professional. He was now ready to return to the center of his universe, Boston, heralded by the sounds of *Rip Van Winkle,* which was performed there before his arrival in the spring of 1880. The December 20, 1879, *Musical Record* reported the performance by the Harvard Musical Association orchestra at the Music Hall:

> The "Rip Van Winkle" overture which followed, was a treat. The work is quite melodious, and is remarkable for its rich and full instrumentation. With the exception of an undue predominance of brass there is little to complain of in its effects, while on the other hand there is much that deserves highest praise. It achieved a great success for its composer, who gives promise of a brilliant future. While we accord the full credit to the Association for its recognition of this composer's ability, we wonder if his work would have been given by them if it had not previously received the stamp of approval of Leipsic.[66]

Chadwick left Munich for Boston in March 1880 and was welcomed with the following personal notice: "Mr. George Chadwick, organist, composer of the overture to "Rip Van Winkle," which has been enjoyed so much, will make Boston his home. He will make a great accession to our body of resident musicians."[67]

Chadwick was entirely on his own. His only capital was the publicity of his German triumphs.

During the next seventeen years, the not-so-young composer, who turned twenty-six that November, pursued a life plan typical for the time and place. His professional activities were to be concentrated in teaching, playing the organ for various churches, and conducting when the opportunity arose. His personal life would involve the search for a mate and family as well as the fellowship of kindred spirits. His aesthetic imperatives and his desire for immortality would greedily devour the time left over in the composition of music.

CHAPTER 7

Boston

The Boston to which Chadwick returned in 1880 was a thriving commercial and cultural city. No longer just a regional hub, it had, after the great fire of 1872 and the reclaiming of Back Bay as a fashionable residential and public center, taken on the elegance and modern style of Paris. Copley Square, named for America's first great painter and constructed on the site of the monstrous wooden shed that had housed the World Peace Music Festival in 1872, was soon adorned by H. H. Richardson's romanesque Trinity Church, built in 1877, and later by the Boston Public Library and the hotel bearing its name. The large, level area of new land by its side, stretching up to the south bank of the Charles River, was divided by Commonwealth Avenue with a wide median strip of promenade garden. A grid of parallel and intersecting streets provided a novelty for the 250-year-old town: the thrill of walking or driving down straight and level roads. Surely it must have been the goal of any success-driven young man to live in a town house on one of these streets some day.

With an inexorable movement, the center of population moved in an ell down Washington and Tremont streets, around the bend of the Common at Boylston, and up to the new square. Aside from its developing physical beauty, the city still could boast that it was the intellectual "hub of the universe" and the "Athens of America." It had long since outgrown its provincialism. As a cosmopolitan town, it drew hundreds of young people attracted to its schools, theaters, concerts, and galleries and thousands more seeking jobs.

With all this in-migration, the population was still largely native. As for foreigners, the Irish, who had begun to come over about the time of Chadwick's birth, were mostly concentrated in South Boston. Another decade was to pass before Italians and Eastern European Jews were resident in statistically significant numbers. The ancient community of blacks was not to become a social-political force for almost a century.

In his novel *The Rise of Silas Lapham,* William Dean Howells seems to describe the young Chadwick on his return from Germany:

> A man has not reached the age of twenty-six in any community where he was born and raised without having had his capacity pretty well ascertained; and in Boston the analysis is conducted with unsparing thoroughness which may fitly impress the un-Bostonian mind, darkened by the popular superstition that the Bostonians blindly admire one another. A man's qualities are sifted closely in Boston as they doubtless were in Florence and Athens; and, if final mercy was shown in those cities because a man was, with all his limitations, an Athenian or Florentine, some abatement might be justly made in Boston for like reason.[68]

Given such scrutiny and the fact that he did not have the advantage of Boston birth, it is all the more remarkable that two years after his arrival, George W. Chadwick was so well thought of that he was selected for lithographic representation as a member of the pantheon called "Musical Boston." His relative youth was emphasized by his clean-shaven face among a score of hirsute dignitaries including B. J. Lang, Carl Zerrahn, John Knowles Paine, Oliver Ditson, and even his erstwhile teacher, Carlyle Petersilea.

Of the many institutions and organizations that might have afforded a person of Chadwick's talents and desires some kind of living, not all were waiting with offers. It was not until 1882 that he received appointments as organist at the Park Street Church, famous for being the site of the first public singing of "America," and at the New England Conservatory of Music. In the meantime, he advertised himself in *Dwight's Journal of Music* as a private teacher, a "Conductor and Solo Organist . . . who will receive pupils in pianoforte and composition," in a rented studio on Tremont Street.[69] At the same time, he was living in Malden, a suburban town, with his brother Fitts Henry, the bookkeeper for the old-line hardware firm, Wilkinsons, on Washington Street. The most prestigious institutions—Harvard College's Department of Music, the Boston Symphony Orchestra, new in 1881 under the sole patronage of Henry Lee Higginson, and the Handel and Haydn Society under the direction of Carl Zerrahn—and even such lesser opportunities as the Cecelia Society and the Apollo Club, both controlled by B. J. Lang as conductor, were all closed to Chadwick for lack of proper credentials, experience, or social position.

With typical Chadwickian luck, however, one of his first private pupils was Horatio Parker (1863–1919), who recorded in his diary in 1881:

> February 13: Carried Chadwick at 10:00 A.M. (the) first movement, slow movement, Scherzo and as much of the Rondo as I had done He liked the first three but not the last. . . .
>
> March 10: . . . Saw Chad about going to Germany.[70]

Parker's reference to Chadwick by nickname indicates a rather informal relationship right from the beginning between these two subsequently influential composers.

Evidently, Chadwick's teaching was not as renumerative as he might have wished, for he sent out an engraved card with somewhat irregular prose style later that year:

MR. G. W. CHADWICK

> begs leave to remind his Pupils and Friends that his advanced Pupils take great pleasure in recommending him as a Teacher of Harmony and Composition to the impecunious or suburban public, or to others who cannot afford to pay their prices. Also, that he had returned from Europe.
>
> Boston, Oct. 1, 1881[71]

Besides teaching, Chadwick also began a career as church organist at the Park Street Church. Never a particularly outstanding performer, he would hold posts at churches of only second rank, but as a composer he got off to a great start. In addition to the Handel and Haydn Society's 1880 performance of his *Rip Van Winkle* overture, which he himself conducted, the Boston Philharmonic performed his *Waltz-Symphonique* (*Schoene Muenchen*), and his second quartet for strings was given at a concert by Arthur Foote. In March 1881 the Arlington Club performed his *Marquerita* for men's chorus. And at the end of the season, the Apollo Club, under B. J. Lang, presented *The Viking's Last Voyage*, which was very favorably received. His first symphony was given in

February 1882 at the Harvard Musical Association's fourth concert at the Boston Museum, with Carl Zerrahn conducting. Chadwick even found time to join a newly organized Musician's Club, among whose members were some of the best known musical people of the city, including the critic William Foster Apthorp; Louis Elson, a later colleague; the composers Arthur Foote and John Knowles Paine; the conductor B. J. Lang; and Arthur P. Schmidt, the music publisher who brought to the world most of the best works by the Boston School. The searching out of kindred spirits was also documented the next year, in May 1882, in the lithographic representation mentioned earlier, published in John C. Freund's nationally distributed journal *Music and Drama,* which gives one the impression that, like Silas Lapham and despite a newcomer's usual difficulties in being accepted, Chadwick must have had what it takes to gain recognition as a composer even if he was not appointed to a prestigious position.

His ambitions as a conductor were obvious from the opportunities he seized here and there. But whatever chances he might have had were, ironically, lost by the founding of the Boston Symphony Orchestra. It had sprung, like Athena, fully grown, with the best musicians money could attract world wide. Higginson, the founder, built his orchestra in much the same way professional baseball teams were organized. "Boston" in the title referred only to the place of its concerts and residence of its benefactor. With relatively cheap tickets and its virtuostic performances, it was not long before the orchestra would monopolize orchestral music in the Hub, reducing the already limited opportunities for any local aspirant to conduct. Despite the demise of the two main competing groups, the Philharmonic Society and the Harvard Musical Association, Chadwick honed his skills and kept in the public eye by conducting an amateur ensemble, the Boston Orchestral Club, and later directed the Springfield and Worcester festivals. It was not until he became director of the New England Conservatory that he had the power to organize a permanent orchestral instrument, albeit of students and alumni, on which he could play and realize his lifelong desire.

Whether Chadwick had any ambitions of teaching at Harvard is not known. Certainly he readily accepted the invitation to make an appearance there in 1882 as conductor of Paine's music for the Greek production of *Oed-*

ipus Tyrannus at Sanders Theatre in Cambridge. The *Musical Record* reported that "Mr. G. W. Chadwick has few equals as an orchestral conductor,"[72] a statement that must be read in the context of comparison with the new conductor of the Boston Symphony, George Henschel, a singer whose brief tenure was not without controversy. Chadwick also conducted Paine's dramatic music in Boston, New York, and Philadelphia. But nothing else resulted in Cambridge from this showcase of his executive talents.

Thus, when the rumor began that "one of the largest conservatories of music in this city is to be removed to the South End and established at one of the great hotels in that part of the city,[73] Chadwick must have perked up his ears. Eben Tourjée, the director of the New England Conservatory of Music, had decided to expand the facilities of the conservatory, which he had begun in 1867, primarily by enlarging the faculty and acquiring dormitory space for its growing number of students. The St. James Hotel, an immense mansard-roofed pile, provided the space and dignity Tourjée wanted. Chadwick had gotten his Olivet job, which permitted him to go to Leipzig, through Tourjée's Summer School in Rhode Island, it must be remembered. If Chadwick was not to be taken on by Harvard, the next best thing was to become an instructor at the conservatory, which some called "the musical Harvard or Yale." At the new New England Conservatory of Music, he succeeded in 1882 in securing a position to teach composition and instrumentation. With this appointment, the composer began an almost half-century association that would last until his retirement in 1930, one year before his death.

In the same year, 1882, Chadwick was made organist of the Park Street Church for three hundred dollars per year, plus use of a small room.[74] Even though he was, by the terms of his contract, severely restricted and warned that his conduct had to be of an exemplary nature, he always remembered this period of his life with fond memories. In a nostalgic letter of June 1923 to the *Evening Transcript,* Boston's semi-official gazette, he wrote:

ET IN ARCADIA, EGO

As the World Wags:
    If your chronicles of the fine arts in Park Street would include music, which would seem to be right, they should begin at the bottom of

the street, namely in the Park Street Church. For in that Church, in the corner room overlooking the Common, dwelt and labored (more or less in 1882 and 1883), a young musician who was beginning to attract some attention as an orchestral composer. He was the organist of the church and the rent of his room was a part of his salary. It was a very satisfactory arrangement for him, for he had made a joyous escape from the purlieus of the Lawrence building (149A Tremont Street), which was at that time infested with voice and piano teachers. All day long the ambient air was filled with the shrieks, wails, thumps and bangs of their pupils. Musical composition was impossible except in the middle of the night, and even harmony lessons were difficult to give except on the keyboard. But in this beautiful, silent room, reached by a short flight of steps from Tremont Street, he found a haven of refuge. It had been used as a study by former pastors of the church, but some of them had not left behind them enough of the odor of sanctity to interfere with musical inspirations of a secular character. The nearest neighbors on Tremont Street—they were of our "best people"—were quiet, very quiet. The silence was broken only by the footsteps of occasional pedestrians or the distant rumble of the horsecars slowly winding up the slope of Tremont Street. To that room came, among others, Horatio Parker and Arthur Whiting, with their fugues and canons. Perhaps they brought with them more than they carried away from their teacher. Many of the good singers of the time came in occasionally and some meetings and rehearsals were held there. The poets and painters came also and the jovial brood of William Hunt, now organized as the Paint and Clay Club, found it agreeable to drop in after the other places were shut up. But if "Mary Elizabeth" could have established her tea room a few years earlier, how convenient it would have been for breakfast. And there was the organ in the church above. It could be played, and sometimes was in the middle of the night.

Ah me! It was 40 years ago. The brimstone has been pretty much eliminated from that historic corner and sometimes I wish I were there yet.

Boston
G.W.C.[75]

Capping the consolidation of his plans for a musical life was an invitation to return to Europe that year. This time he went as the cicerone and mentor to his pupils, Horatio Parker and Arthur Whiting. Chadwick went along to tour and introduce the boys to his teacher, Joseph Rheinberger, with whom they subsequently studied in Munich.

His career now as secure as he had reason to expect, Chadwick began to think of settling down. Given modern curiosity about the relationship between sexuality and the creative process, it is unfortunate that the typical reticence of Chadwick's generation concerning personal matters has obscured this part of the composer's life. However, if there ever was sense to the notion that every work of art is essentially autobiographical, then Chadwick's music, unless gross and deliberate deception was employed in its making, portrays him as a robust, earthy man, fully aware of and propelled by an active male hormonal drive. Without exception, all who knew him, even toward the end when he was slowed and weakened by infirmity, remembered his verbal thrusts, his animation, and his irreverent humor. Harry Newton Redman, the eccentric musician turned painter who came to the conservatory in 1885 as a hayseed from Mt. Carmel, Illinois, recalled Chadwick in his prime. Commenting on Redman's home state, Chadwick said: "Well, that's a good part of the country to be born in and get out of."[76] Warren Storey Smith, the critic for the *Boston Post* and an instructor at the conservatory from about the time Chadwick retired in 1930, confirmed other characteristics of the composer as "brusque," "quick-tempered," and "to the point."[77]

Chadwick was of medium height and, in later years, stocky build (although photographs do not convey this impression), with a head of ample wavy hair, which was sandy-colored before it turned gray. Perhaps the most memorable feature of his face was his twinkling eyes, which were the clue to his delightful, sometimes even impish behavior. Redman mentioned that once, while he was taking a lesson from Chadwick in the office of the organ loft of the New Hollis Street Church (Edward Everett Hale, author of *A Man Without a Country,* was then minister), Chadwick was disturbed by a loud conversation in the church below. He left the office, peered through some staging and saw a couple about to be married in private. Noiselessly, he ran to the organ console, set all the stops, and, just as the ceremony was over, played the Mendelssohn wedding march at galop speed. Then he disappeared, leaving the astonished couple and the venerable Reverend Hale in complete confusion.

It must have been these personal qualities and his celebrity as Boston's newest young composer that attracted Ida May Crocker, a member of the Hollis Street Church. They were married in June 1885.[78] The new Mrs. Chadwick (née Brooks), hailed from Kennebunkport, Maine. Her marriage to

Zenas H. Crocker, a Wareham, Massachusetts, sailor, had ended in divorce only the preceding April.[79] Charles E. Mills, the last of the surviving Duveneck Boys, apparently kept in touch with Chadwick through the years, and some seventy years later he recalled: "Chadwick married a divorcee, her first marriage was an unfortunate one, he was very cruel to her and she later fell in love with George Chadwick."[80] He was thirty and she twenty-eight years old. As if to confirm both his friendship for Horatio Parker and his sentimental feeling for the summer spent in France with the Duveneck Boys, the pair spent their honeymoon together with the just-married Parkers at Giverny, France, where Monet then lived. A contemporary snapshot of the two couples taken at Munich shows a clean-shaven Chadwick casually smoking a cigar while reading a newspaper.[81] His pretty, trim, and obviously taller Ida May, in a high-necked frock fastened with a cameo brooch, is looking down at a paper with a Mona Lisa smile on her lips. Behind the seated pair are the Parkers. Anna Parker, carrying a parasol and hanging on to her new husband, looks into the distance as if detached from the scene, while Horatio, with a black military moustache, looks down at Chadwick's reading matter in such a way as to intersect the rays from Ida May's eyes. The photograph seems to symbolize the nonchalance Chadwick wanted publicly to display, the adoration of his wife, the respect of his best friend, and, unfortunately, Mrs. Parker's standoffishness. In a letter written years later to her husband, then in New Haven, Anna Parker's comments seem to confirm her attitude in the picture. At a Kneisel concert in Boston she had "sat just behind the lively Chadwicks', and they seemed so surprised to see me there. It is really remarkable, I can be with Grace Whiting any length of time, and she never rubs me the wrong way, but Mrs. Chad *will* in five minutes."[82]

That the two best friends, Chadwick and Parker, loved women who disliked each other must have been a constant source of tension between them. In no way, however, did that tension interrupt or compromise their artistic or personal relationship. To Chadwick, who had been deprived of the normal supports of mother love and family life, Parker's upbringing in the home of a doting father, a famous architect, and a brilliant, young mother must have seemed idyllic. For his part, Parker was doubtless envious of Chadwick's early independence and emancipation from family constraints, his boldness, his adventure. At Parker's death, Chadwick's eulogy of his lifelong colleague seemed restrained but did not obscure the depth of his feeling: "As a congenial companion," he said, "a loyal comrade and a steadfast friend, Parker has left a blessed memory."[83] Meaningful as these words were, to plumb the ultimate emotion Chadwick felt, one must rather listen to the music of his *Elegy*, which was dedicated "In memoriam Horatio Parker."

When their honeymoon was over, the Chadwicks returned to Boston, where they rented an apartment at 99 Boylston Street, an address that seemed to point the way to their eventual house in Back Bay.

Forceful as his inaugural *Rip Van Winkle* seemed to the reviewer of Ditson's *Musical Record,* Chadwick's creative powers did not flag after the extraordinary overnight blossoming that took place in Leipzig. It must be remembered that when he left Boston to study in Germany he was quite an average chap with musical hopes greater than any already demonstrated talent would justify. Chadwick's unnoticed departure for Europe in 1877 was a great contrast to the departure of John Knowles Paine, who was sent off for his European experience to the applause and financial support of nearly the whole city of Portland, Maine, and who was shepherded through the maze of foreign travel with introductions to important people by none other than Alexander Wheelock Thayer, Beethoven's biographer. Had Paine subsequently failed, it would have been a great personal embarrassment and disappointment to many. Had Chadwick failed, there would have been few, among even those who knew of his desires, to feel any chagrin.

Rip Van Winkle was followed in the 1880s by a parade of works of increasingly greater stature in almost all genres. They included two choral works, *The Viking's Last Voyage* (1881) and *Lovely Rosabelle* (1889); a dramatic piece, *The Peer and the Pauper* (1884); several orchestral works—Symphony No. 1 in C Major (1881), Symphony No. 2 in B♭ Major (1883–85), the *Thalia* overture (1882), and the *Melpomene* overture (1887); and two chamber works, String Quartet No. 3 in D Major and Piano Quintet in E♭ Major (1887). In addition, Chadwick composed numerous songs, many set to lyrics by Arlo Bates, Henry Wadsworth Longfellow, and Thomas Bailey Aldrich, and keyboard pieces for organ and piano.

This sustained burst of creative energy could not have come at a more propitious time. High-water marks for American music had just been established by Paine's pioneer works—his 1876 Symphony in C Minor, the music for *Oedipus Tyrannus* (1881), which he asked young Chadwick to direct, and the *Spring Symphony* (1882). Paine had proved to Boston that an American could handle the technical and philosophical demands of the symphony as an architectural form as opposed to, say, the miniature, less complex structure of the art song or characteristic piano piece. Then, as it happened, Paine's effort seemed to decline, leaving to Chadwick the task of fulfilling the expectation for American symphonies. In March 1884 the Scherzo of Chadwick's Second Symphony, performed by the Boston Symphony, captured critical imagination by its novelty as well as its craft. Indeed, Chadwick showed that, in addition to technique and large-scale planning, an American could write for such a sophisticated medium as the orchestra with an easily recognizable personal style that sounded American without using either Yankee Doodle-isms for thematic material or banjo.[84] Apthorp, the perceptive critic of the *Boston Evening Transcript*, was quick to spot Chadwick's special manner:

> Mr. Chadwick's new Scherzo is a gem. The themes on which it is built are both original and taking—the first theme, with its quasi-Irish humorousness (it positively winks at you), is peculiarly happy. The working up of the movement sounds clean and coherent, even at a first hearing; the piquant charm of the whole is irresistible! The orchestration is that of a master, and is full of delicious bits of color, without ever becoming outrageous. The impression the Scherzo made was instantaneous, and as favorable as the composer himself could have wished.[85]

Very significant is Apthorp's explanation of Chadwick's musical Americanisms in terms familiar to his readers. The pentatonic, or gapped, tetrachords are identified as "quasi-Irish" and the syncopated accompaniment as "winks." Even more penetrating is his characterization of Chadwick's orchestral sonorities as being "full of delicious bits of color." In juxtaposing this description with the phrase "the . . . impression was instantaneous," Apthorp conveys the notion that Chadwick's new style had something in common with Boston painters of genre scenes. This allusion seems to affirm the importance of Chadwick's early association with the Duveneck Boys and his continuing interest in the work of American Impressionists.[86]

From the beginning, Chadwick showed a talent for musical theater as well as established Leipzig forms. In this way, he clearly set himself apart from most of his colleagues who, besides having in common with him a Yankee musical heritage, study abroad, an academic career, and a church organist position, all shared with their ethnic compatriots a suspicion of the theater. In addition, any right-thinking musician could not be faulted for not expending creative energies in a medium where the probability of performance was negligible, especially for Americans writing in English. But despite his background and common sense, Chadwick was caught up in the enthusiasm for opera in English caused by the "Pinafore craze" after 1878, when Arthur Sullivan's opera was premiered in Boston. Possibly through social connections with members of the Paint and Clay Club or with the new breed of socially conscious writers such as William Dean Howells, Arlo Bates, and Robert Grant, the rising young composer was asked to collaborate on a musical theater project, ultimately called *The Peer and the Pauper.* The *Musical Record* gossiped in June 1884: "A NEW opera, libretto by Mr. Robert Grant, and score by George W. Chadwick, is in the course of composition."[87] Missing from his authorized list of works—perhaps because he had borrowed from it extensively for two later dramatic works, *Tabasco* and *Everywoman*— *The Peer and the Pauper* reveals Chadwick as a composer with a knack for musical characterization, catchy tunes, and sensitivity to the prosody of his text.

These are also obvious features of his songs, which he began writing with fluency in the 1880s. Particularly noteworthy were Tennyson's *The Miller's Daughter* (1881), Bates's *The Danza* (1885), *Two Songs by Thomas Bailey Aldrich* (1886), Lew Wallace's *The Lament (Ben Hur)* (1887), and Amelia Rives's *A Bonny Curl* (1889). *The Danza* sports Afro-Caribbean rhythms; *The Lament,* near-Eastern exoticism; and *A Bonny Curl,* an Anglo-Celtic lilt—all of which Chadwick would pursue in his later musical style.

Besides the Boston Symphony Orchestra, which was to become a medium of expression for most Boston composers, another force, springing up from the larger group, would provide inspiration for a sizable repertory of chamber works. The Kneisel Quartet, led by Franz Kneisel, then concertmaster of the Boston Symphony, premiered Chadwick's third string quartet, his first masterly quartet, in 1888. For the Kneisel Quartet Chadwick would later write his better known fourth quartet and quintet for piano and strings as well.

But of all the works from this post-Leipzig period, when Chadwick was establishing himself as a pedagogue, family man, and composer, none other was more well received and remembered than his romantic overture *Melpomene* (1887), which was lauded even thirty-five years later in a *Boston Herald* editorial. The reasons for *Melpomene*'s success are clear. It reflected the deep vein of tragedy that was part of Chadwick's makeup and so was able to touch the audience immediately. Another reason was the excellence of the Boston Symphony Orchestra itself, which had become, in the few years that Wilhelm Gericke (to whom Chadwick dedicated the score) had trained it, one of the best ensembles in the world. Higginson had freed its members from most of the quotidian concerns of the typical musician: All they had to do was to perfect themselves as artists and the orchestra as an instrument. Moreover, *Melpomene* was a perfect vehicle for Gericke, whose concerts were described as "brilliant in execution, [and] musically moving." With his Viennese experience in conducting both Brahms and Wagner, he was just the right interpreter of a "tragic" overture that evoked, in a convincing synthesis, elements of both masters. That Gericke did not program Chadwick's work merely as a gesture to local talent is indicated by the fact that he performed it no less than six times during his two tenures as conductor (1884–89, 1898–1906), another reason why Boston remembered the work.

By the end of the decade, Chadwick need defer only to Paine as the leading American symphonist, and out of respect rather than reality, for Paine had begun a long decline in his output, possibly due to the onset of diabetes, broken only by his single opera *Azara* (premiered in Boston, 1907), performed in a concert version posthumously. The only other American of equal potential, Edward MacDowell, had not yet made much impact on the American musical scene. He had returned to the United States late in 1888 and had settled in Boston, but he never fully became "one of the boys."[88]

Thus, Frank Van Der Stucken's concert dedicated to works of the leading American composers at the Trocadero Palace during the Exposition Universelle in Paris on July 12, 1889, signalled a milestone for both Chadwick and American musical composition. No matter that the young French music writer Julien Tiersot condescendingly discussed the works, including *Melpo-mene,* between chapters devoted to other "ethnic" musics from Lapland and Bali (music said to have impressed Debussy). Tiersot's great contribution was his recognition, for the first time, of a veritable *"jeune école américaine,"* not just a group of individual composers bound together by time and place. With precision he wrote that they all were inspired by forms of the *"école allemande néoclassique"*—Mendelssohn, Raff, and Brahms. But he noticed also that these models were flavored by Wagnerian harmonies and sonorities. He even heard in the works of some of the young Americans French influence from Gounod, Massenet, and Thomas. Although perhaps not original as yet, the chief characteristics of these Americans' music were craftsmanship and idiomatic orchestral writing. Above all, said Tiersot, the Americans were very productive. Certainly, he expected to encounter more than one of these composers in the future.[89]

CHAPTER 8

The Happy Nineties

For the next eight years, until his appointment as director of the New England Conservatory in 1897, Chadwick's life appeared to advance with predictable speed, though not without some detours. In 1891 Chadwick's first son, Theodore (named for publisher Theodore Presser) was born. Unfortunately, that same year Eben Tourjée, the founder of the New England Conservatory, who had given Chadwick his big chance at Olivet College and also hired him as an instructor at the conservatory when he returned to Boston, died. Consequently, a chain of events was set in motion that eventually led to Chadwick's elevation, but not without his first having to wait for the inevitable failure of Tourjée's immediate successor, Carl Faelten, a German piano pedagogue from Frankfurt.

In the meanwhile, the now thirty-six-year-old composer-teacher-organist continued a productive career. The success of the Exposition Universelle had its effect in America. Chicago sent commissioners to inspect the operations of the Paris fair with a view to sponsoring a similar event, known as the World's Columbian Exposition, on the shores of Lake Michigan during the celebration of the four hundredth anniversary of the discovery of America by Columbus. The importance of American painting at the exposition was assured, but the role of music presented unique problems. Was it to be entertainment or a presentation of artistic and historical significance? Some of the uncertainties about the direction of music at the fair were resolved when Theodore Thomas, who had just been made conductor of the Chicago Symphony, was appointed music director. Questions concerning the role of American music were still unanswered, however. In response to the *Boston Herald*'s inquiry as to the feasibility of a proposed competition for prize money and performance, Paine said he did not believe in the idea and, in any case, would not compete. MacDowell, then beginning his meteoric career as a pianist-composer, dismissed the plan, saying he could recall no great work that ever took a prize. His opinion was seconded by the influential music man B. J. Lang.

Chadwick's answer bears quoting in full because it is an example of his common sense and natural prose style:

> I believe in America for Americans in music as well as in other things, though I say this with no disparagement of the great foreign masters, and I believe in competition insofar as it shows increased interest of the country in music and musicians. About the accomplishment of this there are several difficulties. If the competition should be open to all, it is altogether likely that the prizes would be borne off by foreigners, and if restricted to native composers, then there would be very few to compete. Then, as regards the judges, another difficulty would arise; it would be well nigh impossible to find impartial ones. For instance I don't think it would be possible for a German to regard a French composer like Massenet seriously, he puts him on the same plane as Offenbach; on the other hand a Frenchman holds that Brahms and Rheinberger are dull and prosy indeed. Competition is not a good way to bring out the most musical compositions; the moment a composer feels that his work in order to attain a certain result must reach a certain standard in a certain time, he feels insecure. But there are plenty of American works already written under different circumstances which would easily be brought forward into this proposed competition. In regard to performances of native musical works, I have always felt that they should take their chances by the side of the works of foreign composers. As yet we can be said to have no school of American music, and the concert programs made up entirely of American music show a distinct lowering of the proper standard. The production of an American work at a concert where only the best music is heard—as our symphony concerts here— means a great deal, and recognition there should give the composer great encouragement.[90]

From the projected concert plan, which insisted that the Music Bureau be independent of any commercial interests, it would seem that Chadwick's ideas were adopted. Recognized American composers were asked to choose representative works of their own for performance. Only two were actually commissioned to compose music for the exposition—Paine, who wrote the *Columbus March,* and Chadwick, who composed music for Harriet Monroe's *Dedication Ode.*[91]

In the end, however, the World's Columbian Exposition proved that nationally the United States was not yet ready or disciplined enough for a genuine exposition of the arts in what was a commercially controlled enterprise. Because of pressure mainly from Western piano manufacturers, who were leading exhibitors at the fair, all Steinway pianos were excluded after Steinway chose not to participate. When Thomas, defying a directive, had a Steinway smuggled in for an appearance of the great Paderewski, he was threatened with dismissal. Boston mobilized when it received a plea for help from the critic W. S. B. Matthews:

THE WESTERN UNION TELEGRAPH COMPANY
Received at 109 State Street, Boston 1056a
May 12, 1893

Dated: Chicago
To: Arthur Foote
   2 West Cedar St. Boston

EDDY [Clarence] AND I ARE PREPARING CARD OF CONFIDENCE IN THEODORE THOMAS ATTACKS WHOLLY UNJUSTIFIABLE PLEASE WIRE TODAY ALL GOOD NAMES, POSSIBLY CHADWICK MC DOWELL ETC.
                                           WSB MATTHEWS[92]

Further souring this experiment in mass aesthetics was the Panic of 1893, which threatened the salaries of the orchestral musicians. Thomas resigned with the suggestion that the only music needed at the fair was that which would be sure to "please the shifting crowds in the buildings and amuse them." With Thomas absent and morale low, the performances that were given were of little artistic value. A magazine report of the May 23 concert gave an accurate impression of the dissensions and uncertainties in the orchestra:

This afternoon an American symphony concert was given in Music Hall. It was a Boston program: Symphony No. 2 in B-flat, G.W. Chadwick, op.21; Serenade in E, op. 25, Arthur Foote; Suite, op. 42, E.A. MacDowell.
    The affair was a species of musical outrage. Neither Mr. Thomas [who was ill] nor his *chef d'attaque* were present, the hall was nearly empty and during the performance of Chadwick's symphony the members of the orchestra talked and tittered while Mr. Mees tried to elicit some music from the band. Mr. Foote conducted his own *Serenade* and

by knowing exactly what he wanted he succeeded in commanding sufficient respect to insure a tolerable performance. . . .

I had not the heart to stay and hear MacDowell's romantic suite
performed under such circumstances, and so I made my exit. Yesterday's
official program made no mention of this American concert, and few
were aware that it took place. These facts together with the absurd
charge of one dollar for admittance, were sufficient to insure an empty
house.

Americans may well be proud of the achievements of these three
young representative musical creators, and it is to be hoped that they
will turn their attention to native folk-songs and thus supply what is
most lacking in our high-class music—national character and individual
coloration. . . . [93]

Under the circumstances, one may excuse the reviewer for not paying attention to the "national character and individual coloration" of Chadwick's Second Symphony. Certainly the exposition left bad feelings among leading
American musicians. Perhaps more than any other event, it created suspicion
among composers about the motives of business-oriented festivals and fairs.
The days of the more naive Peace Jubilee of 1869 and the World Peace Festival
of 1872, which had inspired thousands of citizens like Chadwick himself, were
over. The disillusionment widened the gulf between those who strove for a
music of aesthetics and the mass of the people who, more and more, were
left to be manipulated by the growing music industry. It is difficult not to
recall the tyro musician's jeremiad seventeen years before when Chadwick
warned the Music Teachers National Association about commercialism in
music: "Have we the right to debase our music simply to earn bread and
butter?" When Theodore Thomas was invited in 1904 to be the musical director of the St. Louis Fair, he promptly declined, saying that the fair should
confine its music to the bandstands in the open air.

Chadwick now actively pursued his conducting career, begun in the
1880s. He led the amateur but respectable Orchestral Club, which performed
with soloists and chorus to present such novelties as Gounod's *Philemon and
Baucis,* Niels Vilhelm Gade's Symphony No. 4 in B♭ Major, and even a revival
of his own overture, *Rip Van Winkle.* In 1890 he became music director of the
Springfield Festival, a rival to the summer series in Worcester and self-
dedicated to "a somewhat more severe standard." It is significant that as a

conductor, Chadwick elected to program many non-Germanic works at this time, among them Gounod's *The Redemption* and Verdi's *Requiem,* as well as such contemporary American works as Parker's *The Kobolds.* In these choices Chadwick was reflecting a trend already noticeable in literature, painting, and architecture, and one that was about to influence the programming of the Boston Symphony Orchestra. In an article entitled "Boston's Musical Bigotry" the *Boston Home Journal* commented: "A plea for more French music and less German is demanded. . . . we grope about in German mists . . . and say it is purer and healthier than clean air and a blue sky. We pay American money for the privilege of submitting to German dictation. . . ."[94]

It was during the 1890s that Chadwick, ever more aware of Romanic (even Slavic) taste in music as revealed in the works of French and Italian composers, began with purpose to cultivate his unique style, which might be termed populist realism.[95] Not that he shed or wished to shed the constructive methods of neoclassical German technique or the sonorities of chromatic voice leading. These were, after all, accepted as universal rather than as ethnic property. But the idea that music did not always have to be "pure" to be valid aesthetically began to direct him. Certainly choral works such as *Phoenix Expirans* (1891), the World's Columbian Exposition *Ode* (1892), and even the prize-winning Symphony No. 3 in F Major (1893–94) easily demonstrate their academic credentials. They also show, together with such theatrical works as the operetta *A Quiet Lodging* (1892), the burlesque opera *Tabasco* (1894), and especially the String Quartet No. 4 (1896) and the *Symphonic Sketches* (1895–1904), that Chadwick was finding his own path. Although it was in the same direction as the New England School, of which he was a loyal member, it ran on a separate track. Perhaps this path reflected his special gift for orchestration; perhaps it was the facility with which he conjured up tunes, as did his maternal relative the tunesmith Asa Fitts; above all, perhaps it was his way with rhythms, especially dance rhythms. At any rate, he allowed inborn tendencies to rise from the forefront of his imagination to be transcribed onto paper. They might not conform to the models of excellence he had mastered, but by this time he had enough self-knowledge and confidence to prevail—always, however, within the bounds of taste. Thus, his popular realist style was well crafted enough for it to be respected by both colleagues and performers and communicative enough for its meaning to be comprehended by any audience without explication. His power to evoke universal emotions and visual imagery as well as the ethnic wellsprings of Anglo-Celtic American music made his art unique in an age of mass immigration. For until Chadwick's works of the 1890s, no other composer in America—not even the more flamboyant Gottschalk, the self-destructive Foster, or the brooding MacDowell—had succeeded in blending together the ingredients of an American orchestral music that could pass the aesthetic muster of Western art music. Symbolic of Chadwick's success was the prize awarded by a committee headed by Antonin Dvořák to his Third Symphony in 1894. This assessment is made not to praise Chadwick at the expense of his colleagues who chose not to compose music immediately identifiable ethnically or nationally but only to define more clearly Chadwick's unique style.

One bond that held together the small but influential artistic and intellectual elite of Boston was informal association in social clubs. Chadwick was involved with two: the St. Botolph Club, the more stolid, and the Tavern Club, the more free and easy. A scene from *The Pagans,* a Boston novel by Chadwick's sometime librettist-lyricist Arlo Bates (which refers possibly to Chadwick or to Arthur Foote), begins:

> At the St. Filipe Club, somewhere in the small hours of the same night, half-a-dozen members were lingering. One was at the piano, recalling snatches from various composers, the air being clouded alike with music and smoke wreaths.
> "I think you fellows are hard on Fenton," the musician protested, in response to some remark of Ainsworth's. "I don't see what he's done to make you all so down on him."[96]

Perhaps a clue to Chadwick's identity lies in Bates's use of the colloquial "down on" to capture the composer's rough and ready speech. The group in the novel was called The Pagans because they "felt that 'Puritanism is the preliminary rottenness of New England . . .' and because they represented 'the protest of the artistic soul against sham.' They stood for sincerity above everything. . . . While they held themselves open to conviction, they refused assent to anything that was offered them *ex cathedra.*"[97]

In *The Peer and the Pauper* (1884), Chadwick and his collaborator, Robert Grant, the novelist and jurist, created Boston's response to *Patience,* Gilbert and Sullivan's exercise in exposing sham. Instead of Bunthorne, the fleshy poet, they satirized an impoverished English duke seeking to restore his fortunes by marrying a wealthy Yankee heiress summering on Mt. Desert island. Later with Bates Chadwick concocted a delightful topical masque, *A Quiet Lodging* (1892), for the Tavern Club, whose first president was William Dean Howells. The occasion, the annual "Narrenabend" on April Fool's Day, permitted the authors to comment without penalty on a wide range of Boston personalities. As with the usual male club casting, all the female roles were impersonated by men. Chadwick was represented, no doubt, as Professor Blowbellow, the unperformed Yankee opera composer. An amorous Italian tenor (who is really a Bostonian forced to change his name because of family objections to his occupation and the general prejudice against American singers) is called Signor Yayelli. An indigent poet, in love with Blowbellow's daughter, is refused consent to his suit because he "knows less about music than the Boston critics." Blowbellow's rivals do everything to hinder the public performance of his masterpiece: "They bribed Mr. Higginson not to have the overture played at Symphony concerts; they got it discredited by having Apthorp say in the Transcript that he admired it. . . ."[98]

Besides producing such gems as *A Quiet Lodging,* the Tavern Club was especially known for its cuisine, created by its Italian cooks. Their dishes, much in demand in the Boston of Charles Eliot Norton and quite a contrast to the normal New England fare, constituted the chief attraction.

One outgrowth of these social relationships was the burlesque opera *Tabasco* (1894), remembered along with *Melpomene* and *Judith* by the *Christian Science Monitor* as one of the main supports of Chadwick's popularity and reputation as a composer who could express the comic as well as the heroic and the tragic. The work was commissioned by the First Corps of Cadets, the acme of Boston Society, as part of its fund-raising activities for the construction of a massive armory in the center of the city.

Not much past his fortieth birthday, the still young-looking composer had more than made up for the late start of his artistic career. With the esteem of his new friends he had gained the threshold of the American cultural establishment. All he needed now to be catapulted to a prestigious institutional position was an error in judgment committed by some complacent executive.

CHAPTER 9

The Faelten Affair

At the time the Faelten affair reached a crisis point in 1897, Chadwick, as in Leipzig, showed himself to be a responsible, presentable chap, even though he lacked academic credentials, a fortune, and family pedigree. He inspired confidence and could be expected to hold a fiduciary trust, raise money, organize and lead, and create communicative works of aesthetic excellence as well.

There can be little doubt that Chadwick had ambitions at the New England Conservatory beyond the teaching of harmony and composition. His own pupil, Horatio Parker, had been called to head the music department at Yale in 1894, and when Columbia established a chair in music, MacDowell was chosen as its first occupant in 1896. Paine had been a professor of music and chairman of the department at Harvard since 1875. Therefore, as Carl Faelten's position as head of the conservatory became increasingly untenable, it was natural for Chadwick to make himself available. But unlike the polite situations in which his colleagues took academic office, his quest was part of an ongoing political storm. When the crisis had abated, one Boston newspaper carried a front-page story on February 1, 1897:

CHADWICK

NEW HEAD OF THE CONSERVATORY

Prof. Faelten Gracefully Bowed Out
Series of Unfortunate Incidents Causes Crisis

Mr. Faelten is a German and did not take kindly to American methods. Other matters, growing out of his manner toward colleagues and subordinates, have alienated a number of faculty, students, and friends of the institution, so that, despite his indisputable high rank as a musician, it became apparent that his continued stay meant constant friction.

The new director, Mr. Chadwick is possessed of faculties which Mr. Faelten lacked and he brings to the position a reputation for ability which is not only national but established in musical centers abroad as well . . . .

Open resistance against him [Faelten] last year, it may be remembered when a paper signed by 18 members of the faculty, and transmitted to the president of the board of trustees, brought matters to a focus.

At a meeting of the trustees, Mr. Faelten was present, as well as some of his opponents, and a compromise was agreed upon. An advisory committee was appointed to consider and bring about reforms.

A few weeks later seven members of the faculty were dismissed on the charge that they had broken faith with the Director by dining at Clark's hotel for the purpose of discussing grievances. . . .

The Alumni Association took up the matter and the sentiment against Mr. Faelten was marked. An investigation was promised by the executive committee of the board of trustees, but the report of this committee upheld Faelten, and maintained that the troubles in the institution were caused solely by certain disgruntled teachers who sought to promote discord.

The alumni were not satisfied with this. Just before their annual meeting in June last, the president of the alumni had a conference.

When the annual meeting came two tickets were put into the field, the old board was re-elected. Ever since that time the movement against the director has been gathering headway.[99]

In its account of the affair, the *Boston Herald* added the following information: "The same evening a meeting of the Alumni association was held in Elocution Hall, and it was alleged that Mr. Faelten had attempted to control the Alumni association and secure the election of officers who were in sympathy with him. This effort failed. . . ."[100]

The exact nature of Faelten's transgressions was never published, but it is possible from personal interviews and reminiscences to reconstruct much of what preceded his dismissal. When Eben Tourjée became seriously ill in 1890, Faelten was chosen chairman of an acting directorate composed of himself, Frank Hale, the business manager, and Henry M. Dunham, teacher of organ. On Tourjée's death in 1891, Faelten took over as director. From the start, his regime was plagued by dissension. According to Dunham:

> . . . Faelten was driving with a little too tight a rein. Many of the faculty were restive under his severe espionage, especially the younger members.

With the faculty as a whole he was gradually making himself unpopular, although, as yet, nothing of the sort showed on the surface. It seems now that there was a feeling astir making for trouble. . . . Hale said: "If Faelten were to resign, the faculty would throw their hats in the air."

I was . . . dumbfounded and as I did not encourage the continuance of the subject, it was dropped abruptly. . . . It proved the opening gun of an internal warfare in the Conservatory that nearly wrecked the whole institution and it was not stopped until the President had resigned and the Trustees had forced the resignation of the musical director, the business manager, and six members of the faculty.

To outsiders, the story of this period, the disintegration of the old regime and the gradual establishment of the new might prove an interesting chapter. . . . [101]

Harry Newton Redman, a Chadwick pupil who had been appointed an instructor in 1890, recollected in his later years:

Faelten, a piano teacher, had the habit of listening to promising piano students practice and then enticed them to study with him. This aroused the enmity of Dennée, and other teachers of piano who banded together and tried to stop his practice of pirating students. But once Faelten overstepped his bounds in saying that he had the Board of Trustees in his pocket and that he could do anything that he wished. Finally the Alumni Association got into the quarrel and invited Faelten to a banquet in order to bring the issue to a head. Faelten, recognizing the situation, refused to go even after a cab had been sent for him. When Faelten finally arrived, he was confronted by the man to whom he had made his boast. He admitted it and was fired a few days later. Chadwick, then famous as a composer, was chosen director.[102]

Faelten was not without his partisans. Particularly incisive was the editor of the *Boston Home Journal,* who wrote a cutting editorial that gives us special insight into a public perception of Chadwick's rugged personality:

The personal reputation of the director as a conscientious and upright man has all along been above suspicion. . . .

— —

The serious and at the same time unique feature of the whole affair is that a conservatory faculty has been endowed by the action of a board of trustees with an unmistakable vote power which in the present case indirectly made itself felt by the impelled resignation of Carl Faelten.

— —

It had been said that the present director is no diplomat.

There is a tribute in this very charge that is highly creditable to Mr. Faelten's sense of honor.

No strictly honest musician was ever conspicuous for his diplomacy.

Mr. George W. Chadwick has been chosen as Mr. Faelten's successor.

The conservatory, to its credit, had no diplomat as its musical director, and a diplomat was desired in his place.

Consistency, thou art indeed a jewel.

Please name the date when Mr. George Chadwick has conducted himself after the manner of a diplomat. Mr. Chadwick's genius is for music.

How if he accepts the appointment in question, the cause of music as to a limited extent represented by the New England Conservatory may gain a diplomatic director of that institution, although we may much doubt this, but this gain in an unimportant direction, comparatively speaking, will be at the unavoidable expense of a splendid composer's best work.[103]

The last statement may have been prophetic. Of course, it is impossible to say whether or not Chadwick would have written more or better if he had not taken on the time-consuming responsibility. Predictably, though, the development, planning, and administration of such an enterprise must have been a full-time occupation in itself.

News of the affair and appointment reached London and was noted in the pages of the *Musical Times:*

Speaking of Boston, there have lately been radical changes in the personnel of the faculty of the New England Conservatory of Music, the latest of which is the retirement of Mr. Carl Faelten. . . . Mr. Faelten's place has been filled by the appointment of Mr. George W. Chadwick—a selection which seems to give general satisfaction. It has been known for some time that there was friction among the faculty and trustees of the Conservatory, but details have been kept from the public with most commendable discretion. A rival institution has been started in Boston.[104]

The "rival" school was to be known as the Faelten Pianoforte School. Together with his brother Reinhold, Carl Faelten conducted the school on a unique method, one of whose features, along with other notational innovations, was the transcription of piano music from the conventional two-staff system to a single eleven-line staff. The school lasted until the outbreak of World War II.

CHAPTER 10

Director of the
New England Conservatory

For both Chadwick and his wife, his investiture as director of the New England Conservatory must have been the highest point of his career. Born to only a humble position in society, Chadwick was the prototypical self-made man of whom such novelists as Howells and his own friends and librettists Robert Grant and Arlo Bates had written realistically. Like Howell's Silas Lapham, Chadwick, propelled by his merit and industry, had risen to a position of parity among his peers and even higher, since he was not simply a department chairman but also a chief executive officer. Also, like Silas Lapham, Chadwick gravitated toward Back Bay. True, his town house was a modest structure, located on Marlborough Street rather than Beacon Street, without a view of either the Charles River or Commonwealth Avenue. Commendably, although Chadwick, like Lapham, grew in sophistication, he never forgot the virtues of his native speech and tastes, common though they may have been. As he grew more secure and more social, he began to explore consciously the roots of his art. No longer was he necessarily concerned with living up to the expectations of his betters. He was now ready to do only that which made sense to his own taste. He would begin to develop his long-held populist views, his sympathy for realist art in the modern American novel and impressionism in painting, and his talent for composing musical metaphors of these styles.

From Chadwick's election as director of the New England Conservatory of Music in 1897 to the end of World War I, he assumed a position of leadership in academic life equal to his prestige as a composer. Immediately he set about to convert what was, despite its name, essentially a glorified singing and boarding school for young ladies into an educational institution of national significance. His first move was to raise funds for a new, functional building to meet instructional and performance needs. This handsome neo-classical building—together with the Symphony Hall, Horticultural Hall, Northeastern University, the Museum of Fine Arts, the Gardner Museum, and the Boston Opera House—helped form an unofficial cultural center on Huntington Avenue.

Originally domiciled in the Music Hall, which had been the locus of serious musical activity in Boston, the conservatory had moved into quarters at the sprawling St. James Hotel in Franklin Square, which had, besides space for teaching, facilities for boarding women students. But these two functions were not easily reconciled. To create truly academic, professional surround-ings, Chadwick conceived of a new structure, in a prestigious location, that would provide the indispensable amenities for teaching and performing ar-tistic music: a recital-concert-opera hall, a music library, a modern organ, practice studios, and classrooms. Needless to say, there would be *no* dormi-tories! With the generous support of men such as Eben Jordan, the heir to a department store fortune for whom the concert hall was named, Chadwick's dream came true.[105]

With the physical plant assured, Chadwick went about creating his new institution. A symphony orchestra was established, an opera workshop be-gun, and a whole series of pipe organs installed. The curriculum was modi-fied. As a result of Chadwick's experience in Leipzig, lessons in singing and piano playing took back seat to courses in harmony, counterpoint, orchestra-tion, and composition. Orchestral instruments were taught by members of the Boston Symphony, the one outside activity that Henry Lee Higginson actually encouraged. Professional singers from the Boston Opera Company were hired as coaches.

Allen Lincoln Langley, a symphony violinist, remembered Chadwick as a gruff but basically fair man. Although impatient with students who exhib-ited unprofessional habits in orchestra rehearsals, he was always willing to take the time to explain and inspire. "He made the orchestra play better than it had any reason to." Chadwick once confessed his real feelings, his frustrated ambition to become a conductor of a professional group. "One day nothing went well. Suddenly Chadwick laid down his stick and surveyed the scene with a curious mixture of sorrow and anger. . . . His eyes roamed the stage; then he slumped heavily in his chair and shouted: 'Do you want to know something? This orchestra is my life blood—do you understand? My life blood! You're hardening my arteries—that's what you're doing.' And then, a bit ashamed of his revelation, 'Well, let's get to work.' "[106]

While taking into account the limitations of a student orchestra when choosing a repertory, when possible Chadwick read music rarely played "across the street" at Symphony Hall. New works by contemporary French composers such as Bruneau, Louis Aubert, and Emmanuel Chabrier and by Americans such as Arthur Shepherd, Edward Ballantine, and Edward Burlingame Hill were given first performances. To be sure, Chadwick could not resist the temptation to hear his own scores. He was especially interested in trying out works scheduled for performance by the Boston Symphony Orchestra and other professional presentations. In this way, he was able both to make alterations and corrections and to give the students the privilege of being the first to perform works such as *Tam O'Shanter*. What might have been merely an exercise in amateur fiddling turned out to be a real experience in professional music making, and the sense of participating in a musical movement had lasting meaning.

Chadwick's performance plans went beyond orchestral repertory. He also envisioned the development of a native musical-operatic theater not dependent upon European impresarios or performers for its existence. The first American opera workshop, the New England Conservatory Opera School, with coaches, directors, and other professionals drafted from the newly organized Boston Opera Company, offered the kind of stage experience American singers lacked. As it also turned out, the faculty of the opera school were helpful in Chadwick's composition of the opera *The Padrone*. In addition, Chadwick created an independent conservatory chorus, which unfortunately did not become a permanent organization until much later, after he had retired.

Because of personal friendships, Chadwick maintained close ties with the Harvard music department. As a result, many student composers who were studying with Archibald T. Davison, E. B. Hill, and Walter Spalding were made welcome at the conservatory. Hill had already been a visitor to

Huntington Avenue, attracted by Chadwick's novel course in orchestration, a subject usually taught only by experience or by treatise. "Chadwick's approach to this subject," Hill wrote,

> was comprehensive and practical as well as enlightening on many points untouched by textbooks. He enlisted the cooperation of his students by insisting that they choose the pieces for orchestral transcription. Through this process he stimulated the perception as to what pieces were suitable for use. He was particularly resourceful in pointing the manner in which piano accompaniment figures could best be adapted to specifically orchestral devices, another branch of the subject neglected by the textbooks. . . . Chadwick's keen sense of humor was an active ingredient in awakening the pupils sense of fitness in the appropriate choice of instruments. I recall particularly his mordant wit in decrying the long oboe solo at the beginning of the slow movement of Brahms' Violin Concerto, not always in the best range of the instrument instead of contrasting two or more wind instruments as prudence and euphony would suggest. His comment upon this passage was: "Any violinist would sound good after that." Similar musical quips, far removed from the average pedagogic or pedantic injunctions, not only enlivened the criticism of our exercises, but they gave point to Chadwick's observations far more compelling and illuminating than pages of a text-book.
>
> I look back over a half century to this course under Chadwick as an exceptionally valuable contact, in that he communicated knowledge and in a most persuasive manner, developing the judgment and self-reliance of the student to an extraordinary degree.[107]

Portrait of George Whitefield Chadwick, 1917, by Joseph Rodefer De Camp. Courtesy of the heirs of George Whitefield Chadwick.

Chadwick homestead in Boscawen, New Hampshire, built in 1765. Courtesy of the heirs of George Whitefield Chadwick.

Alonzo Calvin Chadwick, father of the composer. Courtesy of the heirs of George Whitefield Chadwick.

Chadwick before he went to Leipzig, c. 1876. Photo by A. N. Hardy, Boston. Courtesy of the heirs of George Whitefield Chadwick.

The Chadwicks and Parkers in Munich, c. 1886. From Isabel Parker Semler's *Horatio Parker: A Memoir for His Grandchildren* (New York: G. P. Putnam's Sons, 1942).

Chadwick, c. 1884. Courtesy of the heirs of George Whitefield Chadwick.

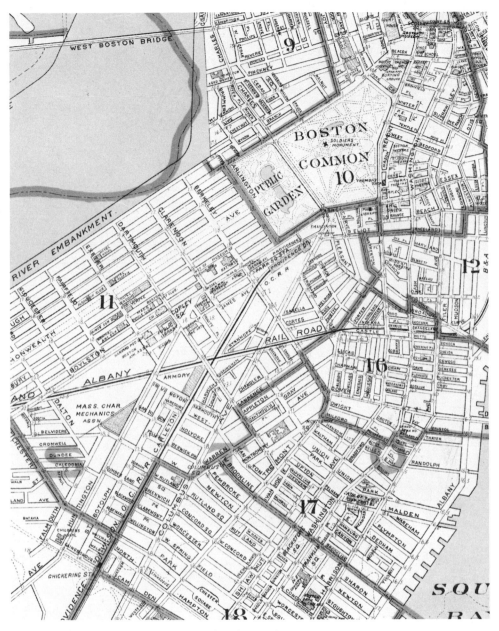

Map, downtown Boston. From *Atlas of Massachusetts* (Boston: George H. Walker & Co., 1891).

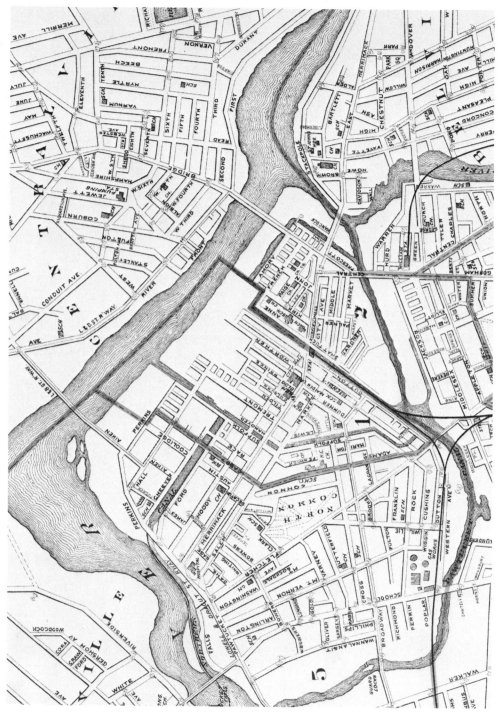

Map, city of Lowell. From *Atlas of Massachusetts* (Boston: George H. Walker & Co., 1891).

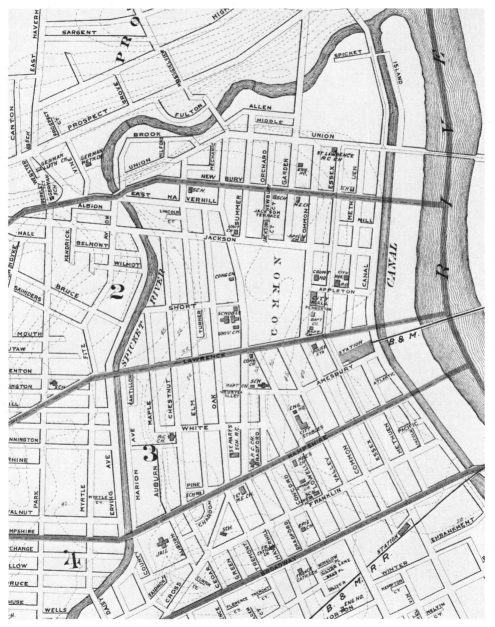

Map, city of Lawrence. From *Atlas of Massachusetts* (Boston: George H. Walker & Co., 1891).

The Peer and the Pauper, title page from original manuscript.

Chadwick and Victor Herbert wearing each other's hats, in Springfield, Massachusetts, spring 1890. Photo by George H. Van Norman, Springfield. Courtesy of the heirs of George Whitefield Chadwick.

Chadwick, c. 1910.

Horatio W. Parker. Photo by Pirie MacDonald, New York.

Chadwick at play with a cat, West Chop, Martha's Vineyard, Massachusetts. Courtesy of the heirs of George Whitefield Chadwick.

NEW ENGLAND
CONSERVATORY OF MUSIC

A CONCERT

IN MEMORY OF

GEORGE WHITEFIELD CHADWICK

NOVEMBER 13, 1854   APRIL 4, 1931

Director Emeritus

JORDAN HALL

MAY THE NINETEENTH

NINETEEN HUNDRED AND THIRTY-ONE

New England Conservatory Memorial Concert, May 19, 1931, title page.

CHAPTER 11

Dean of American Composers

During this period the conservatory director added to his duties a most prestigious but ill-starred position. In 1899 he resigned as director of the Springfield Festival to assume the directorship of the Worcester Festival, a post Carl Zerrahn had held for many years. Zerrahn, whose conducting career had begun the year of Chadwick's birth, was one of the members of the Germania, the first professional symphonic orchestra in America. Along with B. J. Lang, he was a leader of Boston's musical renaissance. In 1872 Zerrahn served as the conductor of P. S. Gilmore's World Peace Jubilee chorus, and in 1866 he had taken over the direction of the Worcester Festival.

The Worcester critics and chorus never quite took to the younger man from Boston. Those qualities that had gained Chadwick respect among a wide spectrum of musicians—from professionals to conservatory students— were not calculated to endear him to adult amateurs. Besides, he had to overcome the thirty-year Zerrahn tradition. Not until his third season did he achieve "total acceptance by a chorus that had been firm in its devotion" to the former leader. The critic for Worcester's *Evening Gazette* condescendingly confirmed both Chadwick's initial difficulties and their tentative resolution: "Mr. Chadwick seems to have justified his appointment as conductor about which there was some discussion after his first year of service. . . . The chorus now understands him better." [108]

As if appeasing amateurs was not enough, Chadwick also encountered problems with the orchestra. Although its members were drawn from the Boston Symphony Orchestra and therefore were the best players available, far too few rehearsals were budgeted. Consequently, the music suffered, especially the novelties. Frederick R. Burton, covering the premiere of Chadwick's *Judith* for the *New York Times,* describes a typical situation:

> The Orchestra was the Boston Symphony, which is saying a good deal, but there should have been some more rehearsals. Not once were the chorus, soloists and orchestra brought together until the hour of performance. In other words "Judith" was not played and sung through once before its critical trial on the audience. . . . [109]

Not until the Berkshire Festival, at Tanglewood, Massachusetts, would it be possible to perform music in the summer according to winter standards.

In spite of these conditions, the composer-conductor was able to present an array of important but generally neglected works, illustrating his catholic taste in music: Berlioz's *The Damnation of Faust;* MacDowell's *Lancelot and Elaine;* Glazunov's Symphony No. 6 in C Minor; Brahms's *German Requiem;* Dvořák's *Scherzo capriccioso;* Verdi's *Te Deum;* and the first performance in English of Franck's *Les Béatitudes.*

Nevertheless, Chadwick found it impossible to continue in a position where his popularity with an amateur chorus was the major criterion for success. He resigned after the 1901 season and handed over his baton to his protégé Wallace Goodrich, who would later also succeed him at the conservatory.

In the last creative period of his life, from about 1897 to the end of World War I, Chadwick turned out a series of works mainly for orchestra and the theater. Works like the operas *Judith,* based upon a feminist biblical theme, and *The Padrone,* a tale of lovers thwarted by the politics of immigration; the orchestral *Symphonic Sketches,* with their genre scenes of contemporary American life (painterly music presaging the unique combination of realism and humor of Norman Rockwell's art); and the symphonic ballad *Tam O'Shanter,* an orchestral poem of Anglo-Celtic imagination—all presented Chadwick's final and mature auralizations. They should have helped form a national repertory because, beyond the skill and craft they exhibited, these pieces demonstrated constructive and textural elements that, taken together, might be defined as a recipe for an American style in the novel or in art. This recipe was based upon a subconscious inclination toward modal-pentatonic tunes, the lilt of Celtic song, the rhythms of prosodically derived syncopation and Afro-Caribbean dance, a tilt toward subdominant harmonies, and the sonorities of the organ and brass band.

Perhaps the best example of this natural American formulation is heard in "Jubilee," the first of the *Symphonic Sketches*. It can be found in the curious combination of the habanera rhythm, used as an accompaniment, with a pentatonic tune harmonized in the subdominant and colored by harmonica- and guitarlike sonorities in the orchestra. The evocation of the loneliness of broad spaces traversed by a rider and horse at a trot is banished by raucous cornet and tambourine sounds.

With *The Padrone,* an ill-fated work doomed, so it seems, because of its rejection by the Metropolitan Opera, Chadwick reached a peak in the history of American opera. Despite the fact that it was never proven in an actual stage (or even concert) performance, the completed orchestral score bears all the hallmarks of a noble, viable work. Aside from other considerations—musicality, dramatic interest, scenic design, vocality, all of which *The Padrone* displays with flair—it is the composer's sensitivity to the intimate relationship between the prosody of the words and his musical invention that is most noticeable. His derivation of the rhythm from language, which alone assures immediate comprehension of sung words, should have been, along with Chadwick's "American" recipe, the vade mecum of every subsequent American composer.

However, it was not. The very process of immigration, which *The Padrone* sympathetically examined, was to be the cause of a gap in the continuity of American musical history between older composers of Yankee stock and young modernists, many of whom were first- or second-generation immigrants. As the Yankee "fathers" tended not to recognize the ethnic (i.e., American) legitimacy of the upstart "sons," the sons, in turn, denied their musical "parents" the usual filial affection and respect and even, at times, their existence.[110]

To this ethnic and aesthetic antipathy must be added, as reasons for the failure of works such as Chadwick's to become the basis of a classical American musical repertory, the gradual loss of Boston's preeminent musical and cultural position to New York and the increasing importance of theatrical, mechanical, recorded, and movie music. Thus, the continuity of American creative musical history was effectively severed. Ironically, when the American style was demanded during the New Deal days, it had to be reinvented, this time by reference to material found in library books rather than from mother's milk.

Finally, in Chadwick's case, performance of his works declined, even in Boston, as the older, sympathetic German conductors of the Boston Symphony were replaced by directors of French and Slavic origins. Especially during the quarter-century reign of Serge Koussevitsky, from the 1920s onward, performances of works by the Boston School ebbed until, given the almost absolute lack of recording, the only way in which such music survived was in silent scores on the shelves of a few libraries.

As a man and as a creative artist, Chadwick was greatly rewarded and honored at the crest of his career. He lived comfortably enough both in his 360 Marlborough Street townhouse during the academic year as well as in his West Chop summer home on Martha's Vineyard, where he did most of his composing. His happy marriage had borne him two sons, Theodore and Noel, who survived him up to the third quarter of the twentieth century. He must have been proud of both. Theodore had achieved all the social and business goals that the grandfather he never knew, Alonzo Calvin, had wished for his son. It was Theodore, rather than his father, who was the classic Bostonian of the Marquand novels: a graduate of Harvard, a soldier in the Yankee Division in World War I, a broker with the prestigious firm of Paine, Webber, Jackson and Curtis, and (like his father) a Son of the American Revolution. Noel, the second son, if not the achiever his older brother was, must have been the more adorable as a child. He was the inspiration for two tender and sensitive works that Chadwick wrote—"Noel" the slow second movement of the *Symphonic Sketches* and *Noel,* the oratorio with its texts arranged and selected by the composer and Mrs. Chadwick.

Besides the personal satisfaction of a happy marriage and children, Chadwick received all manner of public recognition. In 1905 Chadwick was honored by the Concordia of Leipzig, where he traveled to conduct a concert of his works. The *Boston Globe* reported the event:

LEIPSIC DISCOVERS A BOSTON COMPOSER

. . . last month [November] in Leipsic, where he studied years ago, the Concordia Choral Society gave a concert in his honor, at which he conducted his familiar overture, "Melpomene"; his hymn for male chorus "Ecce Jam Noctis"; and his third symphony in F Major, that we heard for the first time ten years ago. As he had only an orchestra from one of the regimental bands of the garrison, the performance must have proceeded under some difficulties, but one of the Leipsic reviewers writes warmly of this symphony in this wise:

"I declare that I consider this symphony the best of all that have been written since Brahms. It is extraordinarily rich in tone color and masterly in construction and instrumentation. It is hard to say what most strongly seizes the listener—the joyous energy of the first movement, the original humor of the third, or the sturdy manliness of the last which closes in such splendid pomp. The rhythmic variety, in harmonic detail, the superb tone-coloring and the wonderfully clear part-writing all demand unstinted praise. . . . From this symphony I hold George Chadwick the most important living Anglo-American composer, Elgar not excepted. . . ."[111]

Another memorable event was a transcontinental trip in 1915 with Ida May and the composers Mabel Daniels and Horatio Parker to Los Angeles, where Parker was to receive a prize from the National Federation of Women's Clubs for his opera *Fairyland*. After the ceremony for his erstwhile student, Chadwick and the troupe turned north to San Francisco for an American Composers Day given in connection with the Panama-Pacific International Exposition. There in front of the neoclassical facade of Festival Hall, leaders of American music posed momentarily for a photograph. With Mabel Daniels and Mrs. H. H. A. Beach occupying the center, ten American composers lined up on the steps. The photograph gives us a revealing indication of Chadwick's physical stature and condition at age sixty. Clearly supporting his right leg with a cane, injured, according to his son Theodore, as early as 1898 aboard a transatlantic steamer, he appears the shortest of the group save Mrs. Beach. By contrast, Horatio Parker, wearing an up-to-date turned-down collar (Chadwick wore a conservative wing collar) stands lanky and tall, a model of robust health, a fact that may explain Chadwick's shock when Parker suddenly died only five years later, in 1920.

During the last years, gout and heart disease increasingly restricted

Chadwick's activities and output. Besides the daily exertions as an administrator, instructor, and conductor, he still found energy for composition as attested by the *Anniversary Overture* (1922), commemorating his twenty-fifth anniversary as director of the New England Conservatory, and *Tre Pezzi*, a suite for orchestra written later. But it was evident that his main creative force was spent. No matter. He had achieved more than he had ever dreamed of, and he could console himself as well by taking pleasure in his expanding family, his friends, and in the many tokens of recognition he had received. Chadwick had already made up for dropping out of high school by receiving honorary degrees from Yale (A.M., 1897) and Tufts (LL.D., 1905). He was a member of both the American Academy of Arts and Letters and the National Institute of Arts and Letters, which awarded him its Gold Medal in 1928.

In 1930, at the close of his public career, he was given a banquet and retrospective concert billed as "The fiftieth anniversary of his first professional appearance as conductor and composer."

> For almost two hours last night G. W. Chadwick sat as a guest of honor at a banquet . . . and heard a half a dozen or more speakers eulogize his career and works. And as the final speaker . . . Mr. Chadwick gave a simple, gracious account of himself . . . he did so extremely well. For without rebuffing the encomiums so heartily proffered him, and avoiding complacency, he turned what began as a brief outline of his own musical experiences into a thoroughly engrossing tale of the musical history of Boston during the past fifty years.[112]

A year later, on Thursday April 4, 1931, Chadwick died in his sleep of complications due to arteriosclerosis. He was seventy-six. Funeral services were held at Trinity Church in Copley Square. His body was cremated, and the ashes were buried in Mount Auburn Cemetery in Cambridge on the Charles, not far from the site of the homestead of the first Chadwick in America, thereby completing a cycle of exactly four centuries.

The following Monday, the editorial pages of all the Boston newspapers were devoted to obituaries of the composer and educator:

> He found the New England Conservatory a singing school and left it a national institution of the highest standing. President Eliot accomplished no more for higher education than Mr. Chadwick in his own field. . . . Although he received a severe formal training in Germany—

he used to regret that he had not studied in Paris, also—he was American to the very core. That American spirit which has recently gone to such extremes in jazz was in him. . . . He was one of our great American pioneers of the spirit.[113]

Although a conservative he was by no means lacking in humor, as is witnessed by the fact that his burlesque opera "Tabasco" won popularity no less certain than his serious opera "Judith" or his overture "Melpomene"—to name two of his more important works—won critical recognition. The influence of his artistic integrity and personal character on the musical culture of the United States will be permanent.[114]

Olin Downes in the *New York Times* confirmed Boston's estimates of the man's importance: "When all is said and done, he more than any other one man gives his creative period its stamp and character and represents most completely the body of serious American music."[115]

Sadly for Chadwick, Downes's perceptive opinion did not represent the views of the new generation of tastemakers who would shape cultural history during the four-term reign of Franklin Roosevelt. The New Deal not only brought with it such liberating programs as Social Security, the institutionalization of trade unions, and the forty-hour week but also helped elevate an entirely new class of Americans into positions of power and influence in government, academia, and the arts. For these "new" Americans, history was not so much a matter of genealogy or instinct, as it was for Chadwick, who was a Son of the American Revolution (his national number was 13980).[116] It was, rather, a required school subject. Many of them were themselves first- or second-generation immigrants who had little reason to be sympathetic to the old-timers who had often erected barriers to their advancement through preference for family name and religion over merit. The antipathies generated by ethnic fears and economic rivalry spilled over into social and aesthetic realms. People began to fear dilution of traditional American values, which the nativists tried to prevent by founding such organizations as the Sons of the American Revolution, dedicated to the fostering of "true patriotism and love of country" and therefore limited to only "such persons who can *prove their descent* from well-authenticated patriot Revolutionary ancestry."[117] Ultimately, Congress passed the first comprehensive Immigration Act of 1924 to stem the flow of non-Protestant populations, the multiplication of foreign linguistic enclaves, and people with darker skins. In music the popularity of ragtime, jazz, and melodies and performers with Jewish mannerisms was seen as the result of an insidious conspiracy to infect and destroy the white, Anglo-Saxon melos. Even on more elevated planes of discussion, conservatives rallied against modernist tendencies in music as typified by Debussy, Stravinsky, and Schoenberg and spread by the new immigrant-dominated generation as an indication of the breakdown of long-held aesthetic principles.

Chadwick's reputation began to suffer during the 1920s. Seeing the victories he and his native-born colleagues had won for American music being snatched out of his grasp and being increasingly ignored as irrelevant must have been bitter medicine to swallow in spite of the kudos of his friends. And the rub was that only he knew of his humble social and economic origins—that he came from New Hampshire peasantry, had experienced the trauma of maternal loss and separation in infancy from family, and lacked any of the advantages he might have been supposed to have, on account of his name, from old-school ties. Perhaps he might have been expected to have more than a little sympathy for the new breed of Americans coming from people uprooted, deracinated. Indeed, his populist realism in such works as his Second Symphony, *Symphonic Sketches,* and, especially, *The Padrone* prove to anyone who cared to know his progressive emotional and intellectual attitude toward the common man, Yankee or immigrant. Yet it cannot be denied that, like others of his native ancestry, he may have worn his prejudices like badges of merit.

Warren Storey Smith, the Boston critic and teacher, related an anecdote that illustrates such seemingly logical inconsistencies. During a meeting one day in his office, Chadwick noticed Smith looking at a marking in the margin of a student's record: "B D W." Upon Smith's inquiry as to the meaning of the notation, Chadwick smiled as he replied: "Born dat way," indicating the student's color.[118] Nevertheless, it was William Grant Still, the most important academically trained black American twentieth-century composer and conductor, who freely credited his success to Chadwick's concern and encouragement. Chadwick thought so much of Still that he gave him private lessons at no cost.

For Chadwick, the label of "conservative," too, must have been difficult to bear. Given that he was born only twenty-seven years after Beethoven's death, it should not be surprising that his works are marked by an adherence to common-practice harmony, regular metric division, and vocal melody. He was indeed conservative. Using the same logic, however, when one does hear irregular, syncopated rhythms, parallel voice-leading, and the ubiquitous presence of pentatonic melody, all part of the modernist canon, he should be credited all the more for his creative individualism. But the complexities or even contradictions of Chadwick's life and music never became questions to be mulled over by his successors.

Aided by conductors such as Pierre Monteux and Serge Koussevitsky, works of the newer composers such as Aaron Copland and George Gershwin seemed suddenly to displace the compositions of the Yankee school from symphony programs. In the first age of music broadcast over the radio, recordings, and motion pictures, composers allied with the League of Composers and their journal, *Modern Music,* supplanted the previous representatives of American art music in the eyes of the media. As a result, very little music of Chadwick's generation was perpetuated in actual performance or on discs. For all practical purposes, its repertory was dead.

Chadwick's formulations of an American-sounding music, and through it an artistic pipeline into the rich thesaurus of American dance music, popular melody, and hymn tunes, were effectively hidden or ignored. When the New Deal called for art both to express the aspirations of the common man and to teach the socially beneficial uses to which it could be applied, hundreds of unemployed intellectuals, artists, and performers were put to work rediscovering the roots of liberal cultural Americanisms. In music, they bypassed the already proven recipe for an American style in serious music and proceeded to reinvent it through research into published vernacular or historic forms. Then, with the awesome power of theater, movies, recordings, concerts, critics, and finally the academy, they also created a new history and repertory of American music that, in effect, began with themselves. By the 1950s the Yankee musicians were labeled Europeanizers, as if they had committed musical adultery. John Knowles Paine's two noble symphonies were dismissed as being "primarily of historical interest." Chadwick's populist realism was merely "toying with the seamy side of life" and had "no real roots in the cultural traditions of his own land."[119] Such opinions betrayed a lack of aural knowledge of the music and an indifference to the populist artistic motivations of a composer like Chadwick. Commissioned to compose an oratorio, *Noel,* for the Norfolk Festival in 1909, Chadwick accepted, saying:

> [I]t is my conviction that if musical art and taste is to be kept alive in this country, it will be not alone by performance of grand opera, symphony concerts, and great schools of music, but by the cooperation of the people themselves as singers and players in the performance of good music. In the earlier days of New England there were many flourishing musical societies containing both singers and instrumentalists. The singing school was ubiquitous. In the year 1836 one of them was taught by my father, and one of his students was my mother. It is this kind of work which is now fostered and nurtured by societies like the Litchfield County University Club, and it is, therefore, a matter of particular pleasure and pride as a New Englander and descendant of New Englanders that I should be invited to compose this work for you.[120]

In the 1960s the Music Library Association found that of the total number of recordings of American art music, very few were devoted to works written before 1920.[121]

Nevertheless, Chadwick's legacy survives. The New England Conservatory is flourishing half a century after his death. His music is now being made available in reprint editions, and through the medium of concerts and recordings more and more of Chadwick's compositions can be heard in sympathetic performances of varied quality. Less well known and understood, perhaps, is the way Chadwick's gifts and ways of thinking were preserved and continue to influence American musical culture.

One tangible impact on American music was as a teacher. During Chadwick's fifty years as a master of music, he was responsible for training phalanxes of musicians. He imbued them, above all, with a new spirit of professionalism and with an artistic vision that transformed America from a provincial outpost of sectarian hymn singers to the center of world musical activity. His particular blend of traditional Western standards of excellence with Yankee practical pedagogy produced flexible musicians of varied outlook. His famous *Harmony: A Course of Study,* first published in 1897, achieved the stature of a classic during his own lifetime and went through seventy-four editions.[122] It was one of the first texts to present the facts of harmonic voice-leading through examples drawn from the masterpieces of music rather than the usual abstractions of rules. These he expected to be mastered through actual performance at the keyboard rather than in imaginary choirs. He even dealt with "polyharmony," modal progression, augmented triads, parallel voice-leading, and enharmonic notation, all technical features of the avant-garde music of his day.

Always seeing himself as a liberating force rather than a guardian of purity, Chadwick urged his students to explore.

> If, as has been repeatedly stated, the rules forbidding consecutive fifths, octaves, and augmented seconds and false relations, are broken with impunity or even ignored altogether by modern composers, the question arises, why were these rules ever promulgated? To this we may answer, if the effect justifies the means, *any* rule may be disregarded. This usually involves considerations other than purely harmonic ones; orchestral color, rhythm, and the dramatic effect often give striking significance to harmonic combinations and progressions which would otherwise be offensive, or at least unsatisfactory to the normal musical ear. . . . The works of modern masters are full of such example and such justification.[123]

Again, note his progressive attitudes toward such elements as orchestral sonority and rhythm as fundamental elements of form in addition to harmony. He was also one of the first to emphasize practical experience in the performance of orchestral music and opera over graded lessons in piano and voice.

As a professional artist, Chadwick distrusted above all those in American education who would elevate pedagogy and its numerous methodologies to a position of power. Rather, he was sympathetic to the notion that education, especially musical, was most successful when a proficient master was brought in contact with a willing student. To anyone who would listen, he said, "If you can play, you can teach."[124]

The success of Chadwick's teaching and its significance to American music history today is obvious in the number and quality of his students. Any casual reading of our music history will disclose that many of its important personalities were Chadwick's pupils or their "descendants."

In particular was his relationship to music at Yale, for example, through Horatio Parker and his musical progeny, Charles Ives, David Stanley Smith, and Quincy Porter, who later became director of the New England Conservatory. Similarly, Chadwick maintained a lifelong connection with Harvard as a friend of John Knowles Paine and through composition students who attended the college: Frederick Shepherd Converse, also later a director of the New England Conservatory, and Edward Burlingame Hill, a professor of music and a teacher of Walter Piston, Leonard Bernstein, and Irving Fine. Daniel Gregory Mason, a most influential and widely read writer on music, a composer, and MacDowell Professor at Columbia, studied with Chadwick while attending Harvard. His successor as chairman of the Columbia music department was Douglas Moore, a student of Parker and Smith at Yale. Another Chadwickian, Arthur Shepherd, was the leading composer and professor of music for almost a quarter of a century at Western Reserve University in Cleveland. Henry Kimball Hadley, a prolific composer of instrumental music and opera who long before Bernstein was dubbed an "Ambassador of Harmony" because of his youth and peripatetic ways, conducting all over Europe and America, was one of Chadwick's prize students. Settling in New York, he became a major musical and cultural personality during the two decades following World War I. Ethelbert Nevin's younger brother, Arthur, who composed the Indian opera *Poia* (Berlin, 1910) and who was professor of music at the University of Kansas, Lawrence, and later a director of music in Memphis, was taught by Chadwick, as was Leroy Robertson, a composer and professor at Brigham Young University of Utah. Margaret Ruthven Lang, daughter of the Boston music arbiter B. J. Lang; Mabel Daniels, long associated with music at Simmons College, Radcliffe, and Harvard; Helen Hood, the song composer; and Anna Priscilla Risher, who won the Presser Prize in composition—all were Chadwick pupils. Or, consider the tie, perhaps obscure, of Samuel Barber to Chadwick via his aunt, opera singer Louise Homer, and uncle Sidney Homer, composer of American art songs, who studied in Boston with Chadwick. Last, although he never actually worked with Chadwick, Walter Piston credited the older composer with introducing him to works of the modern French orchestral school at rehearsals of the conservatory orchestra in Jordan Hall, where Harvard music students were always welcome.

Through his position as the administrator of America's leading music educational institution, his textbooks, and his teaching, Chadwick, more than any other composer of his generation, influenced the progress of American music far into the twentieth century. But it is as composer that he must be judged if he is, at last, to be recognized and revered as one of America's great creative artists.

PART TWO ❧ CHADWICK *The Music*

It is difficult, even today, to make a proper aesthetic evaluation of Chadwick's music without an understanding of musical activity in America during his creative years. Such special pleading is called for because, paradoxically, although music was widespread in America since the settlement in Jamestown in 1607, neither it nor its practitioners were regarded with any particular awe. One could say with license that the American polity, originally based in Protestant Christianity, was founded on the premise that in order to be in good standing, its citizens had to be musicians or at least singers of psalms, hymns, and spiritual songs in the meetinghouse. Music was among the first studies at Harvard College, as indicated by seventeenth-century theses or commencement propositions. In the eighteenth and nineteenth centuries, singing schools were, in effect, the first public schools. Much of what that great educator Horace Mann wrought in creating a public school system was influenced by the earlier enterprise of America's premier musical organizer, Lowell Mason.

Unlike European music, compartmentalized and stylistically influenced by the church, the nobility, the bourgeoisie, and the folk, American music reflected the social and economic contradictions of its flexible class structure and thus resembled a patchwork quilt. Early American music is characterized by the lack of a predominant style. Any style might be employed for a particular function.

So, too, its composers were not specialized. At the beginning, they were merely artisans, merchants, or professionals in other fields. Having a calling for musical expression superior to their compatriots, all of whom as Americans could read music, write it down, and sing, they exercised their right to publish without the necessity for royal patent or noble subvention. Every tune book always began with a how-to section on the rules of music and thus sowed more seeds of musical composition. For love or money many hundreds of such books were published, the most successful of which went into many printings and editions.

After the Revolutionary War, with the establishment of theaters dominated by British personnel, music became, in addition to a religious or secular rite, a home entertainment ritual. Music took on the function of today's cassette player or television as a leisure activity. The piano was the console of family get-togethers, and a music industry as vigorous as today's consumer electronics business grew up to supply the demand for instruments, printed music, and music teachers. In music stores the installment plan made it easy for almost anyone to own a piano. Soon, also, churches were demanding more than congregational singing. Trained vocal "quartettes" and elaborate pipe organs became the new media for God's praises and prayers.

By the time Chadwick was a teenager, had quit high school, and was working in his father's insurance office as a clerk, music was an activity with the promise of a living for anyone who dabbled as an amateur (and everyone did) and who, in addition, resented working for his father.

But the very availability of music lessened its value. As the cheap drives out the dear, music was not generally considered a fine or respected art. This may have been one reason Alonzo Calvin opposed his son's aspirations toward a music career. Anybody could be a Yankee fiddler on the roof. At this advanced stage of his youth, when he was about twenty-two years old, Chadwick probably still had no idea of the metier of a composer in the European sense of the term—that is, a person who dedicates himself to the pursuit of music as a medium of artistic expression and is good enough at it to make an adequate living. Chadwick's conception of the occupation was most certainly teaching and, perhaps, making a little money on the side by writing piano pieces, songs, or dance tunes that might sell. One should remember that his putative career models were not so much Mendelssohn, Schumann, Meyerbeer, and Verdi as Lowell Mason, Carlyle Petersilea, and George F. Root. The ideal of the gifted artist appreciated and supported by a noble patron, a reality in European cultural history even until the twentieth century, was never practical for American musicians.

Thus, it was probably not until his European experience in Leipzig, Dresden, Giverny, and Munich that the pragmatic New Englander, by then almost thirty years old, had an inkling of a career directed by artistic guidelines. Still, it would have to be combined with an income-producing job. Teaching in an institution of higher learning such as a conservatory would remove the ignominy of having to give private lessons. He could also earn a bit more with relatively little expenditure of time and thought by playing the organ on Sundays at a nearby church. Such an olio of jobs would still leave some free time, especially during the summer months, for composition. In a way, then, the American system patronized the serious composer. He would even have some time for performing and conducting, another good way of keeping his name before the public.

By now, one fact should have become clear: There was no such profession as "American composer." Yes, there were many—too many—part-time composers who were essentially amateurs, since they earned their bread doing other things. But, in the classical sense of the term, America had no composers.

Here is the central reason why any comparison between European and American music always tends to be invidious. Here, too, is one reason why any consideration of Chadwick's music must take into account the effects of amateurism as well as that other side of American musical amateurism—academism. The way one earns a living cannot be divorced from one's manner of expression.

Today, after a century of sophistication, this blend of amateurism and academism still stamps American composition. The one area where Chadwick and his confreres might be considered professionals was in education.

Without the tradition of professionalism of his European counterparts or even of his American contemporaries in the fine arts, literature, and architecture, Chadwick's creative output must be judged realistically as the work of an artist oppressed by destructive demands on his time and psyche. An imaginative mind occupied daily with politics, compromise, or the sham of fund-raising cannot suddenly invent remarkable designs in musical sound. The same energy needed for mental concentration in solving problems of sonority cannot be expended on ingenious methods of instruction and concern for the acquisition of knowledge by often recalcitrant pupils without a negative effect on creativity. Compared with their opposite numbers in the other arts, composers of Chadwick's generation must have felt that they were working with insuperable handicaps.

Chadwick and his composer friends had also to struggle for simple respectability. Ironically, that status, so long denied them, is still used by some today as a club with which to beat them after they had achieved it not only for themselves but also for future generations of American composers. The Harvard faculty debates of the 1870s on music as a proper subject for academic credit[1] and the later conflict at Columbia between MacDowell and President Nicholas Murray Butler concerning music as a fine art should be remembered.[2] However, did not this struggle to achieve social parity with their peers tend to separate them from the common wellsprings of their music?

Respectability, amateurism, and academism were the three most significant forces working against the American (i.e., part-time) composer. That Chadwick walked tall despite these millstones, that his best work shed the negative shells such forces tend to erect between the artist's imagination and his art is much to his credit. The same cannot be said of many of his colleagues. Partially freed from these bonds of local circumstance, Chadwick created an American-sounding music of original rhythmic vitality, melodic verve, and orchestral brilliance that has served as a model for his followers and, indirectly, for some subsequent composers who mistakenly thought they had invented it.

CHAPTER 12

Symphonies

As an avowed member of the musical academy, Chadwick naturally and enthusiastically maintained his position as an instrumental composer of abstract designs. In this category, with no less than five string quartets, one piano quintet, and three symphonies, he was unsurpassed in sheer quantity among his coevals. Besides his own drive to meet the challenge of the great masters whose works were his models during the intensive course of study at Leipzig, at least one other factor must be mentioned: the foundation by Henry Lee Higginson in 1881, almost simultaneously with Chadwick's triumphal return to Boston after his student days were over, of the Boston Symphony Orchestra on a professional basis, an entirely novel idea. The presence of this magnificent assemblage of the finest players in the world must have acted as a constant prod to Chadwick's creative imagination, for he knew that any piece he might bring to term would be assured a performance of excellence and that he himself might even expect to conduct from time to time. While the Boston Symphony players were not allowed to accept other employment or do anything to disgrace themselves musically, such as by playing for dances or the theater, they might spread the gospel of good music by teaching and giving recitals. The orchestra not only offered the possibility of performance of orchestral music but also spurred the production of chamber music, especially after the founding of the Kneisel Quartet, named for the symphony's concertmaster.

The two of the three Chadwick symphonies that have been recorded show a remarkable personality. Symphony No. 2 in B♭ Major (1883–84) and Symphony No. 3 in F Major (1894), which was awarded the National Conservatory of Music prize by no less an authority than Antonin Dvořák, are easily identified as Chadwickian even though they were written in the shadow of such symphonists as Brahms, Tchaikovsky, and Dvořák himself. Of the three masters Brahms seems to have been the most influential, especially in Chadwick's Third. A perusal of Boston Symphony programs shows that the interested composer certainly had the opportunity of not only reading the Brahms scores but also hearing them played more than once by one of the best orchestras in the world.

Having said that Chadwick, a product of Leipzig, was writing in an academic style in his symphonies and chamber music (the most academic of forms) does not say much that is surprising. What is significant about these works is that within their accepted rules, Chadwick was able to create a national or, even better, a personal manner comparable to any in that instrumental tradition.

❧ Symphony No. 2 in B♭ Major, op. 21

1883–84
For 2 flutes, 2 oboes, 2 clarinets, 2 bassoons, 4 horns, 2 trumpets, 3 trombones, timpani, and strings
I. Andante non troppo (B♭ major, $\frac{4}{4}$; Allegro con brio (B♭, $\frac{3}{4}$)
II. Allegretto scherzando (F major, $\frac{2}{4}$)
III. Largo e maestoso (D minor, $\frac{3}{4}$); Assai con Fuoco ($\frac{2}{4}$); Tempo I
IV. Allegro molto animato (B♭ major, $\frac{4}{4}$)

The B♭ Major Symphony was not presented to the Boston public all at once. The Scherzo, which became the second movement, was premiered independently in 1884; the first movement was heard in 1885; and then the whole work was given in 1886. The dates are important, for the work sounds to some ears like the "From the New World" Symphony (1893) of Dvořák, whom many writers have touted as a missionary teaching the natives how to weave musical baskets out of their local materials. Quite to the contrary, it was Chadwick's piece, almost a decade earlier, that pioneered the blend of a cosmopolitan symphonic vehicle with American melody, rhythm, and sonority.

The fact that the Scherzo was performed two years before the rest of the work is one indication of the order of composition. But another, internal characteristic confirms the fact that the first, third, and fourth movements

EXAMPLE 1   Symphony No. 2, first movement

were conceived as a group: They are the only movements thematically integrated by the quotation of what may be called the motto motive of the symphony (ex. 1) announced at the very beginning as well as by the recapitulation, in the last movement, of the main themes of all the rest, save the preexistent Scherzo. Another sign of this thematic integration is the close relationship between the main allegro themes of the first and fourth movements, which seem to be mirror images of each other. Of more than just technical significance, this cyclical, or transformative, connection among the movements gives the entire symphony an audible and satisfying organic unity that, important though it may be structurally, is only hinted at by the logical tonal scheme. A penultimate clue to this unusual order of composition is the fact that only the Scherzo lacks the full complement of brass of the other movements. Finally, in regard to the helter-skelter fashioning of the work, it is interesting that the first movement was presented separately in 1885 and originally labeled "Overture B-flat" or "Introduction and Allegro."[3] One may speculate, then, that having composed a jaunty and successful orchestral scherzo in F major and then an overture in B♭ major, the composer made them into a symphony by adding a slow movement in D minor and a finale in B♭ major.

As in Chadwick's other orchestral works, his native, natural sense of instrumental sonority and driving rhythms dominates the mere tonal and thematic organization. The skillful execution of the required four-movement structure in the traditional sequences of tempo and mood—rhetorical, comedic, elegiac, and triumphant—notwithstanding, the symphony's chief attraction lies in its notable American melody (ex. 2) and the kaleidoscopic orchestral sounds that propel it. These qualities were not hidden from contemporary audiences.

EXAMPLE 2   Symphony No. 2, first movement

When the Scherzo was first performed in 1884, William Foster Apthorp, writing in the *Boston Evening Transcript*, called it a

> gem. The themes on which it is built up are both original and taking— the first theme, with its quasi-Irish humorousness (it positively winks at you), is peculiarly happy. The working up of the movement sounds clear and coherent, even at first hearing; the piquant charm of the whole is irresistible. The orchestration is that of a master, and is full of delicious bits of color, without ever becoming outrageous.[4]

That "quasi-Irish" main theme, so called by the critic, is also a clear description, in other words, of its pentatonic, syncopated melodies accompanied by syncopated rhythms (exs. 3, 4).

When the entire symphony was performed in 1886, the *Transcript* described it as anything but pedantic or classic. Instead, it was called

> so unexpected in character that one hardly knows how to take it. . . . We, for one, cannot remember any music of this character being written in the symphonic form. . . . The light, almost operatic character of the thematic material; the constant changes of rhythm; the frequent solo passages—not merely incidental phrases for this or that instrument, but often full-fledged solos of considerable length—all contributed to make the work fall short of what may be called symphonic dignity.[5]

EXAMPLE 3 Symphony No. 2, second movement

EXAMPLE 4 Symphony No. 2, second movement

It is difficult to link the critic's remarks to specifics. However, it may be observed that the composer's symphony made quite an impression on its listeners as an imaginative and novel solution to well-understood symphonic problems.

❧ Symphony No. 3 in F Major

1894
For 2 flutes, 2 oboes, 2 clarinets, 2 bassoons, 4 horns, 2 trumpets, 3 trombones, tuba, timpani, and strings
I. Allegro sostenuto (F major, $\frac{3}{4}$)
II. Andante cantabile (B♭ major, $\frac{3}{4}$)
III. Vivace non troppo (D minor, $\frac{6}{8}$, $\frac{2}{4}$)
IV. Finale: Allegro molto energico (F major, $\frac{6}{4}$, $\frac{4}{4}$)

The first orchestral score by an American published by an American house, Arthur P. Schmidt, without subscription in 1888, Chadwick's Second Symphony may very well have been perused by Dvořák before he wrote his historic "From the New World" Symphony in 1893.[6] Notwithstanding this possibility, it was Dvořák himself who sent Chadwick the news that his Third had won a prize:

> Mr. George W. Chadwick
> 903 Boylston Street
> Boston, Mass.
> I take pleasure in announcing that your symphony offered for the second annual competition of the National Conservatory of Music has obtained the prize. In view of your desire to produce it without delay, we have decided to waive our right.
> > Antonin Dvořák
> > Director
> > National Conservatory of Music[7]

Chadwick's Symphony in F Major, written before he was forty years old, was only his third, but it was to be his last. Curiously, Brahms, whose Third Symphony in F (1884) Chadwick seems to draw on, did not begin his symphonic career until he was about forty-three. Why Chadwick abandoned at so young an age the genre that had won him such favorable comment is puzzling. Although he would continue composing works for symphony orchestra, he would never again concern himself with the symphony proper.

Quite different in atmosphere from the Second, the Third Symphony seems to have been composed in one integrated burst of creative force. But the total effect of the work is attenuated by the first subject of the first movement. It begins with a splendid chordal motto that combines the American flavor of a chromatic subdominant cadence with the blues-like ambiguity of its third degree as well as the noble sound of a royal fanfare (ex. 5). But directly following is a melodic line that vitiates this powerful thrust in fussy elaboration; like a once-powerful stream in a sandy desert, all the force is absorbed in this welter of busy notes going everywhere at the same time. The movement does not regain a definite thematic character until the handsome, waltz-like second subject, introduced by the horns in close harmony (ex. 6). Fortunately, Chadwick emphasized this idea in the subsequent development and episodic section. Like any sonata form in triple meter, this one pays homage to Beethoven's "Eroica," via Brahms, in the clever manipulation of meter and rhythm. Perhaps it was this aspect to which Chadwick referred in a letter to the conductor Theodore Thomas, to whom the symphony is dedicated: "It was very well received here & condemned by some of the news-

EXAMPLE 5   Symphony No. 3, first movement

EXAMPLE 6   Symphony No. 3, first movement

EXAMPLE 7   Symphony No. 3, third movement

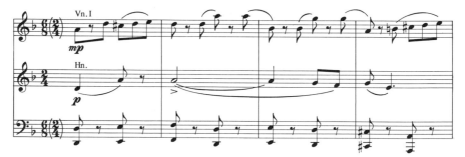

paper men as a 'dry and uninspired work' by which you may guess that it had some features which were not altogether trivial."[8]

Whatever sarcasm Chadwick felt the reviewers deserved for their estimation of the first movement, he certainly had no grounds for dissatisfaction with either the rest of the symphony or its reception. Without resorting to the cyclical devices of his Second Symphony for unity, the movements of the Third present together a coherent whole, the expressive and personal nature of the themes balanced by ingenious interpretation of the standard abstract designs that symphonic movements require. Particularly noticeable is the way

EXAMPLE 8   Symphony No. 3, fourth movement

EXAMPLE 9   Symphony No. 3, fourth movement

in which the scherzo's main horn theme, in $\frac{2}{4}$ meter, is presented only after the listener has been duped very convincingly into thinking that its accompanimental countermelody, a bonny $\frac{6}{8}$ reel, was the principal subject (ex. 7).

In the Finale, Chadwick pummels the accents of his $\frac{6}{4}$ meter into every conceivable grouping, thereby creating syncopated rhythmic designs of great propulsion and energy (ex. 8). Balancing these features is the regular, common-time march of the second subject, hymnic, smooth, and reverent (ex. 9). It may have been this theme that inspired a German critic to aver, "From this symphony, I hold George W. Chadwick to be the most important living Anglo-American composer—Edward Elgar not excepted. . . ."[9]

CHAPTER 13

Chamber Music

One aspect of Chadwick's versatility is vividly demonstrated by his chamber music. Of the five string quartets and one piano quintet, only the quintet received relatively widespread performance and was published both in score and parts. Nevertheless, the third and fourth quarters and the quintet, together with the works of Arthur Foote, Mrs. H. H. A. Beach, Arthur Whiting, and Daniel Gregory Mason, to mention only a few, have come to be recognized as a treasure trove of intellectual music composed during a period not generally known for its devotion to the chamber.

As an adept orchestrator, Chadwick might be considered to be at a disadvantage in a medium whose limited possibilities for instrumental color place a high premium on thematic invention, contrapuntal skill, and architectural design. Then, too, the realm of chamber music presented a knowledgeable audience that might be ignored by a composer only at the peril of invidious comparison with the masters of the form.

Yet from the very beginning Chadwick seemed impelled to produce in this field and did so for almost a quarter of a century. Then, just when one might have expected him to continue composing chamber music because of his mastery of the form, his academic position, and the growing introspection usually associated with age and experience, he stopped. As in his production of symphonies, which ended when he was a mere thirty-nine years old, he ceased the composition of chamber music for all practical purposes. He was just past forty-four and was to live on for about thirty-three more years.

❧ String Quartet No. 3 in D Major

1886
For 2 violins, viola, and violoncello
I. Allegro di molto (D major, $\frac{3}{4}$)
II. Tema con variazione: Adagio (D minor, $\frac{2}{4}$) Tempo risoluto, Moderato piu mosso, com moto
III. Allegretto simplice (G major, $\frac{3}{4}$)
IV. Finale: Allegro vivace (D major, $\frac{6}{8}$)

Chadwick's first two string quartets (1878, 1879), student works that helped launch his career, attracted much favorable comment in German, English, and American musical periodicals. The third quartet, his first masterly essay in the genre, however, seems to have been shrouded in obscurity. It was never published. Its holographic score was missing. Only a set of copyist's parts, a few concert listings, short notices, and the later fourth and fifth quartets indicated its existence. For a long time, even the date of composition and its dedicatee were unknown. Then, in 1986, a sharp-eyed graduate student spotted the fading manuscript among leaves of secondhand music in a New York City shop.[10] It indicated that the quartet was completed one hundred years earlier, on May 25, 1886, and was dedicated to Chadwick's friend and colleague Arthur Foote. Foote, coincidentally, was the secretary of the Euterpe chamber music organization, which sponsored the work's Boston premiere on March 9, 1887.[11]

Together with the piano quintet, this charming quartet established the thirty-one-year-old composer as a master of chamber music. With newfound confidence Chadwick here crafts a work with both a hint of his personal "American" manner to come and tokens of his talent for designing music in the traditional developmental forms. Each of the four movements conveys a distinctly different mood, although the second—a theme and variations in which some saw the influence of Schubert's "Death and the Maiden" Quartet[12]—displays further the many possibilities of its hymn tune subject (ex. 10). Still reflecting the impact of southern German culture, the third ("dance") movement, presents a lilting *ländler*. The Finale, with a spectacular fugue in the development, is a large-scale tarantella in sonata form. And the first movement oscillates between a main theme that sounds like the initial four notes of the *Messiah's* "Hallelujah" Chorus (ex. 11) and a pretty waltz.

EXAMPLE 10   String Quartet No. 3, second movement

EXAMPLE 11   String Quartet No. 3, first movement

Having failed to achieve publication, as did the contemporaneous Second Symphony, the piano quintet, *Melpomene,* and the succeeding fourth quartet, the third quartet fell in between the cracks of time. After a couple of performances, including one in New York on November 22, 1887,[13] given by his friend Gustav Dannreuther's group, the Beethoven String Quartette, the professionally copied parts gathered dust on Chadwick's desk, and the score, on slowly oxidizing paper, ultimately found its way to the secondhand bins of a music seller.

As a transitional work, the third quartet signals Chadwick's mature style. Although far from the easily recognizable American cut of the fourth quartet, written a decade later, in 1896, it has the features of a serviceable suit of clothes: good material and fine tailoring.[14]

String Quartet No. 4 in E Minor

1896
For 2 violins, viola, and violoncello
I. Andante (E minor, $\frac{4}{4}$); Allegro moderato
II. Andantino semplice (A major, $\frac{3}{8}$)
III. Giocoso, un poco moderato (C major, $\frac{2}{4}$)
IV. Finale: Allegro molto risoluto; Lento espressivo; Allegro con brio; Presto (E minor, $\frac{6}{4}$)

With the Quartet No. 4 in E Minor, according to William Foster Apthorp in the *Transcript,* Chadwick arrived at a proper balance between the "Irish"-sounding high-jinks of the Scherzo of his Second Symphony and the brooding seriousness of his tragic overture *Melpomene.* The reviewer heard in the quartet the "genially humorous Chadwick again, but with his sense of humor refined, ideallized, and held within artistic bounds."[15] Instructive, as well, was the writer's identification of Chadwick's American flavor as Irish. But he simply could not let go of this apperception. He had to rub it in: "The characteristic Irish brogue still remains—we believe Mr. Chadwick has a drop or two of Gaelic blood in him, and the Gael and the Kelt are cousins—." Now, Chadwick was pure Yankee back to 1631 and English on both sides even beyond. Still the critic had to continue his flawed explication of the ethnic roots of the quartet: "But the Irish turn of this or that phrase has nothing of vulgarity in it, neither does it impress one as indicating a with-malice-prepense dive into volkslied; it all sounds wholly instinctive and natural."

What is one to make of this insistence that the joviality, the skylarking, the sly winking, the jollity, the geniality, the humor of Chadwick's personal style were imported from Erin or perhaps Scotland (any place but New England); that Chadwick deserved praise for avoiding Irish vulgarity, however; and that, certainly, one should not consider these characteristics native American? How should one interpret all this semiserious casting of aspersions upon Chadwick's ancestry in a society that valued pure blood lines unadulterated by non-English mixtures above all?

Maybe it was this kind of criticism that moved Chadwick away from the standard genres. In a way, as a composer of sonata form, he was like the Olympic figure skater who is damned if he dares to be too original and damned if he executes too perfectly the compulsory figures. Such animadversions, no matter how jocularly intended or charitably made by the patrician Apthorp, could not but get under the skin of Chadwick, who had at last won a degree of equanimity and self-confidence after long struggle. For his part, even Apthorp admitted this ingrained suspicion of the lighter side of art. "I much fear," he once wrote, "that what sorely troubles most of us Anglo-Saxons, in our relations to the fine arts, is that precious tendency of ours to take everything by its ethical side first."[16]

Heard today, a century later, one wonders what exactly Apthorp was getting at. Chadwick's now-distinctive Yankee melodic style in the fourth quartet does not sound even vaguely Irish. With its gapped tetrachords and prosodic syncopations, accompanied by the typical subdominant model harmonies, it presents classical models of typically American tunes from the same mold as William Billings or Stephen Foster. Right from the beginning of the first movement, this formulation dominates the sound of the piece and, for the moment, obscures and makes irrelevant the conventional tonal sonata design (ex. 12). So fresh is the effect of hearing these beautiful and distinctive tunes that one need not focus on the tonal organization or other details of composition. Yet the contrapuntal working out of these themes and

EXAMPLE 12   String Quartet No. 4, first movement

their constituent phrases demonstrates Chadwick's natural ability to manip-
ulate, rearrange, and redefine aspects of his two main subjects in the tradition
of sonata form.

Besides developmental displays, Chadwick also demonstrates his ear for
extending the normal range of string sonorities. At the end of the slow second movement is a completely unexpected use of artificial and natural harmonics as an obbligato to the theme in *pianissimo* pizzicatos.

After a typical Chadwickian scherzo full of driving rhythms (ex. 13) and
especially a syncopated close-harmony phrase (ex. 14) that sounds as if it was
excerpted from a comic opera comes the archetypal Finale.

A series of variations on a hymn tune, the form of the fourth movement
is novel.[17] It consists of four basic tempo sequences. The first, Allegro molto
risoluto, introduces in unison the amazing facsimile of a Yankee tune, at once
betraying its roots by a modal and gapped tetrachordal series of tones. The
monophonic presentation reminds one of the old-fashioned singing of
psalms led by a deacon in a meetinghouse (ex. 15). Chadwick leads his quartet
of strings through a chain of variations: a dazzling display of his perception

EXAMPLE 13 String Quartet No. 4, third movement

EXAMPLE 14 String Quartet No. 4, third movement

EXAMPLE 15 String Quartet No. 4, fourth movement

of the harmonies, figurations, textures, and rhythms inherent in the hymn tune motive; and a variation that counterpoints a lilting fiddle tune with the hymn tune. After a cadence, the Allegro is transformed into a Lento expressivo. Then, one hears what seems to be a new, sentimental song with a varied repetition only to realize that this is nothing but an imaginative transformation of the original theme. Ending abruptly, a third tempo, Allegro con brio, returns to the literal version of the hymn tune, now energized rhythmically as a fugue subject and countersubject. There is a complete exposition, an episode, and one entry in augmentation, all sophisticated reminders of the aboriginal fuging tunes of Jeremiah Ingalls and Jacob French. The tempo changes a fourth and last time to an even faster Presto, in which the main theme is compressed by diminution. A final statement, accompanied by chordal punctuation, ends the piece.

Where Apthorp got an impression of Gaelic humor in the quartet as a whole or particularly in this Finale is difficult to say, for the movement itself stands as a textbook example of a late nineteenth-century piece that, in effect, recapitulates the whole history of American music from its origins in the tunes of the Anglo-Genevan Psalter and the Bay Psalm Book, through the singing schools, and to its reunion with continental academism of the romantics. Unlike some of the American composers a generation or so later, Chadwick did not find *his* American melodic material in a library. He wrote the way he sang, the way his folks sang in Nathaniel D. Gould's singing school in Boscawen, New Hampshire, and the way all the other Fittses and Chadwicks had sung for generations.

❧ Quintet in E♭ Major for Piano and Strings

1887
For Piano, 2 violins, viola, and violoncello
I. Allegro sostenuto (E♭ major, $\frac{4}{4}$)
II. Andante cantabile (A♭ major, $\frac{4}{4}$)
III. Intermezzo: Allegretto ma poco risoluto (C minor, $\frac{3}{4}$)
IV. Finale: Allegro energico (E♭ major, $\frac{4}{4}$)

A good indication of Chadwick's reputation in Boston cultural circles for jollification in the years immediately following his triumphal return from

Europe in 1880 comes from a *Boston Evening Transcript* review of his Quintet in E♭ Major. It is quite clear from the writer's choice of words and allusions that, in those years at least, the young man from Lawrence was considered somewhat of a cutup, a provocative gadfly. He was criticized for flavoring

> some of his earlier works . . . with a certain, easy-going joviality of humor that not only verged dangerously on the trivial, but even made it, at moments, hard to believe that the composer was really taking himself seriously. Certain passages in the first and second symphonies almost made one wish that Mr. Chadwick would have done with the sonata for good and all, and, like Sir Arthur Sullivan, content himself with a more easily won success in the field of comic opera.[18]

The *Melpomene* overture (1887) had gone a long way to quiet such fears as to Chadwick's probity, but it was not until this quintet, following quickly in succession, that "all doubts of this sort" were dissipated. Even though, the reviewer admits, some of the thematic material is still "light-hearted, jovial and rollicking . . . the treatment is always dignified and earnest in musical purposes. The composer had kept himself as clear of triviality as possible."

The *Transcript* critic (perhaps Apthorp?) did not quite seem to accept Chadwick's quintet as a *bona fide* of his conversion to seriousness or believe that it completely "gave assurance of the composer's having conquered what was at one time his besetting fault. . . ." Amusing as these insights into Chadwick's character and style may be a century later, they also reveal that among his Boston School contemporaries he stood out as quite a personality and that even in his academic essays his American style, characterized by "rollicking musical material" treated in a dignified way, was unique. Forty years later, another *Transcript* evaluation by H. T. Parker praised Chadwick, in barnyard lingo, for "his skill with the matings . . . of piano and strings."[19] Curiously, Parker failed to hear "the American quality that usually seeped into his chamber, as well as his symphonic, pieces." Be that as it may, the quintet, published by Arthur P. Schmidt in 1890, together with the fourth quartet remain the two most popular of Chadwick's chamber works.

The quintet follows the standard scheme of four movements in contrasting tempos and tonalities related to its stated key. Beyond conforming to a general tradition, there appear to be some specific reflections of Brahms's

EXAMPLE 16   Quintet for Piano and Strings, third movement

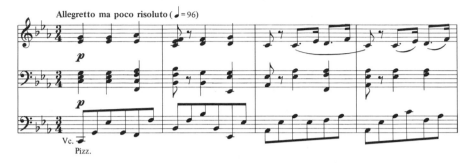

Quintet, op. 34, and his Fourth Symphony, both of which were performed in Boston before the completion of this piece in 1887. The opening theme of the Intermezzo, the third movement, for example, seems to recall the second movement motive of Brahms's Fourth (ex. 16), and the beginning of the last movement (ex. 17) exhibits the same rhythmic relationships between the *perpetuum mobile* accompanying figure and the main melodic idea, as in the last movement of the Brahms quintet. Nevertheless, every movement of the Chadwick piece shows his own personality through the unique thematic and harmonic emphasis on gapped-scale melody and subdominant harmony. So also does the Boston quintet define itself rhythmically in terms of syncopations and the dance-like lilt of uneven notes. These were, perhaps, the personal moods of the "rollicking musical material" that created the sentimental "theatrical" affect noticed by the *Transcript*.

The Finale is by far the best of the four movements. Its bustle and snap were recognized by contemporary audiences and critics. The first theme, particularly, establishes what one listener called "a rushing, stirring movement, carried through with admirable force and energy."[20] The engine of this energy is the *perpetuum mobile* figuration, which, while reminiscent of Brahms's works for its function, sounds more like a fiddle tune, say, "The Devil Among the Tailors." Over this rides a syncopated tune that, in time, will allow Chadwick to indulge in his favorite horn-call intervals, going up the diatonic scale of the harmonic series. The less rhythmically active secondary theme similarly

EXAMPLE 17 Quintet for Piano and Strings, fourth movement

telegraphs Chadwick's intention to later display his nimble fugal skills. In this he does not disappoint. He leads his thematic steed through all the best of the possible contrapuntal capers, including very close stretto.

Then, precisely at the climax of the speeded-up coda, the composer reveals—with only eight notes—the hidden purpose of the whole quintet. A descending scale, clearly in the shape and rhythm of Mendelssohn's "Wedding March," relates the music to its dedicatees, "Mrs. and Mr. Gustav Dannreuther, New-York," recently wed friends.[21] Apparently the reviewer of the *Transcript* who had so questioned Chadwick's seriousness and who finally and grudgingly had accepted the quintet as an earnest of his reformed ways, missed this musical pun, a symbol of Hymen.

CHAPTER 14

Orchestral Music

Chadwick stopped writing symphonies in 1894 with his Third Symphony, but he did not stop writing in symphonic form. The *Symphonic Sketches,* the *Sinfonietta* in D Major, and the *Suite Symphonique* in E♭ Major are, in reality, symphonies in the conventional four movements, with organic tonal relationships and tempo sequence, and intended for symphony orchestra. Why Chadwick felt uneasy about using the title *symphony* is hard to say. It may be that as he matured and became more knowledgeable in the ways of journalistic criticism, he shied away from a name that might make him more vulnerable to invidious comparison. His use of the derivative adjective, *symphonic,* or the diminutive, *sinfonietta,* might have been motivated by a desire to deny reviewers a weapon. But if the last three symphonic works are considered together, an answer may also be found in the novelty of the musical material. In contrast to the three named symphonies, they tend to be influenced less by the Teutonic and more by an American style: a greater emphasis on rhythmic and pulse modulations, exploration of nondominant harmonies, and orchestral sounds in which individual timbres sparkle. As such, they lie outside the domain of the Central European symphony. Another explanation for such labels may be that Chadwick himself considered his last "symphonies" musical entertainments conforming aesthetically more to the original late eighteenth-century models than to the late nineteenth-century secular liturgies that all seem to deal with ultimate questions.

❧ Symphonic Sketches

"Jubilee," 1895; "Noel," 1895; "Hobgoblin," 1904; "A Vagrom Ballad," 1896
For 2 flutes and piccolo, 2 oboes and English horn, 2 clarinets and bass clarinet, 2

bassoons, 4 horns, 2 trumpets, 3 trombones, timpani, bass drum, cymbals, side
drum, triangle, tambourine, xylophone, harp, and strings
I. ("Jubilee"): Allegro molto vivace (A major, $\frac{6}{4}$, $\frac{4}{4}$)
II. ("Noel"): Andante con tenerezza (D♭ major, $\frac{3}{4}$)
III. ("Hobgoblin"): Allegro vivace (F major, $\frac{3}{4}$)
IV. ("A Vagrom Ballad"): Moderato. Alla burla (A minor, $\frac{2}{4}$); Molto vivace—
Prestissimo (A major, $\frac{6}{8}$)

Written between 1895 and 1904, the *Symphonic Sketches* were neither tone
poems such as *Tam O'Shanter* nor formal sonata-form movements as in the
symphonies. Halfway between the abstract and the representative, the
Sketches nevertheless may be considered a perfectly respectable symphony,
Chadwick's Fourth, as it were. The conventional four movements—fast,
slow, scherzo, and finale—all demonstrate coherent tonal design. But because
of the evocative generic elements of the music, signalled by Chadwick's own
epigraphic titles and preambular quotations, these *Sketches* must also be
placed within the orbit of program music.

The title itself is ambiguous. It may refer to the literary and dramatic as
well as the visual arts. In the case of the first three movements or sketches—
"Jubilee," "Noel," and "Hobgoblin"—there is a question as to whether the
composer's intention was to tell a story or paint a picture. But the last sketch,
"A Vagrom Ballad," definitely may be understood only as a vaudeville or music hall act.

In any case, the extramusical quotient of the *Sketches* echoes such American artifacts as Currier and Ives prints, derives from the same sources as the
works of the Ashcan school of painters, and parallels the realism of such
authors as William Dean Howells and Stephen Crane. Unlike *Rip Van Winkle,*
they do not celebrate nostalgia for a mythic past but convey the view, through
Chadwick's mind, of aspects of contemporary American life. H. T. Parker
understood fully Chadwick's musical realism and, as a representative listener,
speaks to the way the composer's audience perceived his musical metaphors.
After identifying Chadwick as "the most American of our composers, because oftener than with the rest in mood and spirit sounds distinctively
American," he goes on to point out in his 1908 review in the *Evening Transcript* that the Yankee composer caught in his music such American traits as
"fooling around" and "jollying" as in "The Vagrom Ballad." In "Hobgoblin"

Chadwick writes, so Parker says, "bluff music with an unmistakable sturdy American tang and has taken his boy-fairy out of English farm steads to set him in American farm houses." "Jubilee," which to Parker echoes "Negro tunes," relies more on "the high and volatile spirits of the music, the sheer rough-and-tumble of it at its fullest moments. . . . the music shouts because it cannot help it, and sings because it cannot help it, and each as only Americans would shout and sing."[22]

Perceptive as these comments are in recognizing Chadwick's musical realism, the musical complement to the artistic and literary realism of his aesthetic peers, they fail to tell us what musical materials the composer employs or how they are combined to create the work of art. Of course, if H. T. P., as he usually signed his reviews, were writing about a novel or reporting on an exhibition, he might mention specific narratives, dialogue, and objects to make his point. He might even have said, "Here is how Stephen Crane describes an American music hall":

> The chief element in the music of the orchestra was speed. The musicians played in intent fury. A woman was singing and smiling upon the stage, but no one took notice of her. The rate at which the piano, cornet, and violins were going seemed to impart wildness to the half-drunken crowd.[23]

But how does a composer, writing already in an abstract medium, compose realistic music?

It would seem that one way in which Chadwick was able to join the realist movement of his friends was to use a visual image or scenario, much as Modest Mussorgsky used pictures at an exhibition, as a point of departure. Thus, in varying degrees, from "Noel," the most visual and static of the *Sketches,* to "A Vagrom Ballad," the most dramatic and active, the composer recreates the essence of four characteristically American scenes in music. Again, it is as if Chadwick had written music for imaginary movies.

While not conveying the seedy ambience of a turn-of-the-century music saloon as described by Crane, Chadwick's first sketch, "Jubilee," does emphasize orchestral speed and the cornet. Following the suggestion of the double quatrains, posted by the composer at the beginning of the movement, it conveys the power of vivid colors, red and green, by means of the cornet and

tambourine. Only in the two temporarily reflective passages does the movement display prominently flutes and oboes:

> No cool gray tones for me!
>> Give me the warmest red and green,
>> A cornet and a tambourine,
> To paint MY jubilee!
>
>> For when pale flutes and oboes play,
> To sadness I become a prey;
> Give me the violets and the May,
>> But no gray skies for me!

This sketch is less a story than a pair of moods—one boisterous, one contemplative—derived from the lines of the poem. The first stanza is the recipe
for the recurring first tutti motive dominated by the sounds of brass and
percussion (cornet and tambourine). The contrasting mood comes from the
second stanza. In Chadwick's musical scheme, the boisterous section appears
four times, separated by the more reflective music, creating thus a rondolike
form in which the idea of Jubilee wins out. It was the perceptive Parker who
first pointed out the American quality of this device, which Chadwick uses
twice in the *Sketches,* "to turn suddenly serious, and deeply and unaffectedly
so, in the midst of its fooling to run away into sober fancies and moods, and
then as quickly turn 'jolly' again."[24]

The secret of "Jubilee"'s success is not so much this formal "American"
twist as the musical materials themselves. The most obvious Americanism of
the melodies is the Stephen Foster–like, close four-part harmonies of the
horn motive that introduces the main contrasting theme. Reminiscent of the
chorus from "Camptown Races," it exhibits three important American features—a habanera rhythm, prosodic syncopation, and the gapped tetrachord
(ex. 18). The following *cantabile* theme in the violins echoes the style with
variations. This time the habanera rhythm, first heard as part of the Foster
horn call, becomes the bass accompaniment to a gapped tetrachord melody.
The combination of this Afro-Caribbean dance figure and the Anglo-Celtic
tune magically transforms these two seemingly disparate musical elements

EXAMPLE 18   *Symphonic Sketches,* "Jubilee"

into a sonority that has come to be accepted as a metaphor for the wide open spaces of the West: horse and rider cantering into the setting sun. Incidentally, the consequent phrase of this sweet theme is assigned to the "pale flutes and oboes" of the preambular poem.

Another touch of musical Americanism comes at the end of this nostalgic section. Here, Chadwick introduces the flatted third degree of the tonality, C major, the so-called blue note (ex. 19). Returning briefly to Parker's estimate of the *Sketches,* Chadwick must have successfully communicated such extramusical ideas in "Jubilee":

> Here, as now and then elsewhere in Mr. Chadwick's later music, is the echo of Negro tunes; but the American quality of the music lies little in that. Rather, it is in the high and volatile spirits of the music, the sheer rough-and-tumble of it at its fullest moments [ex. 20].[25]

EXAMPLE 19 *Symphonic Sketches,* "Jubilee"

EXAMPLE 20 *Symphonic Sketches,* "Jubilee"

EXAMPLE 21 *Symphonic Sketches,* "Noel"

"Noel" is more like a Currier and Ives print than a short story or vaudeville skit. Timeless as a rustic snow-covered landscape under a clear night sky with a full moon, the movement depicts rays of warm light coming from a farmhouse window that frames a mother and child. The slow tempo, sustained notes, and legato muted strings create the musical image of an unchanging landscape. The sonority acts as background for the pastoral tones of the solo English horn, which stand for the emanating beams of light (ex. 21).

The genuine sentiment of the picture, doubtless reflective of Chadwick's deep feelings for his second son, Noel, and his wife, Ida May, are encoded not only in the central melodic phrase but also in the evocative orchestration. Chadwick's penchant for the timbre of such instruments as English horn, harp, and solo violin is clear. And he assigns one sequence of the "Noel" melody to octaves of trombones and trumpets, an unusual combination for such a sweet tune but nevertheless a memorable example of his unique sense of instrumental sound. Also noteworthy in "Noel" are the harp harmonics and solo violin of the last cadential measures, reminiscent, in a way, of Debussy's *L'après-midi d'un faune* coda. Yet just as Debussy evokes the fleeting remembrance of an erotic experience, so does Chadwick recall the equally

EXAMPLE 22 *Symphonic Sketches,* "Hobgoblin"

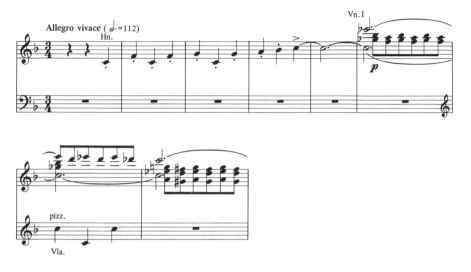

potent emotions of maternal love. Perhaps the difference between the two metaphors in music may be attributed to such a simple thing as the absence in "Noel" of the sensuous ring of antique finger-cymbals, which clearly would have been out of place.

The title "Hobgoblin" and the preliminary quotation from *A Midsummer Night's Dream* might appear to indicate a revelry on a June evening. But Chadwick's sprite seems to be the kind that becomes active in New England during the crisp nights at the end of October. He domesticates the English Puck and transfers him to Massachusetts, where youngsters are permitted to imitate the antics of Robin Goodfellow by demanding treats and performing tricks.

Very clear from the beginning of this Scherzo capriccioso, as the author subtitles his movement, is an unmistakable Gallic flavor in both harmony and orchestration (ex. 22). Shades of Emmanuel Chabrier and Paul Dukas, especially in the former's orchestral rhapsody *España* (1883) and the latter's *Sorcerer's Apprentice* (1897), seem to be cast over this American genre scene. But a quick check of the dates of the Boston Symphony's first performance of these works—*España* in 1897 and the *Sorcerer's Apprentice* as late as 1904—tend to rule out anything but a casual familiarity with scores rather than a full or-chestral experience. Whether or not the composer intentionally borrowed from this or that source, the "Hobgoblin" movement definitively contradicts the oft-stated simplistic description of Chadwick as a romantic composer in the German academic mode.

As in the other parts of the *Sketches,* the thematic stuff locates the scene in time and place. By now, two easily recognized traits of Chadwick's Yankee style abound. Gapped tetrachordal lines with hemiola syncopations charac-terize the chief motives, as well as such passage work as the figuration of the final cadence (ex. 23). Crisp, energetic rhythms provide the musical equiva-lent of crackling leaves underfoot, brisk winds, and even the touches of frost associated with Halloween.

"A Vagrom Ballad" is pure vaudeville. Chadwick must have seen tramp and hobo acts dozens of times in such Boston theaters as the Bijou or the Tremont. Dressed in a costume of artfully oversized and tattered formal wear, including large ill-fitting shoes and a battered derby, the soft-shoe dance man would tell his tale of woe in pantomime. At the acme of his spell-binding presentation, he figuratively pulls the emotional rug from under the audience and scampers off the stage. This kind of vaudeville skit may not have been Chadwick's only model. The prefatory verse reads:

> A tale of tramps and railways ties,
>   Of clay pipes and rum,
> Of broken heads and blackened eyes
>   And the "thirty days" to come!

This verse may be considered a correlative source. But, according to Warren Storey Smith, the Boston music critic who was also an instructor at the New England Conservatory during Chadwick's tenure as director, the composer mentioned to him the proximate incident for the ballad. While the conductor of both the Springfield and Worcester festivals, Chadwick remembered al-ways seeing an informal encampment of hobos in the Worcester yards as his outbound train stopped to let returning trains pass. Thus, he was intrigued

EXAMPLE 23 *Symphonic Sketches,* "Hobgoblin"

by a slice of life, the same real scene that might have been described by a Stephen Crane or painted by a John Sloan.

But how does a composer who appreciates the aesthetic possibilities of such a genre scene write the music of realism? One explanation may be that Chadwick saw the vaudeville sketch as an intermediate model of reality. It was usable because the theatrical scene, unlike reality, is associated with music

EXAMPLE 24 *Symphonic Sketches,* "A Vagrom Ballad"

as accompaniment to dance, gestures, and mime. By referring his symphonic music to the vaudeville accompaniments, Chadwick could evoke the actual visual performance and communicate the "tale of tramps and railway ties" to his audience.

And because his audience was composed of Boston Symphony subscribers, he could also afford to make musical allusions to an even wider spectrum of the musical repertory and in so doing increase the possibilities for humor or musical punning. Thus, he introduces his invisible tramp with a parody on a Meyerbeer scene complete with a bass clarinet cadenza similar to that in Act V of *Les Huguenots,* recalling his earlier use of a clarinet recitative in the comic overture *Thalia* in 1884. Instead of the traditional aria, one hears a soft-shoe shuffle in the bassoon, a lilting gapped tune with ragtime syncopations accompanied by off-beat accents (ex. 24).

All kinds of interruptions, including a trumpet and snare drum fanfare, try to prevent the forward progress of the dance. When it resumes, its ending is transformed into a quotation from Bach's Fugue in G Major for organ, assigned for comedic effect to the most unlikely instrument for baroque music—the xylophone. The dance tune, now in the brass and thus given the stiffness of a military march, continues for a third time. After a stirring tutti,

EXAMPLE 25 *Symphonic Sketches,* "A Vagrom Ballad"

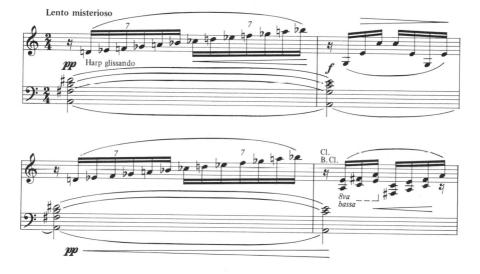

another pitband fanfare cadences with a stereotypical dominant-seventh chord. Suddenly, the farce is over. A *lento mysterioso* musical scrim, woven from gossamer-like harp glissandos, soft woodwind trills, and *sul ponticello* string tremolos, introduces a "pathetic" melody of great emotional depth (ex. 25). Of course, this "new" theme is nothing more than a skillful transformation of the tramp's soft-shoe tune. As it falls lower and lower, it leads back to the beginning pleading bass clarinet recitative (ex. 26). The rug is then pulled. Chadwick ends the sketch with a rollicking finale, fast and loud. As the ultimate comedic gesture, he directs the horns to bray a few notes of the well-known jingle "Shave 'n a haircut, two bits!"

As Arthur Sullivan downplayed the artistic merit of his Savoy operas earlier, so Chadwick seems to have undervalued his most original and evocative orchestral work. In a letter to Theodore Thomas, the conductor, he offers the *Sketches* as a possible second choice to his elegiac overture, *Adonais,* in somewhat apologetic terms: "I could send you . . . my *Symphonic Sketches.* . . . they are not serious, but they sound."[26] Perhaps he was being sensitive to Thomas's taste for "serious" art and was trying to mitigate the music director's possible initial reaction. Nevertheless, he felt he could always

EXAMPLE 26   *Symphonic Sketches,* "A Vagrom Ballad"

reach the conductor by assuring him that the pieces were effective orchestrally, for Chadwick never needed to doubt his imagination and control of instrumental sonority.

❧ *Sinfonietta* in D Major

1904
For 3 flutes (piccolo), 2 oboes, 2 clarinets, 2 bassoons, 4 horns, 2 trumpets, 3 trombones (ad lib.), timpani, snare drum, bass drum, triangle, cymbals, harp, and strings.
I. Risolutamente (D major, $\frac{3}{4}$)
II. Canzonetta: Allegretto (A minor, $\frac{2}{4}$)
III. Scherzino Vivacissimo e leggiero (F major, $\frac{9}{8}$)
IV. Finale: Assai animato (D major, $\frac{2}{4}$)

If one of Chadwick's reasons for not calling a symphony a symphony was, indeed, to make the critics listen to his music with fresh ears, then he was right on the mark with the *Sinfonietta*. The reviewer of the *Boston Transcript* got the idea immediately.

> In Mr. Chadwick's compositions where a keen sense of rhythm, humor, brilliancy and warmth of emotion have play, as in the Scherzino and the

finale of the Sinfonietta . . . , we at last have music by an American composer that is more than skillful, intelligent, earnest work after the pattern of French and German musicians who happen to be in fashion. These movements are as distinctive, as peculiarly "American," one may say, as Richard Strauss's music is peculiarly German, as d'Indy's is French.[27]

And, certainly, the whole *Sinfonietta,* not just the last two movements, is suffused by the ingredients and method of Chadwick's American style.

In the first movement, identified only by its tempo indication—*risolutamente* ("boldly")—rather than by a specific subtitle, the principal theme is a typical Chadwickian syncopated, gapped tetrachordal melody (ex. 27), followed by a more lyric phase in an altered phrygian mode for woodwinds accompanied by a syncopated figure in the strings (exs. 28, 29). A third, more sensuous theme plays with the chromatic relationship between two chords: a tonic and its lowered sixth-degree triad (ex. 30). A special moment occurs in final cadence with its very Anglo-American–sounding progression from the minor subdominant to a triad on the lowered (modal) seventh degree to the major tonic in D major.

Probably what interested the *Transcript's* reviewer in the Scherzino was the gapped tetrachordal theme, the singular use of parallel augmented fourths in a rapidly descending sweep, and the plain fourths of the cadential section, which seem to have been repeated after their successful appearance at the end of "A Vagrom Ballad."

The Finale begins with rustling sounds of a rainy night, which are whipped up into dynamic and rhythmic peaks of a storm (ex. 31). A *Doppio piu lento* ("twice as slowly") section, which also, curiously enough, parallels "A Vagrom Ballad," introduces the contrasting element of pathos only to cause it to evaporate in the strains of the country dance–like secondary theme.

Chadwick's manipulations of most of the possibilities of duple, compound duple, and triple meter give the movement constant but smooth shifts of pulse. An additional nice touch in the coda is the seeming quotation of the main theme from Mrs. H. H. A. Beach's Credo in her *Grand Mass.*

EXAMPLE 27 *Sinfonietta,* first movement

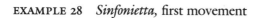

EXAMPLE 28 *Sinfonietta,* first movement

EXAMPLE 29   *Sinfonietta,* first movement

EXAMPLE 30   *Sinfonietta,* first movement

EXAMPLE 31 *Sinfonietta,* fourth movement

❧ *Suite Symphonique* in E♭ Major

1909
For 3 flutes (piccolo), 2 oboes, 2 clarinets, 2 bassoons, alto saxophone, 4 horns, 3 trumpets, 3 trombones, bass tuba, timpani, bass drum, small drum, cymbals, triangle, glockenspiel, xylophone, harp, and strings
I. Allegro molto animato (E♭ major, ¢)
II. Romanza: Andantino espressivo (B♭ major, ⁴⁄₄)
III. Intermezzo e humoreske: Poco allegretto (G minor, ²⁄₄)
IV. Finale: Allegro molto e energico (E♭ major, ⁶⁄₄)

Like his Third Symphony, which Dvořák awarded the National Conservatory Prize of three hundred dollars, the third of the nonsymphonies, which Chadwick entitled *Suite Symphonique* in E♭ Major, won the not inconsiderable sum of seven hundred dollars as the first prize given by the National Federation of Music Clubs in 1911. Perhaps he was impelled to use a French appellation by the ambience of Lausanne, where he began to sketch the work. Maybe, too, his movement subtitles, Romanza (for the second) and Intermezzo e Humoreske (for the third), were inspired by his subsequent stay in Italy during his sabbatical year, 1905–6. Nevertheless, the total effect of this symphony is of a thoroughly American style in the Chadwickian manner, displaying boisterous cross-rhythms, beautiful, sentimental tunes, solid subdominant harmonies, brilliant orchestration, and ironic contrasts of mood. Certainly, the composer is, as always, committed to the tonal system, but within this common-practice scheme Chadwick takes some liberties, recognized by contemporary commentators, that indicate he wished to show his audience he knew a thing or two about modernisms or, at least, that he did not entirely depend upon the Leipzig crowd for his inspiration.

Before the February 1912 performance of this piece by the New York Symphony Society, Walter Damrosch, the conductor, called attention to the third movement, which he said featured "a 'Cake Walk,' in ⁵⁄₄ time, and a bit of parody of the modern French style, the 'whole tone' scale of Debussy, the consumptive frogs in dismal pools of the decadent poets."[28] Later, on February 18, 1924, in a significant revision of an earlier, negative opinion of the work, H. T. Parker of the *Boston Transcript* praised the saxophone-led Romanza as "gentle, tender, musing, half-smiling, quite honest, making no parade of its warmth. It does not drool Germanically or after the manner of the English. It is free from Gallic rhetoric, listening for the audience. It puts by Italian passion and Slavic frenzy. In other words, it is truly and characteristically American."[29]

Any comparison between the *Suite Symphonique* and the *Symphonic Sketches* or the *Sinfonietta* shows deliberate reconciliation of the strong tonal architecture of classic recapitulatory forms and the novelties of American popular music and the latest sonorities from Paris and Milan. The piece follows the traditional four-movement tempo scheme without question: fast, slow, scherzo, finale. Chadwick even employs an E♭ major–B♭ major–G minor–E♭ major series of tonalities, and each movement begins and ends in the same key. But within these basic formats are the fresh musical materials that typify the composer's personal style and foreshadow the concerns of American art music until the middle of the century.

Memorable highlights, such as the sentimental E♭ alto saxophone solo of the Romanza (ex. 32), link the unique sonority of the melody (which is purely Anglo-Celtic) to the past—to Bizet's *L'Arlésienne Suite* (1872) and perhaps to William Henry Fry's 1861 opera, *Notre-Dame of Paris*—and to the future—the too-numerous-to-mention saxophone evocations found in American symphonic music of the succeeding decades. The contrasting section of the second movement is all shimmer and scrim written in the early twentieth-century manner of rapidly oscillating pianissimo thirds in flutes and clarinets, open-fifth bass intervals and natural harmonics in the strings and harp arpeggios with muted horns accompanying an indolent, reedy oboe tritone melody that inevitably recalls Debussy. Yet, also, it should help recall

EXAMPLE 32   *Suite Symphonique,* second movement

EXAMPLE 33   *Suite Symphonique,* third movement

those other aesthetic blends of American subject matter and French style in contemporary paintings by Childe Hassam and Maurice Brazil Prendergast, so admired today by art historians and dealers. A particularly bittersweet flavor is created for the final cadence by flatting the sixth degree of the Bb major scale.

The Yankee Doodle parody in whole tones of the Humoreske section and the $\frac{5}{4}$ meter seem to dominate the third movement (ex. 33). Relatively simple instrumentation—including xylophone, triangle, cymbals, harp, and bass drum—is skillfully deployed to enhance the pixie-like quality of the orchestral sonority, already familiar from the *Symphonic Sketches*. Like the Romanza, the movement ends with a subdued cadence characterized by the G minor scale with double leading tones. They create two piquant augmented steps: B♭–C♯–D and E♭–F♯–G.

The first and fourth movements, the two outside movements, depend less on such arresting thematic and sonoral ideas than on sheer energy and, sometimes, bluster. For these two qualities Chadwick works up crescendo (or, as Virgil Thomson once said, non-accelerating crescendo) thrusts propelled by two Afro-Caribbean rhythms—the habanera tango and the Antillean cinquillo. Since writing the song *The Danza*, Chadwick had been fascinated by such south-of-the-border beat patterns that he, like many other Americans, must have assimilated from the characteristic piano pieces by Louis Moreau Gottschalk. These two rhythms accompany the main theme and, together, seem to make the American sound so noticeable to audiences then and today. A contrasting slower, noble melody of the marching hymn variety gives the animated opening repose and adds dignity to the movement. With its major sixth leap upward, it adumbrates the touching saxophone theme of the following Romanza.

The Finale is a reflection of the first movement. This time Chadwick writes in his favorite ⁶⁄₈ meter with its potential duple or triple accent patterns and its inherent cross-rhythms. A descending gapped theme, accompanied by only the first half of the cinquillo beat, stamps the opening phrase. It soon changes kaleidoscopically into a more legato music that toys with the whole-tone scale in the oboe, atmospheric harmonics, and *sul ponticello* arpeggios in the strings and the harp, sustained by soft, muted horns (ex. 34). A lilting syncopated rhythm then ends the Allegro section. It is succeeded by a quiet horn section solo. The recapitulation repeats the opening musical gestures, and the work is brought to a climax with the previously obscure lilting syncopated rhythm, now in a marchlike *molto vivace* coda in duple meter.

Although Chadwick would live for another twenty years, he would write no more symphonies. Never as popular as the *Symphonic Sketches*, the *Suite Symphonique* generally remained on the shelves of orchestra libraries. The Romanza, however, was revived for a nostalgic all-Chadwick concert in

EXAMPLE 34 *Suite Symphonique,* fourth movement

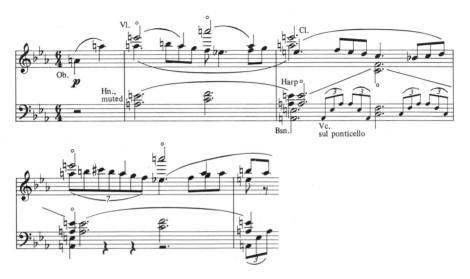

Boston in 1924, when it received H. T. Parker's unquestioned praise for being "characteristically American." But by then the pleasant words must have rung hollow to the septuagenarian suffering from gout, arteriosclerosis, lack of performances, and the growing ignorance of his existence by the young.

CHAPTER 15

Orchestral Music:
Overtures and Poems

Rip Van Winkle, Overture in F Major

1879, revised 1930
For 2 flutes, 2 oboes, 2 clarinets, 2 bassoons, 4 horns, 2 trumpets, 3 trombones, timpani, and strings (original version); revised version also calls for piccolo, tuba, bass drum, triangle, and xylophone

In 1855, when Chadwick was just a year old, George Frederick Bristow of New York City presented his opera *Rip Van Winkle* there. Ten years later, in 1865, the young actor Joseph Jefferson, scion of an old American theatrical family, on the way back from an Australian tour asked Dion Boucicault in London to tailor a *Rip Van Winkle* play for him based upon his suggestions for dialogues, setting, and action. As a result, Boucicault constructed a dramatic vehicle for Jefferson that would make his interpretation of Rip the most widely known American stage character of the nineteenth century. Of course, all of these Rips were descended from Washington Irving's short story of 1809 concerning the quaint Dutch New Yorker whose propensity for hard liquor and vagrant ways led to an encounter with the ghostly crew of the discoverer Henry Hudson and, subsequently, to a twenty-year sleep lasting through the years of the American Revolution.

Without a doubt Chadwick was not influenced by the Bristow opera. He may very well have read the tale in Irving's *Sketch Book.*[30] However, the form of the legend that most likely impressed him was Jefferson and Boucicault's popular theatrical version. Jefferson himself denigrates the importance of Irving as a model for his play by mentioning (as did Irving) German origins for the main character and by complaining that, after all, in the original narrative Rip had but ten lines of dialogue. Even more to the point of

German ambiance was the fact that Jefferson gave to Rip a pseudo-Dutch ethnicity by using the more rapidly recognized dialect of the Pennsylvania Dutch, who were Germans. When Rip, as an aged man, returns to his hometown he asked in German, not Dutch: "My friends, kanst du Deutsch sprechen?" Last in this summary of the sort of symbol *Rip Van Winkle* must have been for Chadwick is Jefferson's explanation of the way his play is transformed from the realism and comedy of its early scene to the fairy idealism of the later scenes after Rip meets the ghosts of Hudson's crew: "The Fairy element in play seems to be attached to it as the fairy element in a Midsummer Night's Dream."[31]

Jefferson first appeared as Rip in Boston in 1869, and his troupe returned in 1870, 1872, and 1878. Thus, Chadwick could have witnessed any number of performances during his periodic visits to Boston for lessons and to see his brother before leaving for study in Germany.

Accordingly, when he began to plan a Leipzig Conservatory graduation composition, a piece that, if successful, would be performed in the famous Gewandhaus, the powerful impact on his imagination made by Rip Van Winkle, the most recent and popular symbol of American character, must have determined his choice. In fact, Chadwick dedicated his manuscript score to Joseph Jefferson.

Doubtless, Rip's easy-going personality, the mystical elements, and the romantic setting also found sympathetic responses in his Leipzig mentors, Salomon Jadassohn and Carl Reinecke. For although the story was authentically American, it rang many German romantic changes, especially those whose musical metaphors had long since been explored by composers such as Weber, Mendelssohn, and Wagner: the mountain forest, the fairy atmosphere, and the ghostly crew of seamen.

Scored for woodwinds by two, four horns, two trumpets, three trombones, timpani, and strings, the overture is cast in a tripartite sonata form with an introduction and coda. Most of the descriptive musical material (ex. 35) is introduced at the slow beginning and briefly returns just before the recapitulation. A solo cello seems to portray Rip and places him in the forested Catskills, a scene conveyed by a horn melody accompanied by rustling, muted-string tremolos. An acceleration leads to the first theme of the prin-

EXAMPLE 35   *Rip Van Winkle,* introduction

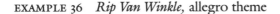

EXAMPLE 36   *Rip Van Winkle,* allegro theme

cipal allegro section, a lilting dance tune with the unmistakable Yankee flavor of the gapped tetrachord harmonized with a typical plagal cadence (ex. 36). Even as early as this first public orchestral work, Chadwick established a distinctive musical speech that he would retain as a mark of both his personal and national melodic style for half a century. A more lyrical secondary subject written for clarinets and cellos in octaves provides rhythmic contrast because of its longer and even note values (ex. 37).

The development manipulates various phrases of the first theme, as is to be expected. Then, slowing down the forward momentum, Chadwick tem-

EXAMPLE 37   *Rip Van Winkle,* secondary theme

porarily brings back the introductory programmatic andante with its recitative-like cello solo. Another acceleration pattern returns to the dancelike first theme of the recapitulation. Built on this theme is a sturdy coda that ends the overture but not before the young American seizes the irresistible opportunity to state the Yankee tune one last time in *fortissimo* trombones in augmentation.

Chadwick's first orchestral essay was the kind of work that inspired smiles, admiration, and, especially, applause. In contrast to *Hamlet* and *Julius Caesar,* the apparently lugubrious and pretentious overtures offered for consideration by his classmates, *Rip Van Winkle* was heard by the many German critics as "original," "charming," and "bustling." Its orchestration, particularly, was praised for its color and effectiveness, which to the critics sounded fresh and healthy. And not a little of the favorable commentary was reserved for Chadwick's conducting, which must have had much to do with the enthusiastic reception.[32]

In Boston, as already noted, the overture was hailed with the kind of gusto usually saved for news of military or athletic exploits, even before Chadwick himself arrived home. At the December 11, 1879, concert of the Harvard Musical Association Symphony, although programmed with such masterworks as Schubert's *Rosamunde* overture, Beethoven's Fifth Symphony, and Berlioz's *Marche Nocturne*, *Rip Van Winkle* elicited praise similar to that of the Leipzig critics for its "rich and striking" scoring. The second theme for cellos was noticed as "delightful."[33] One Boston reviewer, though, detected the unwelcome tincture of "Wagnerism in the use of brass."[34]

Dwight's Journal of Music, which accorded *Rip* the most detailed review of all the early reports, "perceived none of those traits of Wagnerism which some have felt themselves called upon to find in his scoring."[35] Obviously, three years before the Bayreuth master died, he was still a controversial figure in Boston, and the detection of his influence or lack thereof upon the young was seen almost as important as an exercise in differential diagnosis. But regardless of this tempest in a teapot, all reviewers were united in the opinion that the young composer had a brilliant future ahead of him.

For those who would think of Chadwick as a Bostonian at this stage of his career is a seemingly innocent remark in the *Journal* review that indicates the distinctions then thought important: "The Overture was received with the heartiest applause and every sign of satisfaction, which must have been gratifying to the friends of *the young man from his native city, Lawrence, of this state*" [emphasis added]. Evidently, while the *Journal* was willing to heap accolades on Chadwick, it stopped short of making him a citizen of the "Hub of the Universe," at least in 1879.

❧ *Aphrodite*, Symphonic Fantasie for Orchestra

1912
For 3 flutes (piccolo), 2 oboes, English horn, 2 clarinets, bass clarinet, 2 bassoons, contrabassoon, 4 horns, 4 trumpets, 3 trombones, tuba, timpani, celesta, harp, tambour militaire, field drum, and strings

More than any other Chadwick work, *Aphrodite* raises an important question: Can a true American, nay Yankee, composer base his art on highbrow subjects without losing his ethnic soul? According to Gilbert Chase, not only was the Bostonian merely flirting "with the shade of Aphrodite" in this endeavor, he was also courting the ancient Greek goddess, perhaps, for the dubious reason of compensating for "his lack of higher education."[36] Only when dealing with the native genre scene of the *Symphonic Sketches* could Chase come to terms with the Boston composer. "Chadwick," he wrote, "was at least on the right track when he broke away from his pseudoclassical preoccupations." For most American composers then, especially those who did not have the benefit of a Harvard education, the railway tramp, for example, was an appropriate subject but not the beautiful marble head of Aphrodite, on display in the Museum of Fine Arts.

Such an assessment of Chadwick's musical poem could not have been based upon actual audition since *Aphrodite* has remained unperformed and unrecorded since its initial performances. Instead, the imaginative historian must needs have relied upon received negative opinion or casual perusal of the score. At any rate, Chase's description of the scenario, coming from Rupert Hughes's opinionated book on American composers (he considered Ethelbert Nevin an "innovator"[37]), is obviously defective as to the nature and sequence of musical events. A close reading of the score itself would have quickly turned up the discrepancies. More important, it would have also revealed that, rather than an exercise of the "cult of the past . . . conceived on a plane of academic conventionality,"[38] as Chase described it, *Aphrodite* was a significant attempt by a mature composer to explore and experiment with new orchestral sonorities as form and structure.

The composer's intentions are evident from both the program of the first performance and the epigraph printed at the beginning of the score:

In a dim vision of the long ago
   Wandering by a far-off Grecian shore
Where streaming moonlight shone on golden sands
   And melting stars dissolved in silver seas,
   I humbly knelt at Aphrodite's shrine
Imploring her with many a fervid prayer
To tell the secret of her beauty's power
And the depths of ocean whence she sprang
And smiling said: "O mortal youth behold!"
Then all these mysteries passed before mine eyes.

One critic, Philip Hale, no doubt basing his statement on information from Chadwick himself, said the composer's inspiration for the prefatory poem came not only from the so-called Bartlett head of Aphrodite but also from the *Greek Anthology*.[39] The words are clearly Chadwick's own. Although they add about as much luster to the music as do MacDowell's quatrains before each of his *Sea Pieces* for piano, they nevertheless help set the scene and establish a mood.

A more immediately valuable explanation of the piece's structure is the composer's description printed in the program of the first performance at the Norfolk, Connecticut, Festival in 1912. According to this account and the score itself, the musical poem begins with an "apostrophe or address to the goddess" and includes eight scenes "which may have passed before the sightless eyes of such a goddess":

1. Moonlight on the Sea	Andante con moto
2. Storm	Allegro con fuoco
3. Requiem	Andante lamentabile
4. The Lovers	Andante amoroso
5. Children Playing	Allegretto semplice
6. Approach of a Great Army	Moderato alla marcia
7. Hymn to Aphrodite	Maestoso
8. Moonlight Scene, partly repeated	Andante con moto
Finale	Molto maestoso

Had Chase based his comments on the epigraphic poem and on the sounds of the music rather than on a flawed description, he could not have accused Chadwick of membership in a cult of the past or of *Aphrodite*'s "academic conventionality."

The best clue to the real inspiration of *Aphrodite* is the fact that it was composed by the sea, on Martha's Vineyard.[40] Seductive and alluring as the Praxitelean goddess may have been to the composer, in the music the moonlight on the sea, the stormy waves, the children playing on the beach remind one more of Nantucket Sound, a nor'easter, and the sands of West Chop. Rather than proving the composer's nostalgia for ancient Greece, the Fantasie demonstrates his newly found manner of descriptive sonority based upon his own recognizable Yankee tune lines and the innovations of the modern French orchestral school. The horn and the violin duet, representative of the lovers, the playing children, and the Aphrodite hymn, are good examples of this synthesis. Certainly, the incredibly beautiful marble structure from the isle of Cnidus captured the imaginations of many Bostonians, including Chadwick. However, its materialization in musical sound was a very contemporary and localized matter, as one critic said, a "musical fabric [that] is beautifully luminous. It is music of sensuous ecstasy."[41]

From the first page of the published score the French influence can be seen. In contrast to Chadwick's previous habits of instrumental identification, he uses the French terms for certain instruments: *cor anglais, bassons, contra basson, tambour militaire,* and *altos* (for English horn, bassoons, contra bassoon, snare drum, and violas, respectively). Other instruments are called by their standard English names except, inexplicably, *violoncelli.* Later, when abbreviations are employed in the score, Chadwick writes *bons* or *tamb mil,* further evidence of the influence of contemporary French orchestral scores.

More to the point of taking his lead from the modern French school is Chadwick's experimentation with simultaneous figuration, novel instrumentation, chromatic harmony, and dynamics modulation to create structure. The sonority of "Moonlight on the Sea," for example, described as "beautifully luminous," is fabricated from intervals oscillating at various speeds, depicting the quick ripples and longer swells. An English horn evocation of the Aphrodite idea travels over this musical metaphor for water (ex. 38). Interruptions by celesta arpeggios and muted horn suggest the play of moonlight on the gently moving water. Here, the graduation from the interior Teutonic moodiness of *Melpomene* to the Cnidian *en plein air* seascape shows how far Chadwick traveled artistically from Leipzig to Paris in the quarter century that separates the dramatic overture and *Aphrodite*. Yet his personal melodic style makes it crystal clear that the author of these modern sonorities is American.

Chadwick's melodic fingerprints may be found in the canonic duet of the lovers (ex. 39). It is followed by an Allegretto semplice scene of children playing on the beach that might easily be visualized by the paintings of William Merritt Chase or Maurice Brazil Prendergast, contemporaries of Chad-

EXAMPLE 38   *Aphrodite,* "Moonlight on the Sea"

wick who similarly wed local American subject matter to the modern technique of creating form through color (ex. 40). The reconciliation of the
contemporary orchestra's flexibilities and virtuosities with Chadwick's unchanging sense of tune was not lost on reviewers, who unanimously considered *Aphrodite* a landmark of American composition (ex. 41).[42] If any dis-
senting voice was raised, it merely confirmed the view that *Aphrodite* places
Chadwick in the forefront rather than in the *arrière-gard.* Richard Aldrich,
writing a favorable review in the *New York Times,* noticed: "Some might be
disposed to find . . . a certain lack of coherence and symmetry in the structure
of the music."[43] What better indication could there be of the popular consciousness of Chadwick's version of the modern twentieth-century orchestral
style?

EXAMPLE 39 *Aphrodite,* "The Lovers"

EXAMPLE 40 *Aphrodite,* "Children Playing"

EXAMPLE 41 *Aphrodite,* maestoso section

Chase's characterization a generation ago of Chadwick as a classicist *manqué* was damaging to the reputation of the artist, especially during the years when only snippets of his work were available in sound recordings. One can only imagine the number of times Chase's judgments were quoted, unawares, as authoritative, further justifying neglect. However, a measure of changing attitudes is the recent admission of this universally admired dean of American music historians, who now writes:

> I once rather snidely described this as "a proper Bostonian flirtation with the shade of Aphrodite." . . . But not all Bostonian flirtations are "proper," and I imagine that Chadwick may have really been in love with Aphrodite. At all events, we should let the music speak both for itself and for him."[44]

Perhaps today, in contrast to thirty years ago, American composers may be allowed to find their inspiration wherever they may.

❧ *Tam O'Shanter,* Symphonic Ballad

1915

For 3 flutes (piccolo), 2 oboes, English horn, clarinet in D, 2 clarinets in B♭, bass clarinet, 2 bassoons, 4 horns, 3 trumpets, 3 trombones, tuba, timpani, bass drum, cymbals, xylophone, glockenspiel, wood drum, Chinese drum, sand-block, rattle, harp, and strings

After the disappointment of *The Padrone,* rejected by the Metropolitan Opera in 1913, Chadwick turned his musical attention to the creation of an orchestral drama, the symphonic ballad *Tam O'Shanter,* based upon the poem by Robert

Burns. Unlike an opera, whose chances for performance are limited, he knew that a Chadwick orchestral work could always find a willing conductor. Besides, the tale of the boozy Scot and his plucky mare was a perfect point of musical departure for a composer who had mastered the art of Anglo-Celtic musical speech and the craft of descriptive orchestral metaphor. So much for consolation!

Tam O'Shanter may also be viewed as a cultural statement. It was a reaffirmation of an ethnicity based on and supporting common American-British values during a period of chaotic change in the United States.[45] The piece represents not only the work of the most identifiably American composer to date but also an English-speaking tradition that transcends geographical boundaries. Hence, *Tam O'Shanter* seems to define its nationalism not just in terms of simplistic, spread-eagle American musical symbols but in the commonplaces of a transnational musical diction. In this, Chadwick was not alone. His colleague Horatio Parker, to whom the ballad is dedicated, made a Druidic princess the heroine of his opera *Mona* (Metropolitan, 1912), chosen by a committee, of which Chadwick was a member, to win a prize and performance. Edward MacDowell's Fourth Sonata for Piano, subtitled "Keltic," was a "commentary" on "Keltic tales of yore, Dark Druid rhymes that thrall," according to the composer's own verse. Mrs. H. H. A. Beach's first widely performed orchestral work was titled *Gaelic Symphony* (1896). To these may be added other contemporary Anglo-American works—(Henry Hadley's lyric drama, *Vivien and Merlin,* and Louis Adolphe Coerne's symphonic poem, *Excalibur*—as further examples of a cultural consciousness that culminated in the United States's entry during World War I on the side of the Allies, against Germany.[46]

Burns's poem fulfilled this need for a broader cultural identity during a period when the term *American* itself was being redefined. It provided a scenario, tailormade for a man such as Chadwick, who was both earthy by nature and sophisticated by training, as was Burns. A master of musical metaphor, skilled in the empirical science of orchestral color, the composer could easily divine in the 224-line misadventure the raw material for an approximately twenty-minute piece: boisterous singing in a tavern on market day, a developing storm, the homeward-bound trotting horse, nighttime bacchanalian dancing in a deserted church, a witches' chase, and escape.[47] Perhaps any adept could fashion a tone poem for such a story line, but Chadwick's musicalization succeeds in a different way because of his sensitivity to its vernacular diction and inflection. It captures the much-admired Anglo-Celtic spirit in the details of thematic material and their accompaniments, in addition to the fascinating sequence of events.

Chadwick's symphonic ballad differs from the Burns narrative in only one important aspect. The poem begins with about seventy lines devoted to descriptions of time, place, and characterization when Tam goes on a drinking spree on a market day to escape his wife, Kate. The storm with which Chadwick begins his ballad is not mentioned until almost a third of the way into the poem. Obviously, Chadwick was using good musical sense and precedent. Only after the storm abates somewhat does the composer introduce the cozy interior of a tavern with its raucous sounds: "The night drave on wi' sangs and clatter" (ex. 42). The remainder of the symphonic ballad then follows the sequence of Burns's events. A drunken Tam mounts his faithful (and smart) mare, Meg, who dutifully trots homeward in the dark, stormy night (ex. 43). Then, on the way past a haunted church, Kirk Alloway[48] (ex. 44), Tam hears and sees the orgiastic dancing of witches (exs. 45, 46). The revels of these old hags do not excite him until he spies the capers of one "winsome wench," dressed only in a short, revealing chemise, or "cutty sark." No longer able to contain himself, he makes his presence known by blurting out a compliment: " 'Weel done, cutty sark!'/And in an instant all was dark!/ And scarcely had he Maggie rallied,/When out the hellish legion sallied" (ex. 47).

The witches chase wildly after Tam and his mount. They are just about to catch Tam, but he makes it more than halfway across the first river bridge and thus, by tradition, is allowed to escape. The escape is not without its toll on Maggie, however; just as she is passing the midpoint of the bridge, a witch rips off her tail.

Burns's seriocomical moral advises would-be tipplers and womanizers to consider first the price of such misadventure: "Remember Tam O'Shanter's mare." Thus, Chadwick's last musical episode is both literally and figuratively a coda (Italian for "tail"), reflective of Tam's tender regard for his horse and

EXAMPLE 42   *Tam O'Shanter,* Tam

EXAMPLE 43   *Tam O'Shanter,* Meg trotting

EXAMPLE 44 *Tam O'Shanter,* Kirk Alloway

EXAMPLE 45 *Tam O'Shanter,* reveling witches

the events she shared with him. Here, there is no doubt of the composer's identification with the "rustic adventurer,"[49] as Wordsworth called Tam.

The symphonic ballad is clearly divided into six episodes, all organized about the tonality of C major, the key associated with the Tam O'Shanter theme and the key in which the piece concludes. The driving force of the composition, however, seems to lie not so much in its themes or tonality but rather in its tempo, orchestral figuration, and dynamics. Listening from this vantage, there seem to be five acceleration sequences: (1) the storm; (2) Tam O'Shanter in the storm; (3) trotting homeward past Kirk Alloway; (4) Tam's observation of the witches' revels; and (5) the witches' chase. The sixth section is the coda, which is constructed upon different principles.[50]

EXAMPLE 46   *Tam O'Shanter,* reveling witches

EXAMPLE 47   *Tam O'Shanter,* "Weel done, cutty sark!"

Thinking of the music in cinematic terms may give a clearer idea of Chadwick's musical conception. Of course, the cinema may be defined as the art of moving pictures according to the principles of music, not the other way around. For an essentially visually oriented culture, however, invisible music may be best understood in terms of pictures in motion.

Accordingly, each of the first five sections is fashioned to represent increasing spurts of power. The power of the storm constitutes the first, second, and third sections and is heard in three distinct patterns of acceleration, increases in orchestral activity, and crescendos. The fourth section, the orgies in the church, is similarly depicted by growing speed, off-beat accents, subdivisions of note values, and dynamic force, all of which reflect the increasing energy of the revels to the point of climax, exhaustion, and release.

Here Chadwick had the benefit of explicit indications in the poem itself:

As Tamie glowred, amazed, and curious,
The mirth and fun grew fast and furious;
The piper loud and louder blew;
The dancers quick and quicker flew. . . . [51]

So the composer instructs his musicians that they are to play with abandon, *energico* and *furioso*, at the height of the orgy, when one nubile witch is particularly noticed by the now-aroused Tam.

The fifth and last section, before the coda, is another acceleration sequence descriptive of Tam's flight and the witches' pursuit, a favorite scenario for today's cineasts, here produced by intercutting two different orchestral figurations. By means of truncation, tempo, and dynamic increase, the sequence arrives at the highest point of power. The superimposition, or montage, of the chasing orchestral figures on the figures representing flight is used to convey the images of the witches almost catching Tom. This chase sequence is abruptly ended by a total and indefinite cessation of all sound.

The succeeding coda presents an entirely different realm of experience. Chadwick himself calls this section "reflective rather than illustrative." It begins with a brief, elegiac statement, again according to Chadwick, "possibly suggestive of Maggie's varied emotions" after her successful flight costing her tail. Continuing, the composer says, "The music now loses it delineative and programmatic character, and becomes more subjective."

Given Chadwick's musical settings of the previous "action" episodes in *Tam O'Shanter* as accelerating orchestral power trains, it is no surprise to see him putting his sonorities in reverse, so to speak, the better to symbolize the cerebral or contemplative aspect of Burns's narrative (exs. 48, 49).

After the abrupt pause, when Maggie's tail is torn away, the coda gets progressively slower, softer, even sweeter, until the final resolution of the varied tonalities into sustained C major triads. The only motion now is provided by muted trumpets playing parallel fourths accompanied by cadential timpani strokes signaling a return to harmonic equilibrium. Between the elegy and final cadence, Chadwick lets the listeners know that he is dealing with mental rather than real images by literally presenting in slow motion

EXAMPLE 48 *Tam O'Shanter,* coda

EXAMPLE 49   *Tam O'Shanter,* coda

the Tam O'Shanter theme, the trotting horse figure, the Alloway hymn tune, and the witches' dance tunes. The resulting dreamlike action is further enhanced by attenuating the harsh, bright, normal sonorities through instructions to the instrumentalists to play *dolce, piano,* and legato and by using mutes, harmonics, harp arpeggios, and sustained string chords to create a musical screen through which such slowed-down melodies are to be heard. Thus, the real musical events of the five acceleration segments are transformed into fondly recollected visualizations.

Masterful as Chadwick's orchestral technique is in organizing a structure of sound for his *Tam O'Shanter,* his musical speech and its accompanimental context gives the symphonic ballad its authentic characterization. Chadwick's recipe for these themes is consistent and therefore easy to analyze. The primary ingredient, as usual, is the gapped tetrachord, most clearly heard in the *Tam O'Shanter* tune and echoed in the cadence of one of the witches' dances.

Wedded to this melodic feature is a syncopated rhythm of prosodic syncopation derived from Anglo-Celtic speech. While there does not seem to be any direct transfer from Burns's text to Chadwick's music, nevertheless examples of this most distinctive rhythm abound in the prosody of the poem:

> While we sit *bousing* at the *nappy*
> An' *getting* fou and *unco happy*. . . . [52]

> And at his *elbow, Souter Johnny,*
> His *ancient, trusty, drouthy, crony;*
> Tam lo'ed him like a *very brither;*
> They had been fou for weeks the *gither* [emphasis added].[53]

These prosodic syncopations find their way into Chadwick's musical fabric in the Tam O'Shanter theme and the Kirk Alloway dances and even as so-called Scotch snaps in various accompanimental figures.

Completing the list of ingredients for this musical Scotch broth is the deliberate use of parallel open fifths and fourths as the harmonic underpinnings for his gapped tetrachordal tunes. These special sounds recollect the drones of the bagpipe: "He screwed the pipes and gart them skirl / Till roof and rafters a' did dirl."[54]

To this list of gapped scales, syncopations, and parallel, open intervals should be added the characteristic uneven lilt of the long-short rhythms and the offbeat emphases in the hymn and dance tunes. And if this recipe seems to taste much like today's country and western music, the similarity is instructive.

❧ Overtures to the Three Muses

Chadwick celebrated three of the nine muses with concert overtures for orchestra: *Thalia,* representing comedy (1882), *Melpomene,* representing tragedy (1887), and *Euterpe* representing music (1903). But rather than elevating his stature as an artist with broad literary taste, these works were later taken by some as evidence of his pretentiousness. One explanation for this appraisal, perhaps, was the misperception that somehow the overtures are an attempt to allude to Greek myth. In reality, Chadwick was merely indicating the general affect of his compositions—comedy, tragedy, and music—by using the names of the muses as symbols; thus, the muses refer not so much to Greece and Rome as to Chadwick's own feelings.[55]

Of course, one need not have a family or academic pedigree to get a license for treating classical or "high minded" subjects. Otherwise, composers such as Beethoven and Brahms would have had lots of trouble. The three muse overtures need no imprimatur to stand as memorable essays by a gifted artist just because he happened not to go to Harvard. Perhaps merely absorbing the atmosphere of the "Athens of America" was an even more valid way of gaining the right to think in classical fashion.

Thalia, Comedy-Overture

1882
For 2 flutes (piccolo), 2 oboes, 2 clarinets, 2 bassoons, 4 horns, 2 trumpets, 3 trombones, tuba, timpani, tambour basque, castanets, triangle, and strings

Composed over a period of more than twenty years, the three overtures provide examples of the way in which Chadwick's orchestral style evolved. In 1882 the then twenty-nine-year-old composer's comedy overture "took all hearts by storm," said the *Boston Evening Transcript*. "It was tuneful, melodious, brilliant and genial. It displayed the richest scoring, an oriental gorgeousness of color." The critic (perhaps Apthorp?) wrote: "The overture was played with that peculiar brilliancy and effectiveness which one notices when composers conduct their own works; it was as if Mr. Chadwick were playing the whole thing himself."[56]

One clue to the spirit and verve of *Thalia* is its dedication. Chadwick writes on the manuscript score: "To Ross Turner, Esq. most affectionately inscribed as a remembrance of many happy days in *OLD MUNICH!!!*"[57] Ross Sterling Turner, a painter, was one of the Duveneck Boys with whom Chadwick spent the summer before studying with Rheinberger in Munich.[58] Clearly this inscription proves that the composer's intention was not to re-create in music the comedic art of, say, Aristophanes. *Thalia,* in fact, is drenched more in the drafts of full-bodied Salvator or Würzberger beers of the Oktoberfest than in the wine and water of ancient Thessaly.

Weaving together the melodic equivalents of events that had occurred only a few years before, Chadwick's overture may be considered a musical memoir of his student days in Germany. But the thematic material, both the sentimental opening melody and the drinking song, are pure Yankee and are ingeniously combined in a rip-roaring finale that in gusto and enthusiasm rivals Brahms's *Academic Festival Overture*. Noticeable, especially to the Boston listeners, was the percussion writing, which included tambourine, castanets, and triangle in addition to the usual timpani. These sounds might refer to an exotic evening's entertainment easily found in the one European town that was considered the most uninhibited and easy-going outside of Paris. All in all, *Thalia* was confirmation of the wild reception earned by *Rip Van Winkle* in 1879 and 1880.

It also proved that the young composer had already developed an easily recognizable style in his first professional essays for orchestra. Interestingly enough, the main theme of *Thalia* would reappear in 1884 in *The Peer and the Pauper* and, twenty-seven years later, in *Everywoman,* Chadwick's great Broadway extravaganza. Furthermore, the composer would remember the effectiveness of his quasi-operatic opening recitative for clarinet when he sat down to compose the "Vagrom Ballad" of his *Symphonic Sketches* in 1896.

Melpomene, Dramatic Overture

1887
For piccolo, 2 flutes, oboe, English horn, 2 clarinets, 2 bassoons, 4 horns, 2 trumpets, 3 trombones, tuba, timpani, bass drum, cymbals, and strings

Before creating *Melpomene,* Chadwick impressed the critics and audiences alike with the Scherzo of his Symphony No. 2 in B♭ Major in 1884 and then the complete performance of all four movements in 1886. Wilhelm Gericke, the new conductor of the Boston Symphony Orchestra to whom the *Dramatic Overture* (as Chadwick called the work) is dedicated, began a long association with the work, which he introduced at the December 1887 concerts. Of all Chadwick's orchestral pieces, it was the most widely performed: in Copenhagen in 1888; in Paris in 1889 at the Exposition Universelle at the American concert at the Trocadero; and by most American orchestras. At the time of his death the *Christian Science Monitor* mentioned it, along with the burlesque opera *Tabasco* and the lyric drama *Judith,* as his most important and memorable work.

Nevertheless, of all Chadwick's orchestral music it is the least representative of his "American" or personal style. More than any other piece, *Melpomene* raises the question of the validity of a musical Americanism index that some have seemingly used to rank the worthiness of American composers of this period. MacDowell, for example, is considered to have redeemed himself by his interest in American Indian music: "It represents at least an attempt to get away from secondhand romanticism and genteel sentimentality."[59] But this attempt could not by itself expiate the sin of genteelness. An even lower score on such a hypothetical index was given the Boston composers of the turn of the century, for their music was generally conspicuous by its lack of true Americanisms.

Chadwick was, as noted, spared the full effect of such reprobation because of his populist gestures from *Rip* to his "Vagrom Ballad." But in *Melpomene* he dares to concern himself with the theme of tragedy. He presents himself not as a provincial craftsman turning out souvenirs for the sophisticated but as a member of a larger, Western culture. He is not limited by artificially imposed restrictions on the artistic expression of his subject matter just because he is working on this side of the water. His musical romanticism is just as firsthand and his sentiment just as genuine as that of his European contemporaries. Chadwick feels himself just as entitled to inherit the mantel of Beethoven and Wagner as any German composer.

The thematic core of *Melpomene* makes this feeling immediately apparent. Its reference to the prelude to *Tristan* is undisguised (ex. 50). The upward minor-sixth motive leads into a chordal sonority passing through the "Tristan chord," ultimately resolving as its dissonant energy is spent. While paying

EXAMPLE 50 *Melpomene,* beginning theme

homage to Wagner's music, however, the young Bostonian makes the music his own. Rather than adopting a Wagnerian apperception of the tragic metaphor, which leaves the musical question in midair, Chadwick's resolution follows a strictly Yankee path, perhaps in imitation of Louis Moreau Gottschalk's "Last Hope," with a strong plagal subdominant cadence in which the third degree of the scale is treated as a blue note fluctuating between the major and minor.[60] Even in this most cosmopolitan of Chadwick's works, the native inflection of his musical speech comes through the chromatic harmony. But if Chadwick's imagination had not been up to the challenge, who is to say that such passionate sonorities have no place in an American's musical expression?

Euterpe, Concert Overture

1903
For 2 flutes, 2 oboes, 2 clarinets, 2 bassoons, 4 horns, 2 trumpets, 3 trombones, tuba, timpani, and strings

Euterpe, a title that recalls the *Euterpeiad,* John Rowe Parker's seminal Boston music journal of the 1820s, was not composed until 1903, sixteen years later. The expression of comedy and tragedy demands certain obvious musical features. How does one write a musical composition about music, except to create a charming piece?

By the first decade of the new century, Chadwick had long since established his idiosyncratic musical manner, and *Euterpe* is a good example of its combinations of gapped tetrachordal melody, syncopation, rhythmic modu-

EXAMPLE 51 *Euterpe,* beginning theme

EXAMPLE 52 *Euterpe,* secondary theme

lation, and orchestral color (ex. 51). The elegant main theme in long note values is propelled by marchlike subdivisions of the basic pulse in the accompaniment in its fully developed form (ex. 52). Fragmented, the thematic material modulates into a kind of Antillean *tresillo,*[61] or syncopated three-beat rhythm within a duple meter bar, identical to the melo-rhythmic figure found in contemporary ragtime. Without establishing the immediate source of Chadwick's syncopated figure, this rhythm adds a further point of distinction to the composer's recipe for an American music derived from organic materials nurtured in this country's own soil.

CHAPTER 16

Songs

Chadwick wrote nearly 150 songs. Yet, in the main, perhaps because of the nature of the genre itself, they lack the profile, the conviction, the character associated with the composer's unique American style in his orchestral and stage works.

From his youth, as indicated by his tirade against the meretricious parlor ballad at the 1876 national meeting of the Music Teachers' National Association, Chadwick despised the musicaster, who parlayed a minimal knowledge of harmony into an enterprise supplying kitsch to the unsophisticated. He was determined to avoid in his songs the kind of commercial sound he grew to hate. Paradoxically, in his instrumental music, where thematic material, once stated, becomes grist for one's compositional mill, he was uninhibited in his invention of popular, whistleable, even vulgar tunes. Songs, however, brought him to grips with the problems of a nondevelopmental musical idiom in which the melodic setting of the text and its accompaniment rather than manipulative musical skills were the twin aesthetic objects. As many contemporaries had early noticed, it was Chadwick's gift for reconciling common ethnic thematic elements with the demands of sophisticated musical forms and techniques that most distinguished his personal style from other New England composers.

Besides, the quintessential place for the art song is the intimate music room or salon, with its small, selected groups of music lovers, rather than the mass market of the popular song or even the theater-sized auditoriums for symphony or opera. The taste of such knowledgeable listeners certainly must have had an impact on the composer of art songs in his choice of subject matter and musical settings.[62]

Denying himself the common touch, Chadwick seems to have cultivated the elegant tastes and gestures of his refined patrons. Thus, the poetic and musical materials of his songs show more of the characteristics of a fin-de-siècle yearning, overemphasis on precious syllables (which has the effect of distorting texts), and fussy changes of tempo and dynamics.

His piano accompaniments tend to be based upon ultrasensitive chromatic harmonies that appear to give almost every syllable special meaning. Many of his rhythmic motives imply the heightened pulsations of growing passion. He employs all manner of harplike figures to create an orchestral sonority on the piano meant to match the quasi-operatic voices for which the songs are intended. And here is possibly another reason why the songs as a whole do not live up to the high level of the larger works: Chadwick was no pianist. While his accompaniments are professional, even artistic, they lack the individuality of a composer-pianist who cannot help reproducing his idiosyncratic way of playing and who invests much of his own personality in the piano part.

A casual survey of the poems and poets of the songs discloses that Chadwick chose as texts poetic themes then most popular: passionate love, exotic locales, nature. Besides his close collaborations with Arlo Bates, other poets whose texts he set included Henry Wadsworth Longfellow, Bayard Taylor, Thomas Bailey Aldrich, Arthur Macy, Lew Wallace, and David Stevens.

❧ The Crocus

The Crocus, the first song of *The Flower Cycle*, by Arlo Bates, is a most charming example of Chadwick's salon style. Bates, who wrote the libretto for *A Quiet Lodging*, Chadwick's satirical comedy written for the Tavern Club, was professor of literature at the Massachusetts Institute of Technology. The two-stanza poem compares "early loves . . . which die so soon in this world's nipping air" to the mission of the brave crocus: not to endure "but to make springtime fair" (ex. 53). Chadwick captures the simple image with a restricted tessitura, syllabic setting, and flat dynamic levels. What lifts the music above the standards of his own repertory is the accompaniment that flows

EXAMPLE 53   *The Crocus*

effortlessly like a sharp-edged spring breeze. To accomplish this, he seems to have had the inspiration of a Bach *perpetuum mobile* prelude with its arpeggios and small-note figurations. Almost valid by itself, the piano part enhances the vocal line by embedding the chain of pearly notes within its own fabric. And as with all good music, *The Crocus* demonstrates a sense of timing: It is over before its true effect is felt.

❧ *Allah*

Contrasting with the delicacy of the songs of *The Flower Cycle* is *Allah*, Chadwick's setting of Longfellow's poem.[63] Today it seems ponderous, perhaps because of the stolid repetition of a syncopated rhythmic figure and its pseudo-oriental style, typical of the Western stereotype of Eastern or Islamic melody, sounds that seem rather dated to modern ears accustomed to the real thing. But it fits well with the late-nineteenth century vogue for exotic cultures and the flirtation with non-Christian religions (ex. 54).

Still, the song is redeemed by its dominant Chadwickian features. Written in the 1880s, its chord progression by parallel fifths in the bass, its emphasis on gapped tetrachordal melody, and the sensitive setting of the prosody in syncopations seem to anticipate later developments. Debussy's use of parallel fifths in *The Blessed Damozel* came at least as late as 1888, a year after *Allah* was written.

EXAMPLE 54   *Allah*

❧ *Oh, Let Night Speak of Me*

One of the most popular Chadwick songs was *Oh, Let Night Speak of Me*. It is part of the Arlo Bates cycle of poems *Told in the Gate,* inspired by translations of various Near Eastern lyrics. The song was so successful that Louis C. Elson used the composer's manuscript of the first two bars as the gold-embossed colophon for his influential history of American music, lavishly published in 1904 as part of an ambitious series on American art. Dedicated to the leading American baritone and teacher Max Heinrich,[64] the song was actually introduced in concert by Gertrude May Stein, the dramatic soprano for whom Chadwick wrote the title role of *Judith*.

Arlo Bates's paraphrase keeps to the tradition of translating the exotic style of the original poems into second person singular. But this gives the text a false archaism, a highfalutin cadence that exaggerates the already heightened references to unrequited passion:

> Oh, let night speak of me, for day
> Knows not how breaks with woe my heart;
> Day knows not how I mournful stray,
> Weeping for thee, so dear thou art.

In matching the emotional temperature, Chadwick must also escalate his harmonic vocabulary. Chromatically altered chords and melodic appoggiaturas create the dissonance and tension of yearning. A steady pulsation of eighth notes propels the poetic image of night pleading the lover's case. Little in this song is reminiscent of Chadwick's Yankeeness. The melody—there is no tune as such—oscillates between stepwise motion and tendentious leaps of the seventh and octave. Because of the sophisticated harmonic modulations—for example, from the tonic to lowered-sixth degree and back again—the melody tends to stray, as does the speaker of the poem. Some of the strategic harmonic gestures, going back to the style of Gasparo Spontini's opera *La Vestale* (1807) and subsequently popularized by Liszt and Wagner, add to the feeling of *déjà entendu* (ex. 55). Last in this list of features is Chadwick's adoption of a kind of close harmony with the melody doubled in the

EXAMPLE 55   *Oh, Let Night Speak of Me*

outer voices, shades of the earlier Puccini manner of scoring or even the later Amy Woodforde-Finden's *Kashmiri Song*[65] (ex. 56).

Oh, Let Night Speak of Me is a perfectly good art song, with details of craftsmanship, in displaying to advantage the trained singer's voice and in the propriety of the affect of the accompaniment. Yet its text and its music lack the magic and sensuality of, say, the contemporary French *mélodie*. Nor does Chadwick's romanticism begin to match the insights of despair found in Hugo Wolf or Arnold Schoenberg's early work. One can easily understand how such inevitable comparisons could hurt Chadwick.

❧ *A Ballad of Trees and the Master*

In the more congenial domain of sacred and religious texts, which Chadwick set well and regularly, the composer comes off to better advantage. Particularly his treatment of Sidney Lanier's *A Ballad of Trees and the Master* stands out among the rest as a unique blending of what is an essentially secular form with a deeply religious theme. Considered the most perfect poem Lanier ever wrote, it was said to have been jotted down in from fifteen to twenty minutes without alteration in December 1880. Its inspiration may very well have been Luke 22:39, where it is written that before his crucifixion Jesus retired among the trees of the Mount of Olives, reconciled to his fate.[66] And Chadwick's

EXAMPLE 56 *Oh, Let Night Speak of Me*

The night shall speak of me___ and say All things to thee I

dare not show;___ And to thy dreams my

love___ dis- play,___ Till thou art

melt- ed by my woe.

setting seems to match Lanier's spontaneity. It is simple and free-flowing with a marchlike motion that gives the song a militant quasi-cinematic effect; the images of the poem are realized as a visualization of the narrative through the music. While intended for voice and piano, it is really orchestrally conceived (ex. 57). Some clues, such as the bass tremolo in the piano introduction and the fact that Chadwick subsequently made an orchestral arrangement of the song, support this idea. Otherwise meticulous in his transcription of the text, Chadwick ignores an important repetition Lanier makes with great dramatic effect in the published poem: "Into the woods my Master went, /Clean forespent, forespent."

The melodic style is pure Chadwick, with its gapped tetrachordal structure and its reliance upon Lanier's prosody for rhythmic guidance. Especially memorable is the last line, "When out of the woods he came," in which the upward steps in the bass of the beginning are inverted. Noticeable too, is Chadwick's predilection for resolving the so-called "Tristan chord" as if it were a subdominant-to-tonic cadence. There is little doubt why *A Ballad of Trees and the Master* won the *Musical Record* competition in 1899 and is one of Chadwick's most often performed works.[67]

❧ Joshua

In 1919–20, toward the end of his composing days, Chadwick wrote four songs to lyrics by R. D. Ware, Henry Newbold, and the celebrated Conan Doyle, all of which indicate a definite return to a nativistic celebration of Anglo-Saxon values. *Joshua* and the *Three Nautical Songs* exhibit the sturdy simplicity of Yankee-English dance music, hornpipes, and marches. *Joshua* (pronounced "Josh-u-ay," the composer notes), with the text by Ware and billed as a humorous song, is introduced by a descending hornpipe with its expected gapped tetrachords and continues on with examples of the Celtic lilt and subdominant-plagal cadences (ex. 58). The Yankee musical style is reflective of the vernacular sounding text with its dropped *g*s, the vulgar form of the past tense of the verb do (as in "somethin' must be did"), and such expressions as "It's kinder mean" (for "It's kind of mean").

EXAMPLE 57   *A Ballad of Trees and the Master*

EXAMPLE 58 *Joshua*

In one instance, the relationship between the use of a gapped scale and its harmonic implication is evident (ex. 59). Chadwick's music for the phrase "In the same old way" is the gapped tetrachord harmonized with a tonic-subdominant-tonic progression. Had he, for argument's sake, set the same text with a conventional phrase, a setting that would fit both the text and the rest of the song perfectly, he would have had to harmonize the stepwise melody with a tonic-dominant-tonic combination. Thus, the original Chadwick melodic setting, based on his ethnic musical predisposition, results in a har-

EXAMPLE 59 *Joshua*

monic choice, the subdominant-plagal progression supporting the gapped tetrachord.

It is difficult to say which of the songs represent the essential Chadwick, for he was a complex, diverse, and sometimes contradictory human being. In the rush away from refinement, exoticism, and delicacy as aesthetic goals in art, Chadwick's more basic, aboriginal styles that celebrated earthiness and sturdy ethnicity may be overvalued. Indeed, those characteristics of his music set him apart from the rest of his school.

Nevertheless, the songs of *The Flower Cycle* and *Told in the Gate* cannot be dismissed simply because they do not conform to current notions of what acceptable music should have been. The diminished seventh, the augmented sixth, and even the "Tristan chord" may well come back into fashion. At that time, negative opinions may be taken as further evidence of the general change of musical taste since the invention of sound recording. But unless Chadwick's songs are performed or recorded, no one will be able to make a secure judgment as to their merit.

CHAPTER 17

Works for Soloists, Chorus, and Orchestra

Given the importance of the choral tradition in New England, it should come as no surprise that Chadwick devoted much of his career to writing works intended to be performed by the region's numerous choral societies and annual festival organizations. Subjects of an elevated poetic nature, derived from myths or Bible stories, scenarios that would appeal to choristers and their committees from the grass roots of church congregations, predominated. Drama would be projected through professional solo vocalists, who could add extra excitement to the occasion for the amateur chorus without the drawbacks of staged opera. The accompanying orchestra would be a compromise blend of professional ringers and worthy dilettantes. True, such a mixed medium always presents problems and has the potential for disaster. Success in such artistic adventures, however, must be measured in terms different from the standards usually applied to strictly professional performances. And with all of its uncertainties and political intrigue, the medium of chorus with soloists accompanied by orchestra was a sure outlet for any prolific New England composer who was not content with the occasional possibilities of symphony or chamber music performance and whose dreams of the stage were limited by reality.

❧ *The Lily Nymph*, Dramatic Poem

1895
For soloists, chorus (SATB), and orchestra (2 flutes, 2 oboes, English horn, 2 clarinets, 2 bassoons, 4 horns, 2 trumpets, 3 trombones, timpani, triangle, glockenspiel, cymbals, bass drum, harp, and strings)

A typical Chadwick work in this genre is *The Lily Nymph,* subtitled "Dramatic Poem," set to a libretto by Arlo Bates, the composer's favorite lyricist, and

written three years after their 1892 collaboration on the April Fools' eve con-
fection *A Quiet Lodging* for the Tavern Club. Probing the innermost reaches
of romantic sensibility, Bates takes as his point of departure the idea of the
doomed passion of a Black Forest knight, Albrecht, for an enchanted lake
creature, the Lily Nymph. Borrowing the barest of plot outlines from Fried-
rich Heinrich Karl de La Motte-Fouqué's *Undine,* Bates describes a cohort
of fellow knights escorting Albrecht through the forest on a midsummer's
night en route to his wedding. Dryads and elves are heard singing. A lake
full of water lilies is transformed into a sylvan pool of nymphs on that magical
night until dawn, when they must return to their vegetative form or perish,
and whoever sees them falls madly in love. Albrecht ignores this warning,
claiming that the power of true love may overcome any obstacle. As the night
progresses, the water lilies are transformed into beautiful maidens, and
among them is the fairest of them all, the Lily Nymph. Albrecht, although
betrothed, is transfixed by her beauty and, despite everything, falls in love.
The Lily Nymph's humanity is conquered as well by love. With the certain
knowledge that death will follow their embrace, she yields to Albrecht. The
approach of dawn and the summons of the Lake Spirit to return fail to deter
her. After one last passionate kiss, the Lily Nymph sinks lifeless into the lake,
and the broken-hearted knight drowns by plunging in after her. In an epilogue the elves, dryads, and knights bid the lovers farewell.

Chadwick's setting of *The Lily Nymph* displays many charming elements
of his musical style. Above all is the orchestral sonority, which accurately
depicts the mythic, fairy-like atmosphere. Bearing in mind the limitations
under which Chadwick generally had to work, his scoring is imaginative and
appropriate to the midsummer's night as a background for the emotions of
doomed passion. Also distinctive is Chadwick's personal melding of his
gapped tetrachordal melody with chromatic harmony. He almost succeeds in
transporting the listener from the Black Forest lake to a New England pond
filled with native American water lilies, the *nymphaeae odorata*. Everywhere
in the score, which employs the technique of recurring motives, are the tell-
tale pentatonic inflections that localize the ultraromantic musical flourishes.
In a few cases, certain harmonic touches lift the music above the level of mere
professional competence—for example, the open fifths of the initial *molto*

tranquillo (ex. 60) and the fourths and fifths used to depict the supernatural elves and dryads a little later (ex. 61). Albrecht's first recitative is interrupted by an orchestral metaphor for the enchanted lilies that sounds somewhat like Debussy's symbolist harmonies in that other musical tale of passionate emotion among woodland sprites, *L'après-midi d'un faune* of 1894 (ex. 62). Granted, Bates was no Mallarmé and Chadwick no Debussy, yet the resemblance of these few Boston measures to those written for Parisian ears is uncanny, compelling the listener to speculate about what might have been if Chadwick had indeed studied with César Franck after visiting Giverny, with its pools of water lilies waiting to be immortalized by the other Claude— Monet.

But the reality of Chadwick's career and the Lily Nymph herself is that they were both bound by caution at critical junctures. The ultimate erotic experience, which Mallarmé and Debussy describe symbolically in words and music, is for Bates and Chadwick just a fleeting embrace, maybe only a kiss. Such a moment apparently did not inspire anything more than a brand of institutionalized passion in music. Besides, the plot was a bit too tame and precious even for a late nineteenth-century American audience. After *Tristan und Isolde* and Gilbert and Sullivan, who could believe, even for a moment, that the penalty for an illicit kiss was death?

EXAMPLE 60   *The Lily Nymph,* introduction

EXAMPLE 61   *The Lily Nymph,* elves and dryads

EXAMPLE 62   *The Lily Nymph,* water lilies

Chadwick's audience was unable to accept without question so dated a plot. The *New York Times* said: "It is a pretty, sad story, suitable for the good young ladies and gentlemen of the typical provincial singing school. But Mr. Chadwick has made the music a little too difficult for such organizations."[68] Problems with amateur-professional performing groups were obviously first in the mind of the newspaper critics.

Chadwick did not conduct this premier of *The Lily Nymph,* but he did direct the performance of the musical poem for the Springfield Festival in May 1896. This time the orchestra was prerehearsed, and the soloists included such recognized singers as Emma Juch, Italo Campanari, and Baron Berthald, who were better able to manage the difficulties of the solo roles. Under Chadwick, the chorus responded with great sensitivity. With words of praise, the *Springfield Republican* described *The Lily Nymph* as "full of delicious orchestration . . . it is a real midsummer's night's dream. . . . No American composer, not even Mr. MacDowell, has a surer sense of orchestral color which would have been admired by Berlioz."[69]

But the praise was not unalloyed. The reviewer quarreled with Chadwick about the "Dance of the Lily Nymphs," which serves as an interlude between the sequence of choruses and solos.

> The dance of the lily nymph is piquant and fascinating, in spite of the awful suspicion the "Ta-ra-ra boom de ay" [ex. 63] was being played outside the composer's window while he was at work—it seems that he was writing it as long ago as when that maddening thing was in vogue.[70]

Actually, without knowing it, the critic's words have a kernel of truth. For in *A Quiet Lodging,* that bit of musical high jinks, the composer calls for the hero, Christopher, a cornet-playing poet, to disturb Professor Blowbellow, the would-be opera composer, by sounding raucously a medley of popular tunes, including "Ta-ra-ra boom de ay."

In addition to *The Lily Nymph,* works such as *Phoenix Expirans,* a successful experiment in the modern musical interpretation of medieval Latin lyrics, and the Christmas pastoral *Noel* were well received, published, and often performed. But worthy as they were, they did not make the impact of Chadwick's orchestral, chamber, or stage pieces. And none of them enjoyed

EXAMPLE 63 *The Lily Nymph,* dance

the enormous popular success and international acclaim of *Hora Novissima,*
by his student and colleague Horatio Parker. *Judith,* Chadwick's choral masterpiece and the one work which might be considered in the same league as
Hora Novissima, is in reality a lyric drama intended for but never achieving a
stage performance.

CHAPTER 18

Stage Works

Although Chadwick is known primarily for his instrumental music, through-out his long career he wrote seven works for the stage: *The Peer and the Pauper* (1884), *A Quiet Lodging* (1892), *Tabasco* (1894), *Judith* (1901), *Every-woman* (1911), *The Padrone* (1912), and *Love's Sacrifice* (1923). Not only does this output indicate a lifelong interest in dramatic as opposed to instrumental music, but also the Chadwick stage repertory represents the largest single category of his compositions, approximately fifteen hours of music. More-over, if such unstaged pieces as *Lovely Rosabelle, The Lily Nymph,* and *Phoenix Expirans* are added to these explicit stage works, one can appreciate the sheer volume of Chadwick's works concerned with the drama of the poetic as well as of the theater.

One obvious reason for his relative obscurity as a dramatic composer today is the fact that it is much easer to arrange for the performance of cham-ber and orchestral music than to muster the forces and money necessary to mount complex productions of operas. Unperformed and unheard, works such as *Tabasco, Judith,* and *Everywoman,* which made Chadwick as famous as he ever was to be in his lifetime and upon which a great part of his contem-porary reputation rested, are unknown today except as items in bibliogra-phies.

But these three works especially, together with the ill-fated labor of love *The Padrone,* are not just museum pieces deserving adoration for reasons of national pride. They are all extremely stageworthy. Each one, in its own way, deals with the emotional attitudes of Americans to broad areas of concern in a three-dimensional realization that is virtually unique to the operatic art and that often escapes literature, the visual arts, or architecture. Thus, they may be valued as cultural documents of American history. Nevertheless, it is the music itself, occasioned by the topical scenarios, that demands attention. Depending on the operatic genre, it is, in turn, tuneful, noble, descriptive, and deeply expressive. While it projects these universal qualities, it is always proper to American sensibilities and the prosody of its English texts. An insightful production company that staged any one of the Chadwick dramatic oeuvre would not go unrewarded.

❧ *Tabasco,* Burlesque Opera

1894
For actors, singers, chorus: singers, ballet, and theater orchestra

Tabasco, the burlesque opera for which Chadwick wrote the music, is the sort of piece that makes one wonder about the direction his musical career might have taken if he had not followed the academic groove plowed by American tradition as the only respectable course for a gifted composer. In this regard, one can see the differences between the Boston situation and that of London, which permitted Henry Rowley Bishop and Arthur Sullivan, for example, to pursue the theater as well as the academy. But even this most earthy of Chadwick's stage works had its mitigating features in deference to Boston's general prejudice against the theater.

First of all, *Tabasco* was conceived as the major attraction of a fundraising scheme to build a new armory for the fashionable Corps of Cadets. The theater Satan was, in effect, conscripted by the cadets for a laudable public purpose. The cadet show, as with many Anglo-American academic theatricals, would involve only men, a laudable way of shielding female siblings and sweethearts from the corruption of the stage. And while the show does deal with relationships between the sexes, the chief excitement of its scenario was the perenially popular American hot sauce, Tabasco. Any sexual excess as implied by the presence of a harem of nubile young women was sublimated in the gastronomic passion of an exotic autocrat for the ultimate spicy sensation. All this made for good fun and could be easily accepted in a town not especially known for either its tasty cuisine or unbridled lasciviousness. When *Tabasco* surpassed even the cadets fondest expectations by earning $26,000 during a week's run, it was taken over by the comedian Thomas Quigley Seabrooke for a professional production in that euphemistically named theater, the Boston Museum.[71]

Critical opinion was generally enthusiastic. *Tabasco* was not only one of the best remembered social-theatrical events of the city but also an artistic success. Chadwick, particularly, was singled out for praise. The reviewer for the Boston *Transcript,* among others, predicted that in the future, "given first-class material in the way of a text, the composer would be able to show a comic opera worthy of being rated according to the French standard as an *opéra-comique.*"[72] The Boston *Gazette* praised Chadwick's flair for the theater: "The music is steadily tuneful, it is never on stilts, its melodies fly easily and gracefully, and a popular level has been reached without any sacrifice of artistic dignity."[73] Chadwick must have been gratified, in reading this notice, that his youthful desire to change the course of American popular music (as indicated by his speech before the Music Teachers National Association in 1876) had received recognition. Whether or not he was worrying particularly at this time about his dignity is a question. His music, however, made it obvious he was no mere tunesmith.

Chadwick did not consider *Tabasco* a lark, a change from his priestly vocation as an artist devoted to the religion of aesthetics. And the proof that he took writing stage works seriously may be found in his legal challenge to the piracy of his score. By 1895 the show was apparently so valuable that Seabrooke, the comedian-producer of the commercial version, attempted to avoid the payment of royalties by changing the Tabasco sauce to whiskey and the title to *The Grand Vizier.* Outraged, the author, R. A. Barnet, and Chadwick immediately took action putting the sneaky Seabrooke on notice through strongly worded public announcements threatening all proprietors and managers of theaters with prosecution should they permit the pirate to sail *Tabasco* under any other flag.[74] But Barnet and Chadwick apparently never pursued any legal remedy. Although *Tabasco* was indeed remembered years later in eulogies after the composer's death, along with such elegant works as *Judith* and *Melpomene,* it did not hold the stage too much longer after its initial tour, and the question of its piracy became moot.

Whether Chadwick received other proposals for musicals as a result of *Tabasco*'s notoriety is not known. There are certain indications that Barnet was interested in continuing their association, but nothing concrete ever eventuated.[75] Barnet, unfortunately, was no Gilbert, or else the union of their two names, Barnet and Chadwick, might have rivalled that of their English models.

The original plot, laid in Tangier, involves the quest of the ruling bey for the ultimate in gastronomic excitement, ordinary spices and even his harem having long since bored him.[76] The story is complicated by two pairs of lovers—Marco, a Spanish trader, and Fatima, the latest addition to the bey's harem, and Marco's sister, Lola, and an Irish-American drifter, Dennis, who, having given the bey a taste of a strange new sauce, Tabasco, gets a job as the latest "French" cook in the bey's household. Unfortunately, the Tabasco runs out, and the cook's life is forfeit unless he is able to procure more before the day ends. Additional problems are created by a conspiracy between the Grand Vizier and an aging inmate of the harem, Has-been-a, to undo the bey. But all ends well when a fresh supply of Tabasco, in the form of a five-foot-tall bottle, is delivered to the bey. An idea of the text's literary level comes from the last two lines of the epilogue spoken by the lucky cook:

Don't rise ladies, ye'd better stay below,
And let me, here, in your sweet smiles to bask—oh,
To—bask—oh!

No artistic brief may be made of the text; it goes out of its way to say the obvious. One implication of this and many other chauvinistic scenarios (and a reason they have been so successful, surely) is that they show that even the most powerful potentate of a non-Western land is no match for the lowliest American idler. Besides this jingoistic puffery of American egos, such plots afford many opportunities for topical comment by placing outrageous sentiments in the mouths of exotic personalities.

As in the music of similar shows, greatest emphasis is placed on individual production numbers, and Chadwick's catchy tunes and interesting orchestral accompaniments give the burlesque opera its artistic continuity.[77]

The stage business, dialogue, costumes, and scenery were also entertaining, but only Chadwick's score guaranteed verve and solidity. The fact that Chadwick borrowed some of the material from music he had written almost a quarter of a century before, when he had just quit high school, serves only to enhance his reputation. It shows at that early age, without instruction, Chadwick already had the buds of musical talent. He also borrowed material from his first dramatic work, *The Peer and the Pauper,* which he wrote with Robert Grant.

Tabasco is also a catalogue of contemporary popular music as recorded by a trained composer with imagination. The "March of the Pasha's Guard," a form that may be considered de rigueur for an entertainment commissioned by a militia, is a sterling example of an American parade medley, with its syncopated rhythms and chromatic turns (exs. 64, 65). So are the interpolated genre songs or production numbers of the last act that have little to do with the plot, such as it is. The "Plantation Ballad," in particular, is an obligatory ethnic parody number (exs. 66, 67). Just as typical are the Spanish "Bolero," the Irish "Ditty," and the French "Rigaudon," written as song and dance vehicles for the chief personalities of the show.

More noteworthy are the extended dramatic musical scenes. The opening chorus, for example, involves catchy rhythms and whistleable tunes of vernacular music as well as the tonal and harmonic structure of more formal music with the finale-like contrast between vocal solo and full choral textures.

Finale technique is also used in the other concerted numbers. "Reading of the Mail" displays changes in meter, tempo, key, and orchestration. Interspersed recitative, dialogue, waltz solos, and a vivace ending are good examples of the unusually well-designed dramatic music, rare in such musicals. "Gem of the Orient" is another especially well-crafted scene employing finale ideas in an interior number. Here the plot assumes plausible dimensions as sentiment and surprises are communicated almost totally by the clever unraveling of one musical twist after another. The quartet of Fatima, Lola, Marco, and the Pasha is a moment of sincere emotion in an otherwise slapstick vaudeville.

The explanation for the appearance of such a well-wrought design becomes clear when one realizes that this music was originally written as the

EXAMPLE 64 *Tabasco,* "March of the Pasha's Guard"

*These two measures offer a textbook example of what this author has denominated an *omnibus* progression. It contains all but one of the series of five chords exhibiting stepwise chromatic voice-leading in contrary motion. See Yellin, "The Omnibus Idea" (Paper delivered at the Thirty-eighth Annual Meeting of the American Musicological Society, Dallas, November 2–5, 1972).

EXAMPLE 65 *Tabasco,* "March of the Pasha's Guard"

EXAMPLE 66   *Tabasco,* "Plantation Ballad"

finale to the first act of the composer's earlier *Peer,* which, in turn, was modeled on schemes of the Gilbert and Sullivan operas, notably *Patience.*

However well-written, such musical scenes do not account so much for
the popular success of *Tabasco* as do the simpler numbers: The "Grand Vizier's Song," the "Pasha's Song" ("What Other People Say"), "Fatima's
Song" ("O Lovely Home"), "Has-been-a's Song" ("Hush, Hush, Silent Be"),
and the "March of the Pasha's Guard," which all have friendly tunes and
clever, topical lyrics. The Vizier's song (ex. 68) contrasts a deadpan, mono-
tonal chant over a continually varying accompaniment that quotes Wagner's
Nibelung motive:

The market slumps whenever I take hold;
And gets a boom as soon as I have sold.
To others come the coupons and gold,
But not to me!

EXAMPLE 67 *Tabasco,* "Plantation Ballad"

EXAMPLE 68 *Tabasco,* "Grand Vizier's Song"

me. The mar- ket slumps when- ev- er I take

hold; And gets a boom as soon as I have

sold. To oth- ers come the cou-pons and the

gold, but not to me! I

(*continued*)

EXAMPLE 68 *(continued)*

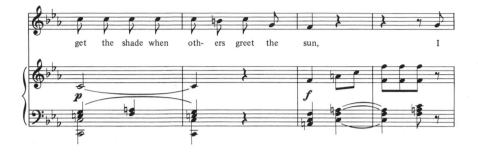

get the shade when oth- ers greet the sun, I

have the crust, the Pa- sha yanks the bun, To

all the rest my fate is on- ly fun, but not to

me!

Later, Chadwick uses a flourish from *Die Meistersinger* as a counterpoint to the words: "I get the shade when others get the sun."

Similar references are echoed in the lyrics of the "Pasha's Song" ("What Other People Say"):

> Brahms and Wagner may be fine,
> But I'll take none of them in mine,
>   And I do not care what other people say.

The lyrics indicate something about the typical Boston audience's level of awareness for comic opera in the 1890s. An interesting sidelight is the fact that the original lines for the Pasha's declaration of independence read: "Brahms and Chadwick may be fine."

Given the vogue today for commercial sponsorship of athletic and artistic events, it may well be that an enlightened chief executive officer of the McIllhenny Company, producer then as now of the famous pepper sauce, might support the revival of a musical that had no small part in spreading its fame.

❧ *Judith,* Lyric Drama

1901
For mezzo soprano, tenor, baritone, bass; SATB chorus: orchestra (2 flutes, 2 oboes (English horn), 2 clarinets, bass clarinet, 2 bassoons, 4 horns, 3 trumpets, 3 trombones, tuba, harp, timpani, cymbals, bass drum, triangle, side drum, and strings).

When William Chauncy Langdon wrote the libretto for *Judith,* he had recently graduated from Brown University.[78] Although Chadwick had made an initial treatment of the story, from the biblical apocryphal story, the published text shows Langdon's youthful flair. The climactic scene of seduction and murder, especially, had moments of high excitement that in its time and place must have appeared quite daring. It inspired Chadwick to write some of his most passionate music.

Langdon had tough standards to satisfy. Thomas Bailey Aldrich, a literary force to be reckoned with in Boston, had already offered the public his *Judith and Holofernes* as a narrative poem in 1896. Three years after the

Chadwick-Langdon *Judith,* the poem was transformed into a stage vehicle, *Judith of Bethulîa* for the rising actress Nance O'Neil. It suffices to say that Langdon (and the composer who gave him a preliminary scenario) had known of Aldrich's earlier version, for both the opera and the Aldrich tale have Judith motivated in her quest by a vision that does not occur in the biblical narrative. In the poem the appearance of a hand merely suggests the direction of Holofernes's camp to Judith; in Langdon's libretto the vision is of Judith's dead husband telling her what she must do.

For all its dramatic qualities, the text is a major stumbling block to the opera's success.[79] It wobbles between conventional religiosity and fin-de-siècle eroticism. Perhaps stylistic tension was inevitable. The minimal prospects for full theatrical production of native American opera no doubt forced composers such as Chadwick, who had strong desires to write dramatic works, to make compromises that might insure performance, at least in the concert hall. As director of the Springfield and Worcester festivals, Chadwick, with some power over choice of repertory, might have skewed his conception of *Judith* toward a musical and dramatic format with significant choral participation. After all, the institutionalized amateur chorus made such summer concert series possible. Not content with the prospect of writing yet another biblical oratorio, however, Chadwick made provisions for a hybrid form, modeled after Handel and the latest French *drame lyrique,* most likely Camille Saint-Saëns's *Samson and Delilah,* which he had recently conducted. Thus, it was also predictable that although a festival performance without scenery, action, and costumes might support, for example, the static oratorio sections devoted to divine supplication, such a production was bound to attenuate the effect of the more explicitly operatic scenes of sensuality, luxuriance, and murder that demanded both action and atmosphere in addition to the music.

In fact, the critics for both the *Boston Transcript* and the *New York Times* came to the conclusion that the stylistic compromise did not work. To test it fairly, *Judith* deserved a theatrical production but did not get one.

Besides such structural problems, the premiere of the opera was dragged down by the intransigence of the amateur singers, whose devotion had only recently been focused upon Chadwick's predecessor as music director and who were rebelling against singing a difficult and unfamiliar repertory.[80] Paying for sufficient orchestral rehearsal time was also a problem. Nevertheless, critical opinion was enthusiastic about the music itself, especially the composer's knack for apt musical characterization, the evocative and exotic orchestral sonorities, the "great climax" of the second act, and, of course, the strength of the choral writing.[81] Mentioned particularly was "Ah, noblest of Judah's women!" sung by Hebrew captives, first with a certain irony when Judith appears in the enemy camp dressed as a seductress and, in the third act, with adoration after Judith's assassination of Holofernes (ex. 69).

The two leading singers, Gertrude May Stein, as Judith, and David Bispham, as Holofernes, were also warmly praised. Curiously, Bispham fails to mention his creation of this role of the Assyrian general in his memoirs, written only a few years later.[82]

After this high point, the history of performances of *Judith* is a tale of decline. It remains unrecorded, and its only recent performance was at Dartmouth in 1977.

Langdon's *Judith* follows the Apocrypha rather literally, with the exception that it fails to present any of the broader symbolic and historic issues that occupy six of the sixteen chapters. In Act I the Assyrians' siege has reduced the morale of the Jews in Bethulia to the point of surrender. Judith, a young widow, asks for divine guidance to save the day. Achior, an Assyrian mercenary, warns the Jews that if they do not surrender immediately, they will be destroyed. Later, the beautiful Judith appears again, dressed in seductive attire, and tells of a vision in which her dead husband commands her to go to the enemy camp to seduce and slay Holofernes, the commander-in-chief. Despite the people's plea to her that "lust digs every grave," she leaves Bethulia.

Act II is divided into two tableaux, the camp of Holofernes and the interior of Holofernes's tent. Separate choruses of Assyrian soldiers, Hebrew captives, and camp followers set the scene of unbridled cruelty and brutality. Holofernes's initial aria commands the stage; Achior's counsel to employ craft rather than force to defeat the Jews earns him the title of traitor. As he is dragged away, Judith enters, much to the despair of the captives, who misconstrue her purpose, dressed and adorned as she is. But the Assyrians, especially Holofernes, are immediately charmed. The general is willing to

EXAMPLE 69   *Judith,* chorus, "Ah, noblest of Judah's women!"

grant her any wish if she will but spend the night with him. All Judith requests is that she and her maid be permitted to leave the camp twice a day to pray.

In the second tableau the revelries of a frenzied orgy are heard in front of the tent of Holofernes. As Judith approaches, the interior of the cavernous tent is revealed. As the celebrations mature, the choruses sing:

Come, taste the dance's wild desire!
Come, touch thy lips with passion's fire!
Come, join our laughing, wanton throng!
While Ishtar woos with wine and song!

Judith coyly strings the willing Holofernes along and asks that he dismiss the orgiasts so that she might serve him alone. The following love scene is a blend of eroticism, teasing, and misdirection, as Judith manages to avoid any sexual contact with Holofernes before he, overcome with wine, "sinks unconscious on the couch." Instead, her passion is reserved for the supreme moment when, guided by her earlier vision, she beheads the sleeping general with his own sword and leaves the camp with the severed head.

In Act III Ozias, the Hebrew magistrate, greets the dawn with foreboding. At the height of his despair, Judith returns with a request to mobilize the people. Displaying the head of Holofernes, she recites her story. The chorus responds with a reprise of "Ah, noblest of Judah's women," this time sung with a new militancy and adoration. Achior, reappearing in the garb of an Israelite, announces his conversion, and the opera ends with a stirring hymn of praise to Jehovah for helping the Jews drive out their now leaderless enemies from the land.

Really, not a bad scenario! Although more cosmopolitan opinion makers might cavil at the mixed genre, such a blend of oratorio and opera proved a viable mix for a culture nourished by high-minded aesthetics yet yearning for music expressive of sexual passion. This search for equilibrium was especially demanded by a society looking for redemption through the arts rather than through religion. Chadwick's effort to meld the hymn-tune harmony of his forefathers with sensuous chromatic orchestral sonorities propelled by the rhythms of erotic love, however, had nowhere to go after it was given its inadequate trial. It was one thing for an American to hold sway at a local summer festival. But it was quite another for him to be able to enter the repertory of professional opera houses at the beginning of the twentieth century.

There are four things to remember about *Judith:* (1) the use of English speech rhythms as the basis for the melodic lines; (2) the American-sounding melodies based on the gapped tetrachordal style; (3) the creation of both exotic and erotic orchestral sonorities; and (4) his ability to depict personality through music. An examination of these four areas shows that they define, in their totality, a personal as well as an American musical style.

One touchstone of Chadwick's native manner is his sensitivity to English speech rhythms in setting Langdon's text. The idiosyncratic syncopations set to certain disyllabic and trisyllabic words are an indication of the composer's attempt to write melodic lines that enhance normal speech patterns rather than obscure them. From the opening chorus the syncopated rhythm dominates the music. When the massed chorus enters on the text "Proud Asshur's host," the listener becomes aware of the origin of the syncopated phrase in the prosody of *As-shur* (ex. 70). These explicit syncopations are heard not only in the settings of *cometh, coward, traitor, Egypt, yonder,* and *Jewess* but also in the settings of such disyllabics as *power, tower,* and *hour* in single tones. Both these syncopated settings contrast dramatically with notations for *to-night, a-way, re-joice,* or *be-hold,* where the syllabic stress is reversed.

Although this is a Hebrew drama, the ethnic origins of its authors cannot be mistaken. Naturally, the English diction immediately gives the piece an Anglo flavor. In fact, Judith appears more of a Yankee paragon—Ida Lewis or Anne Hutchinson, for example—than a beautiful Jewess. Her independence of mind and body and her inability to be corrupted by desire, flattery, or pride place her more in the tradition of the Anglo-Saxon heroine rather than of the continental *Ewig-Weibliche.*

Much of the American ethnic identity is created by the strong pentatonic or gapped tetrachordal melodies. Ozias exhorting the citizens of Bethulia, Judith's plea to Jehovah (ex. 71), the various choruses in Yankee hymn-tune

EXAMPLE 70 *Judith,* act 1, introduction and opening chorus

(In Bethulia. **Israelites, Priests, Soldiers** and **Children** conversing in groups, with despairing gestures. **Ozias** and **Judith** among them.)

EXAMPLE 71 *Judith,* aria, "O show me, Lord"

O show me, Lord, how I may save this____ land!____

Make Thou____ mine arm its du- ty un-der- stand, And

keep me in the hol- low of Thine hand,____

By Thy great might,__ by Thy great might!

EXAMPLE 71   (*continued*)

style, and even the musical high point of Judith's vision (ex. 72)—all exhibit these characteristics of vocal expression rooted in New England's past.

As identifiable as Chadwick's Hebrews are, clothed in Yankee melody, so his Assyrians are dressed musically in a combination of modernistic chords emphasizing the elemental intervals of octaves, fourths, and fifths, driving dance rhythms, and sensual chromatic orchestral sonorities (ex. 73). The second act, with its wild and erotic music, could never have been mistaken for hymn singing at the Worcester Festival. Of all the composers of his generation, Chadwick was the only one to be able to break through the bonds of inhibition and let his imagination go—somewhat (ex. 74). Cross-rhythms, dance-like syncopes, percussive effects, the strategic use of both the high baritone and mezzo-soprano tessituras, and the effective counterpoint of communicative orchestral figures—all join to achieve the great climax of the act when Judith, victorious, slays Holofernes.

This last aspect of Chadwick's musical and dramatic prowess can be better understood by looking at the carefully worked out yet spontaneous-sounding motives. No fewer than thirteen may be ascertained, characterizing everything from Asshur, the pagan god, to Judith's deceit and Holofernes's sword. The sword motive shows that while the composer was obviously aware of Wagnerian operatic practice, his seems to have been based upon an earlier source: the confrontation scene of Giacomo Meyerbeer's *Le Prophète*, where Jean tries to silence his puzzled mother during his coronation by

EXAMPLE 72 *Judith,* Judith's vision

bringing down divine light on her troubled brow. In Judith the heroine suddenly sees Holofernes's brilliantly shining falchion, as if directed to it by divine inspiration: "Thou gleamest in my sight" (ex. 75). Thus, the instrument of Holofernes's destruction, presented as a sharp, heavenly beam of light, is musically characterized by orchestral sonorities of high treble triads similar to the ones Meyerbeer first employed. Wagner's more famous sword

EXAMPLE 73 *Judith,* act 2, second tableau

Before the tent of Holofernes. Sentinel pacing up and down. Music and sounds of revelry from interior of tent.

EXAMPLE 74 *Judith,* act 2, Assyrian chorus

EXAMPLE 74 (*continued*)

Ish- tar___ woos with wine and song!___

Ish- tar___ woos with wine and song!___

motive from *The Ring* simply would not work in this situation: The metallic sound of brass enunciating a military signal, excellent as a metaphor for a weapon to be used by a mere mortal, would be inappropriate as a musical symbol for Jehovah's vengeance. In this way is Chadwick's *Judith* connected to the broad, cosmopolitan tradition of grand opera.

The passion of the music and the mise-en-scène of the love-murder tableau make a full stage production of Judith imperative for American opera. Much as we Americans like to imagine our parents as chaste and pure, as never having capitulated to temptation, we seem to be uncomfortable with an idea of American music written by our ancestors that is not rugged, patriotic, or redolent of Fourth of July oratory. Such erotically charged music as the Judith-Holofernes encounter seems to destroy an illusion. It is now time to expand the restricted canon of American music. The passionate, erotic, chromatic, romantic music of sophisticated sonority and highly trained voices is just as integral a part of American music as of European music. In creating such a unique blend of oratorio and opera, Chadwick successfully made opera American by adding to the music of universal romantic yearning and emotional expressivity the music of a native linguistic ethnic and religious tradition. That is why he picked the Judith story in the first place.[83]

EXAMPLE 75 *Judith,* act 2, sword motive

❧ *Everywoman: Her Pilgrimage in Quest of Love*

1911
For actors, singers, chorus (singing and ballet), theater orchestra

The year 1911, which first resonated to the vibrations of Victor Herbert's *Naughty Marietta* (particularly its hit tune "Ah! Sweet Mystery of Life") as well as Irving Berlin's ditty "Alexander's Ragtime Band," was also enlivened by the appearance of *Everywoman,* with Chadwick's music, beginning on February 27 at Lew Field's Herald Square Theatre in New York City. If any work gives the lie to the simplistic characterization of Chadwick as a Boston classicist, it is this thoroughly modern and stylish Broadway extravaganza in which no effort or expense was spared to produce the most artistic and technologically marvelous theatrical presentation to date on the American stage. Henry W. Savage, its flamboyant producer, a Boston real-estate Croesus, had since 1895 been producing both grand and light opera in English at the Castle Square Theatre. When he came across the English actor-singer Walter Browne's project for a contemporary morality drama that would celebrate the new importance of the modern woman, he instinctively turned to the one composer who could bring to the idea the musical imagination required to transform it into a rite or pageant of the evolving feminine consciousness. Besides, as a Bostonian, Savage must have been well aware of Chadwick's unique populist symphonic style, which could attract the common ear while still maintaining a high level of expressivity and morality. In an interview with the *New York Daily Tribune* on March 5, 1911, Savage let it be known that after hearing Browne read *Everywoman* to him, Chadwick was so moved that he said he would compose the music "as a labor of love." Nevertheless, the composer ultimately had enough presence of mind to accept Savage's generous offer of ten thousand dollars for the score, completed by Christmas 1910.

Although Browne wrote his *Everywoman* as a morality play in which the characters are personifications of abstract qualities, he was a practical enough man of the theater to attempt to achieve a box-office appeal by giving "pleasure and entertainment to all classes of intelligent playgoers . . . hence the music, the songs, the choruses, the dances, the spectacular and scenic effects, and the *realism of everyday life* . . ." [emphasis added]. Here may be another reason for Chadwick's fascination with the project, given his artistic commitment to populist realism as expressed in such pieces as "A Vagrom Ballad," in its own way a kind of symphonic poem about Everyman. Producer Savage further enhanced this realist conception: The sets included a reproduction of a completely furnished sitting room of a country house, the stage of a large metropolitan theater with all its apparatus exposed to the audience, Broadway on New Year's Eve, and the dining room of a luxuriously appointed New

York penthouse. To create the exact mood of a church procession, Savage told the reporter of the *Tribune:*

> I wanted my production to be as realistic in all points. So my acolytes in the church scene in the fourth act are in reality what they seem. Charity, the minister who sings so beautifully in the funeral procession of Youth is impersonated by the bass soloist of an Episcopal Church choir. . . . [84]

His desire for ultrarealism led Savage also to insist on the installation of real church bells weighing several tons. He even had fabricated, for the then enormous sum of six hundred dollars, a "magic" mirror in which the face of Flattery appears while Everywoman and her three handmaids—Youth, Beauty and Modesty, who stand together in front of the glass—are also reflected in it.

Chadwick's contribution was given top billing in advertisements and brochures that were as discreetly extravagant as the stage show itself: "SPECIAL SYMPHONIC MUSIC," "SYMPHONIC INTERPRETIVE MUSIC," "containing all the attractive elements of drama, opera and musical comedy." [85] "It is performed by three companies of artists, viz.: actors, singers and musicians. . . . Accompanying the organization (of over 200) is a complete symphony orchestra," said the leaflet for the western tour. Back in Boston, Philip Hale, the music critic, was quoted in advertisements as saying:

> Not content with elaborate stage settings and handsome costumes, he [Savage] engaged Mr. Chadwick to write music for the play, songs, choruses, dances, melodramatic music—all of real value to the production. The long run of the play in New York is not surprising. As a spectacle with music, "Everywoman" is well worth seeing. [86]

Beyond this not uncommon rhetoric and critical opinion were unusual testimonials from unexpected quarters. Savage was able somehow to garner statements of support from all manner of clergy, public personalities, and feminists. Rabbi Hugo Heyman expressed the hope "that every young woman could see Everywoman and learn the great lesson it teaches." Elbert Hubbard, author of *A Message to Garcia,* said: "I saw it one night and then waited the next day to see it again. The greatest triumph of the American stage." And leading suffragette Ida Husted Harper averred: "I was profoundly impressed. The dignity and beauty of the lines were delightfully refreshing, in contrast to the shallow nonsense which has so largely taken possession of the stage." Even the *Catholic Transcript* claimed *Everywoman* as "three hours of delightful entertainment while teaching a lesson at once needed and salutary."[87]

Sophisticated reviewers such as H. T. Parker of the *Boston Transcript* were more circumspect. Although he saw the play itself as "A Queer Entertainment," dull and tame, nevertheless he grudgingly recognized "the Excellent Declamation, Music and Setting in which the Whole is Clothed." Chadwick was praised for the "Excellent incidental music . . . that often accompanies declamation" and for his songs and dances: "It is effective music heightening text and action, taking color from the scene. . . ."[88]

After its initial New York run, the show came to Boston in November 1911. It then toured the regular circuit of theaters and made an unusual excursion to the West Coast, including Los Angeles, San Francisco, and Denver. On September 12, 1912, *Everywoman* was lavishly produced at Drury Lane in a slightly altered version with London rather than New York locales: Piccadilly Circus was substituted for Broadway's Great White Way in the New Year's Eve scene, for example. The London cast, headed by the beautiful Alexandra Carlisle, was all new except for Patricia Collinge, who played Youth in both productions. Chadwick's score remained intact but did not seem to impress the English critics, judging from the space granted to notice of the music. Still, the *Westminster Gazette,* which mentioned the "real motorcars" in the Piccadilly Circus scene, says, "A great deal of music is given, all of it written for the piece by an American composer of considerable standing named George W. Chadwick."[89] The *Globe* commented enigmatically: "This reminds us to say something in praise of the music of the American composer George Chadwick, who if he has not written anything remarkable, has certainly managed not to rise too high above the level the dramatic orchestration and his melodies have sought to illustrate."[90] The *Times* added: "Of Mr. Chadwick's music not a great deal need be said. It is straightforward, tuneful, and, for the greater part, harmonically moral. There is a pretty song for Conscience with a modal suggestion, but though the score

points the moral sympathetically enough it does not go a long way to en-
force it."[91]

The best synopsis of the allegorical story of *Everywoman* derives from
the Herald Square program:

> Canticle I. Everywoman is shown her quest for love. With Youth,
> Beauty and Modesty she sets out.

> Canticle II. Her travels take her first to the stage of a metropolitan the-
> atre where she mistakes Passion for Love and where Modesty deserts
> her. She learns in time that Passion is not Love and, pursuing her quest,
> leaves the playhouse.

> Canticle III. At a gay dinner party, lasting until dawn, Beauty dies and
> Everywoman, looking at her mirror sees not Flattery as she did at first
> but Truth. Wealth comes to her side, whispers in her ear and, desperate,
> she enters into a mad, drunken dance with him. Conscience seeks to
> dissuade Everywoman, but Wealth temporarily triumphs.

> Canticle IV. Disappointed finally, Everywoman finds herself alone with
> Youth, her body clad in a cheap and shabby dress on Broadway on New
> Year's Eve. Time, the callboy, comes to rob Everywoman of Youth and
> Everywoman, in her plight, tries to regain the affections of Wealth.
> Wealth passes her by and takes up with Vice instead.

> Canticle V. The Truth comes and reveals her Beauty to Everywoman.
> "Love," says Truth "is my son." Everywoman returns to her home and
> there finds Love waiting for her. At first she does not recognize Love,
> but Truth makes her see Love aright and, as Everywoman and Love
> clasp hands, Modesty returns and clings to Everywoman's garments.

When Chadwick accepted Savage's offer of ten thousand dollars for composing a score for *Everywoman,* he ostensibly agreed to supply entirely new music. But like many other theatrical composers faced with the necessity of producing much music on short notice, the composer dipped into his chest of
lesser known scores. Those with good memories in the audience at Boston's
Majestic Theatre must have been quite surprised to hear the main theme of
the Introduction, Everywoman's motive. Chadwick had taken it directly
from the duet between Maud and Lionel in *The Peer and the Pauper* and from
his comedy overture *Thalia,* both dating from over a quarter of a century
earlier!

For the pantomimic and melodramatic scenes, Chadwick creates music that today would be recognized as cinematic, characterized by irregular formal construction and recurring motives appropriate to the atmosphere, action, or dialogue of the moment. A typical Chadwickian protomovie music passage accompanies Everywoman's entrance in the first canticle as she utters: "Farewell, sweet dreamland fairies, fare ye well. At dawn, see!/Everywoman flouts thee. In my dreams I thought myself a flower" (ex. 76). The composer underscores the beginning text with descending parallel six-four chords in *pianissimo* strings. After the mention of Everywoman's name, on *flouts* the strings break into tremolos. Then, as the sound of the word *flower* dissipates, the full orchestra presents the lyric, gapped theme of the Introduction (from *The Peer* and *Thalia*), which symbolizes Everywoman.

Balancing the much advertised symphonic manner Chadwick uses for the Introduction and action music is his musical comedy style as exhibited in the songs, choruses, and dances. Conscience's brief "A Little Star" sounds unusually modern and forward-looking (ex. 77). It avails itself of the typical nineteenth-century repetitive or dance rhythm accompaniment and employs nondominant chords of the ninth and eleventh. This was the one number the London *Times* critic called "pretty." Contrasting such sentimental balladry are Chadwick's energetic songs and dances for the chorus, especially in the New Year's Eve revels on Broadway, where syncopated march rhythms of ragtime dominate (exs. 78, 79).

(NOBODY steps politely aside and exits, as VICE, disguised as an attractive young woman, trips on, singing and dancing.)

VICE
Full of glee, follow me.
Where's the moth loves not the bright light?
Siren, I, Living lie.
I'm the spirit of the White Light.

CHORUS OF GIRLS
Giddy girls, flaunting pearls,
Decked in garments gay and gorgeous,
Laughing loud, swell the crowd
At all bacchanalian orgies.

EXAMPLE 76 *Everywoman,* canticle 1, melodrama

Farewell sweet dreamland fairies fare ye well. At dawn, see! Everywoman

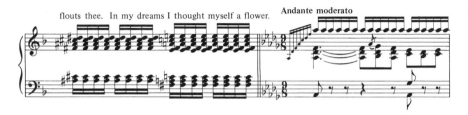

flouts thee. In my dreams I thought myself a flower.

Andante moderato

EXAMPLE 77   *Everywoman,* "A Little Star"

FOOLS

Rah, Rah, Rah,–Rah, Rah, Rah–
We're the rising generation.
Pa you know, made the dough
Which we blow in dissipation.

(ROUGES, GAMBLERS STOCKBROKERS and other
VAGABONDS enter, singing in chorus.)
We are the crooks, but our looks

EXAMPLE 78 *Everywoman,* "Happy New Year" chorus

Hap-py New Year, Hap-py New Year, to the mul-ti, mul-ti, mul-ti, million-

-aire.___ We wor-ship wealth and drink his health, so___

And our manners are deceiving.

Honest graft is our craft—

Impolite to call it thieving.

(FOOLS flirt with VICE, ROGUES, VAGABONDS, etc., cross the stage, each lifting his hat to VICE as he passes. The last one chucks her under the chin. One FOOL resents this. A fight begins. LAW and ORDER, in the uniform of policemen, enter, and seize the combatants. The FOOL gives LAW money. The ROGUE and the FOOL exit, arm in arm, in one direction. LAW and ORDER march off the other. Snow begins to fall.)

EXAMPLE 79 *Everywoman,* dance for boys' and girls' chorus

(continued)

EXAMPLE 79   (*continued*)

All in all, Chadwick's association with a fully integrated Broadway production of a novel musical show, successful on both sides of the Atlantic, should provide a new perspective from which to judge his already versatile career. Given this heady experience, one can easily sympathize with the Boston composer when his *The Padrone,* on which he had been working during this period, was rejected by the Metropolitan Opera the following year.

❧ *The Padrone*, Opera

1912
For soprano, mezzo-soprano, contralto, tenor, bass, baritone; SATB chorus; orchestra (2 flutes, piccolo, 2 oboes, English horn, 2 clarinets, bass clarinet, 2 bassoons, 4 horns, 3 trumpets, 3 trombones, tuba, timpani, bass drum, cymbals, glockenspiel, triangle, tambourine, xylophone, celesta, bell (on stage), harp, and strings)

By contrast with the success and notoriety of *Tabasco* and *Everywoman,* Chadwick's only contemporary lyric drama, *The Padrone,* was doomed from the beginning; it would remain almost unknown even to his own circle. Written in 1912 with the composer's highest hopes of it being produced by the Metropolitan Opera Company (the company had a new policy of producing at least one new American work each season), it was tested by professional members of the Boston Opera, which Chadwick himself had helped found. It had all the ingredients for popularity. It was certainly well-crafted and expressive. Yet it failed even to achieve a concert performance.

For some unknown reason, after its mysterious rejection Chadwick seemed to accept the situation with resignation. *The Padrone* was fully scored and put to bed in his composition drawer.

His apparent lack of desire to push *The Padrone* may be explained by his age. He was fifty-nine, no longer the "young" American composer of great expectations, an image that he retained long after its truth faded. Or it may be explained by his failing health and immobility, documented by photographs that show him with a cane or leaning on a chair arm for support while standing, or by his cynicism, born of his intimate knowledge of musical politics. Perhaps this failure to press for his new opera was simply due to the fact that he had, as a successful academic executive and orchestral composer, other fish to fry. The same expenditure of energy, time, and money realistically required to mount a production campaign for *The Padrone* could be put to better use for his academic duties as well as for the certainties of performance and publication of his concert music.

Whatever the reasons, Chadwick's most stage-worthy opera was conceived, composed, and buried all within less than two years, from 1911 to 1913. But it must be stated that another reason for this seemingly inexplicable failure may lie in the subject matter itself.

The *padrone* system, to which the title refers, operated through the exploitation of poor Italian immigrants by a compatriot boss, or *padrone,* who, in return for the promise of labor, arranged transportation and employment and provided protection and housing. Taking advantage of illiteracy and ignorance, the *padrone* charged such high rates of interest and cost-of-living expenses that a laborer, so indentured, remained in bondage for years. While most such immigrants were men, there were also a relatively few women, thus obligated, who were put on the street as beggars or tambourine girls collecting money for organ grinders or who worked in the kitchens of the numerous restaurants that sprouted up in Boston's North End.

With Chadwick's demonstrated penchant for realism, as in his genre music of the *Symphonic Sketches* and his sympathy for realist literature and painting, it should not be too surprising that he would conceive of the operatic possibilities of a local story that blended the exotic (Italian culture), the real and everyday (Boston life), and the tragic-romantic (thwarted young love and murder). In the verismo opera of the modern Italian and French repertory, he could easily find the structural models that proved the aesthetic potential of similar material dealing with the lives of ordinary people under extraordinary stress.

Chadwick originally thought of his realist opera in one act that would call for part of the cast to sing in Italian, part in English. Such a scheme would reflect the actual language spoken by the immigrants or the immigration officials. It would also make it easier to produce, given the practicalities of an organization such as the Metropolitan and its manager, Giulio Gatti-Casazza. But this formula was soon dropped. The final draft of the libretto, made by Chadwick's friend David K. Stevens, who would later collaborate on Victor Herbert's book *The Madcap Duchess* (1913) and Henry Hadley's *Azora* (1917), was in two acts with an orchestral interlude similar to the layout of Ruggiero Leoncavallo's *I Pagliacci* (1882) and Pietro Mascagni's *Cavalleria Rusticana* (1890).

On December 5, 1912, Chadwick noted in his daybook that he sent a bound copy of the piano-vocal score to the Metropolitan in New York City. This was no speculative gesture. That year saw the performance of his student Horatio Parker's *Mona* at the opera house. Chadwick was a member of the committee that had awarded the opera its prize of ten thousand dollars and its guarantee of production. After MacDowell's death in 1908, Chadwick was certainly the dean of American music. So he had every expectation of receiving more than the perfunctory rejection he got in the mail one day along with requests for the payment of ordinary bills:

> This year [1913] has started off by deserving its reputation as a thirteener.
> First of all I received "The Padrone" back from the Metropolitan Opera House, N.Y. with a polite letter stating that: "it was not found

suitable for production at their establishment." Beyond the conventional editorial phrases, no explanation was given. I found out, however, through H. E. Krehbiel [music critic] that Gatti-Cazzaza [sic] disliked the book because it was a drama of life among the humble Italians,—and probably too true to life,—and that it had been played through by Morgenstern, one of the accompanists, who reported unfavorably on it. So there is the consideration that American composers get from the leading American Opera House. Another cat in the meal is the fact that Victor Herbert has a new one-act opera which he is pushing through Kahn. "The Padrone" is now in the hands of Dippel, who will, I think, at least read it through.[92]

So Chadwick thought his opera failed to be produced, despite the commitment of the Metropolitan to produce a new American work each season, because the company was under the effective control of a foreigner who shied away from a disturbing social theme involving his compatriots and because of the negative opinion of a subordinate member of the musical staff, Hans Morgenstern. Last, there was the political interference of Otto Kahn, the financier, most influential chairman of the ruling Metropolitan board and friend of the composer Victor Herbert. Kahn was strongly in favor of doing Herbert's *Madeleine,* a piece of theatrical fluff set in the salon of an ancient regime French actress in the late eighteenth century. After having her invitation to dine turned down a couple of times by gentlemen friends on the grounds they were obligated to dine with their respective mothers, the heroine decides to follow the example of such paragons of virtue and filial duty by, at last, dining with her own mother! One can easily sympathize with Chadwick's chagrin at having been vanquished by so gripping a plot: "So there is the consideration that Americans get from the leading American Opera House." Although he did not confide to his diary any more details, the twofold use of "American" in the context of the names Gatti-Casazza, Morgenstern, Kahn, and even Herbert (who was still considered Irish) leaves little to the imagination about this Yankee's sense of frustration and powerlessness, at least as far as opera was concerned. The fact that *Madeleine* was not well received critically and did not do well after its New York premiere was no consolation to the Bostonian.

No two operas could have been more different than *Madeleine* and *The Padrone.* Foreshadowing the plot and characterization of Arthur Miller's play

A View from the Bridge (1955), *The Padrone* is a sympathetic outsider's under-standing, far in advance of its time, of the way cultural forces act on the everyday lives of ordinary people of a specific ethnicity. The scene is Boston's North End in the "Summer of the Present Day." The action opens inside an Italian restaurant at night. After a genre scene involving playing a domino game, buying cigarettes, and paying a bill at a cash register, the orchestrally accompanied recitative relates that Catani, the padrone and owner of the establishment, lusts after Marietta, a tambourine girl in his employ. But his passion is unrequited. She is in love with Marco, who plans to marry her as soon as he arrives in Boston, his passage from Italy having been paid by her meager savings so that he will not be indebted to Catani. When Marietta rebuffs Catani, he determines at once to be avenged. Learning that Marco was once jailed in the old country for an assault over Marietta's elder sister Francesca, whom he then was courting, Catani convinces Francesca to pay Marco back for casting her aside in favor of her younger sister by denouncing Marco to the immigration authorities as a felon as soon as he lands. According to Catani's plan, having spent all of her savings to pay for Marco's pas-sage, Marietta would have to remain unwed in Boston, while Francesca, with Catani's aid, would be free to accompany Marco back to Italy with the hope of making up for lost time. After an orchestral interlude of tragic affect, the second act takes place on a steamship pier with the immigration reception areas and the port side and gangplank of the ship visible. As the scene opens, realistic disembarking activities, such as making the gangplank secure, take place. There are three separate choruses: blasé American tourists returning from a Cook's Tour and the immigrants on shipboard, occupying upper and lower decks respectively, and a group of ethnic welcomers and a wedding party on the pier behind barricades. The gangplank down, Marco and Mari-etta are reunited. Francesca, urged on by the padrone, denounces Marco. He is placed under arrest, and as he is led back to the ship, Marietta, in a rage, stabs Catani with the strategically placed chief inspector's knife. The crowd looks on in horror just as the wedding party, singing a joyful nuptial song, comes back on the scene after having fetched the priest. The music more than matches the verismo of the words and action.

As a dramatic composer, Chadwick advances into the big leagues of continuous lyric drama, the most flexible and theatrical medium before the invention of the cinema. He came to the necessary skills relatively late in life. Even though he had already written five stage works before *The Padrone,* he was, after all, thirty when he wrote the first one, *The Peer,* a Gilbert and Sullivan clone. Furthermore, the nature of the earlier dramatic projects, with the exception of *Judith,* demanded either the clever, tuneful numbers of musical comedy or the set pieces of oratorio. Not until *The Padrone* did Chadwick set for himself the challenge of composing in a dramatic style that called for naturalistic flow of musical events, one realistically blending into the other without disturbing the unfolding plot. The obvious models were Massenet, Puccini, Leoncavallo, and Mascagni. But Chadwick had already demonstrated his own flair for orchestral continuity and so was able easily to fashion large-scale structural outlines into believable narrative sequences. In his hands both the necessary plotting as well as the lyric, passionate elements support and balance each other. With *The Padrone* it is as if he had been writing in this continuous dramatic style for years.

Dominated by the ominous motive of Catani's passion, the material delineating the other characters and the tuneful, melodic lines of the arias and ensembles reveal the composer in command of a personal stage manner. Even though his subjects are Italian, the melodic-rhythmic phrases clearly reflect the English text and American locale. The result is an opera as American as *Madama Butterfly* is Italian. The best way to describe the sound of *The Padrone,* thus, is to evoke the sounds of post–World War II American opera. Such an auralization may aid the reader to place the sound and style of *The Padrone* within the spectrum of accepted American repertory. While the orchestra carries the main burden of continuity, it nevertheless does subordinate itself to the singers during recitatives and arias. As in a melodrama or cinematic scores, the orchestra is employed to communicate inner, unarticulated emotions or states of mind; it clues the audience into the innocent or evil motivations of characters; it creates the atmosphere of bustle, as in the restaurant or dockside scene, or of repose; and it projects the audience from the present into a flashback or flashforward existing in the mind.

For these purposes Chadwick uses familiar orchestration: woodwinds by twos, brass, timpani, and strings. Where special sonorities are demanded, he brings in the harp and English horn, for example, but nothing that would create problems for most production organizations. His goal is to provide an imaginative orchestral fabric that contains no self-indulgent surprises. Clearly, Chadwick scored his music so that it could be performed by any competent group. In 1913 the American composer of opera was in no position to give any manager an easy excuse for not mounting his work.

Although the technique or orchestral-motivic continuity throughout the opera is indebted to the then-modern style, the vocal lines are written with the goal of communicating the English dialogue, at the same time grateful to the trained opera singer and resonant with an American melodic style. Evidence of these concerns is everywhere apparent in the score, especially in Chadwick's sensitivity to prosodic syncopation. Such words as *money, chatter, beggar, matters, threatens, finger, little,* and *Marta* all are systematically set to syncopations (ex. 80). This gives the melodic line an American flavor and makes the sung words intelligible.

The melodic lines are typified, as well, by Chadwick's bias toward tunes exhibiting the gapped tetrachord or pentatonicism. Marietta's naive yet passionate song of anticipation (ex. 81), for example, although expressed through the character of an Italian immigrant tambourine girl, is couched in the Yankee's melodic vein, as is her sister Francesca's ballad (ex. 82). Similarly, Marco's desperate "Farewell, my love," sung to his would-be wife as he is led away for deportation, has a noticeable American flavor (ex. 83). It is quite clear that the dramatic situations have a universal appeal, yet the medium of

EXAMPLE 80 *The Padrone,* "Such sums of money"

EXAMPLE 81 *The Padrone,* "I loved my love"

expression is based on Yankee, not Italian, pathos. This is what gives *The Padrone* verisimilitude as an American opera.

Here and there other touches of Americanisms are employed more for their documentary or satirical value than as attempts to make a national style. The dockside setting of Act II, with its specifications for scenic realism and an action scenario, calls for orchestral evocations of sailors and longshoremen at work, the sounds of a donkey engine, and hoisting tackle. When the tourists sing after the excited antiphonal shouts of welcome and greeting among the immigrants, their song is a direct quotation by Chadwick of a well-known ditty called "Home, Again" written by one M. S. Pike and dating from an earlier generation.[93] It is accompanied by a flute and piccolo obbligato on "Yankee Doodle" (ex. 84). Perhaps the most individualistic aspect of *The Padrone* is the orchestral interlude between the acts. Originally Chadwick had conceived of the opera in only one act with two large scenes. But in that

EXAMPLE 82 *The Padrone,* "The wind in the orchard"

version the second scene was too short, much of the dramatic action taking place in an "incidental and apparently spontaneous" effusion of the divided chorus accompanied by the orchestra as if in a realistic pantomime, melodrama, or cinema. But soon only the final version of two acts, more or less coequal in length, was decided upon. The second scene was expanded by realizing the action of the choruses, dockside and aboard ship, into specific composed music rather than left as an improvisatory dumb show. In Chadwick's thinking, this change necessitated an orchestral bridge from act to act, from the gloomy interior restaurant scene at night to the exterior joyful harbor setting under brilliant light. It also gave him an excuse for doing what he did best: orchestrate. The resulting miniature tone poem based on motivic gems of the drama gives a grand emotional scale to the work as a whole as well as provides an orchestral keystone to the arch-like structure of the two vocal acts. Its formal purpose aside, one can easily imagine the psychological

EXAMPLE 83   *The Padrone,* "There's no escape!"

impact of the interlude. It begins by reflecting the passion of the young lovers in the bucolic lyricism of Marietta's aria in the first act and the love duet of the second, only to cloud these smiling feelings by driving orchestral variations on Cantani's theme (ex. 85) and finally to end on the motive symbolizing the hopelessness of Marco's betrayal (ex. 86).

   The Padrone stands out as a missed opportunity for the building of a

EXAMPLE 84 *The Padrone,* dockside chorus

repertory of native works upon which twentieth-century American composers could grow. Ironically, four of America's best-known composers for the stage—George Gershwin, Virgil Thomson, Marc Blitzstein, and Gian-Carlo Menotti (and even a playwright, Arthur Miller)—all worked in ignorance of *The Padrone.* As early as 1912 it had already demonstrated its particularly American solution to such problems as idiomatic text setting, balances between orchestra and voice, choice of a socially realist scenario, and the representation of raw, incestuous passion and betrayal. Lacking such a model, the young composer seeking an operatic recipe had to look to Europe or

EXAMPLE 84   (*continued*)

EXAMPLE 85   *The Padrone,* Catani's theme, orchestral interlude

EXAMPLE 86   *The Padrone*, Marco's betrayal, orchestral interlude

reinvent the wheel, as it were, by examining de novo the peculiarities of English diction or by simply ignoring the problems of intelligibility and relying upon other aspects of musical theater to win over an audience. Although a production of *The Padrone* today cannot make up for the errors in judgment made so cavalierly by Gatti-Casazza, Morgenstern, and Kahn, nevertheless it would add an aesthetically worthy piece to America's still meager gallery of operas and might yet stir the imagination of the growing number of composers interested in learning from this American interpretation of a cosmopolitan form.

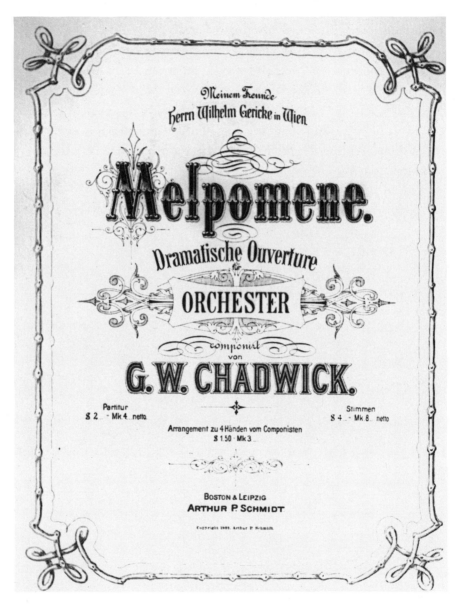

Melpomene, title page from the score published by Arthur P. Schmidt, Boston and Leipzig, 1891.

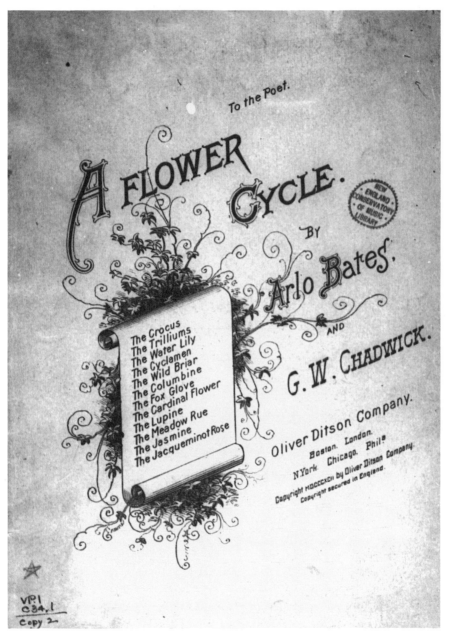

A Flower Cycle, title page from the score published by the Oliver Ditson Company,
Boston, London, New York, Chicago, and Philadelphia, 1892.

The Padrone, first page of orchestral score manuscript (holograph).

"TABASCO"

BURLESQUE OPERA

IN TWO ACTS

Characters

HOT–HED–HAM, PASHA, Bey of Tangier.
MARCO, a Spanish trader.
SID–HAS–SEM, Major-domo.
LOLA, Marco's sister.
FRANCOIS, the chef.
BEN–HID–DEN, Grand vizier.
FATIMA, the beautiful slave.
HAS–BEEN–A, a third-term harem favorite.

Contents

Act I

Act II

* Also published separately in sheet form.

Table of contents for *Tabasco*.

1841   *Boston Museum.*   1894

"A SUCCESS FROM THE START."

BEGINNING MONDAY, APRIL 30, 1894,

Evenings at 8 - - - - - - - - - - - - Wednesday and Saturday Matinees at 2,

LAST WEEK BUT ONE OF

THOMAS Q. SEABROOKE

AND HIS COMIC OPERA COMPANY

—— IN ——

TABASCO

LIBRETTO BY R. A. BARNET.   MUSIC BY GEO. W. CHADWICK.

FRANCOIS, the Pasha's Chief Cook and Supervisor of the Kitchen ....THOMAS Q. SEABROOKE
HOT-HED-HAM-PASHA, Bey of Tangiers............ ....WALTER ALLEN
MARCO, a Spanish Trader...JOS. F. SHEEHAN
BEN-HID-DEN, Grand Vizier...OTIS HARLAN
EXHAUSTED HAWKINS ....ROBERT E. BELL
DUSTY RHODES ....EDGAR SMITH
A-SEL, the false slave...GEO. W. THOMAS
GENERAL MAHOMED ....⎫   ⎧.....................................G. BARDINI
MAJOR-GENERAL MAHOMED ....⎪ The Bey's ⎧.....................................H. C. DAVIS
LIEUT.-GENERAL MAHOMED...............⎬ Body Guard ⎨.......... ....ARTHUR CONCORS
ADJUTANT-GENERAL MAHOMED........ ...⎭   ⎩.....................................WALTER ARLING
AMBASSADOR...D. S. LOEB
ATTENDANT......................... ....JOHN CHANE
BEN-ABED-AB-DER U-HASSEM..WM. S. LAVINE
FATIMA, the beautiful slave ....Miss CATHARINE LINYARD
HAS-BEEN-A, a third term Harem's favorite..Miss ROSA COOKE
SAA-DEE-HASSEM, Court Crier.................... ....Miss GRACE VAUGHN

—— AND ——

LOLA, Marco's sister..Miss ELVIA CROX

ACT I.— Square and Quay at Tangiers.
ACT II.— Scene 1 — Ante Room, Bey's Palace.
Scene 2 — Street in Tangiers.
Scene 3 — The Bey's Palace, Tangiers.

Premiere Danseuse...M'lle PARIS
"DRUM MAJOR JIMMY," composed by...HUBBARD SMITH
Lola's Solo "O'HRIOH!" composed by...LUDWIG ENGLANDER

Musical Director..Mr. PAUL STEINDORFF
Scenery by.... ....HENRY E. HOYT and CASTEL BERT & DODGE
The entire production of TABASCO under the direction of.......................... Mons. C. D. MARIUS

REPRESENTING THOMAS Q. SEABROOKE.

Manager .... Mr. W. F. FALK	Assistant Stage Manager......... Mr. H. B. FAIRCHILD
Business Manager...................Mr. J. J. ROSENTHAL	Master Machinist....................Mr. ALBERT COOMBS
Representative.......................Mr. JAS. QUIGLEY	Master Properties.................Mr. W. A. McCORMACK
Stage Manager............................. Mr. E. S. TARR	Wardrobe Mistress.......................Miss ANNA RICH

Boston Museum program for *Tabasco,* produced in 1894 by Thomas Q. Seabrooke.

Notes

PART ONE

1. City of Lowell, *Vital Statistics, Births,* November 13, 1854. An indication of Chadwick's pride in his non-Boston roots comes from the Boston music critic and colleague Warren Storey Smith, who related that Chadwick told him Lowell had produced only two men famous in the arts: Whistler, the painter, and himself. He added, "The difference between Whistler and me was that Whistler was ashamed of his birthplace, and I was damn proud of it." Warren Storey Smith, interview with the author, October 25, 1955. This as well as other biographical details concerning Chadwick and his family come from the author's doctoral thesis, "The Life and Operatic Works of George Whitefield Chadwick" (Harvard University, 1957).

2. Charles Carleton Coffin, *The History of Boscawen and Webster from 1733 to 1878* (Concord, N.H.: Republican Press Association, 1878), p. xvii.

3. Ibid., p. 297.

4. Ibid., pp. 298–99.

5. Ibid., pp. 195–96.

6. Nathaniel S. Gould, *Church Music in America* (Boston: A. N. Johnson, 1853), p. 42.

7. Ibid., p. 72.

8. Coffin, *History of Boscawen,* p. 299.

9. Boscawen, N. H., Town Records, 3:305.

10. Jacob Bailey Moore, *History of the Town of Candia, N.H.* (Manchester, N.H.: George W. Brome, 1893), p. 429.

11. Louis C. Elson, *The History of American Music* (New York: Macmillan Co., 1904), p. 170.

12. *Lowell Directory* (Lowell, Mass.: Pillsbury and Knapp Turner's, 1845), p. 64.

13. *Lowell Directory,* ed. George Adams (Lowell, Mass.: Oliver March, 1851), pp. 228–29.

14. The pronunciation of Chadwick's middle name has been the cause of some confusion. "Whitfield" is the generally accepted pronunciation of the name of the English evangelist George Whitefield (1714–70), after whom Chadwick was named. Indeed, this pronunciation may have been the reason that Chadwick's middle name was misspelled on the title page of his *Tam O'Shanter,* published by the Boston Music Company in 1917. Basing my pronunciation on the English diction and on the misspelling that I took to indicate the practice among those who knew Chadwick, I began to say "Whitfield" and may have influenced others to do so. In interviews with the composer's grandson Theodore Chadwick, Jr., on July 15 and August 24, 1989, I learned that the family tradition was to pronounce the composer's middle name as spelled, "Whitefield." Since, in matters of taste, fact always should prevail over reason and logic, I accept this quintessential and literal American pronunciation.

15. Horatio Hood, *Annual Reports of the Minister at Large in Lowell* (Lowell, Mass.: Courier Steam Press, 1857–68), pp. 6–7, 22.

16. City of Lowell, *Vital Statistics, Marriages* (1854–60), p. 37.

17. Carl Engel, "George W. Chadwick," *Musical Quarterly* 10 (July 1924):442.

18. John Tasker Howard, *Our American Music* (New York: Thomas Y. Crowell, 1931), pp. 326–27.

19. *The Lawrence Directory* (Boston, Mass.: Adams, Sampson and Co., 1859), p. 65.

20. *Public Documents of the Commonwealth of Massachusetts for the Year 1863*, no. 8. (Boston, Mass.: Wright and Potter, 1864), p. 109. N.B., not the 44th Regiment as stated in Engel.

21. Engel, "Chadwick," p. 442.

22. *Annual Report, School Committee, Lawrence* (1868), p. 52.

23. Elson, *History*, 170.

24. P. S. Gilmore, *History of the National Peace Jubilee* . . . (Boston: Author, 1871), p. 706.

25. Ibid., p. 686.

26. Ibid., pp. 460–61.

27. Engel, "Chadwick," p. 442.

28. Gilbert Chase, *America's Music* (New York: McGraw-Hill, 1955), p. 369.

29. *Register, March 1850–September 1877, Oliver High School*. Incidentally, the school was named after Henry Kemble Oliver (1800–85), a well-known tunesmith and organist who was also a successful politician: mayor of Lawrence in 1859 and Salem in 1877–80 and treasurer of the commonwealth in 1860–65. His most famous hymn tune "Federal Street" was sung at the Peace Jubilee of 1872.

30. George W. Chadwick, letter, in clipping file, New England Conservatory of Music Library.

31. Chadwick, "A 'Touch' of Beethoven," *The Neume* 3 (Class of 1907: The Neume Board, 1907), p. 36.

32. Chadwick, "Edward MacDowell," *The Neume* 4 (1908), pp. 126–27.

33. *The Folio*, 6 (June 1872):187.

34. *The Folio* (September 1873), p. 90.

35. After an exhausting audition for Chadwick in 1893, the young aspiring singer Louise Beatty was asked to return for another test. "This time he requested sight reading of some difficult anthems, and when she had finished he said abruptly, 'All right, I'll engage you, and pay you six hundred dollars a year. Come to rehearsal Friday evening.' Later, after she had married Chadwick's student Sidney Homer, it was Chadwick whom the couple then variously described as a "father-confessor" and "the greatest friend of all." He reminded them that an operatic career for Louise was problematic since "there were no roles in opera for her voice—a statement of fact so undeniable that it fell flat as a stone into the quiet night." See Anne Homer, *Louise Homer and the Golden Age of Opera* (New York: William Morrow, 1974), pp. 87, 119.

36. Wolcott B. Williams, *A History of Olivet College, 1844–1900* (Olivet, Michigan: 1901), p. 92.

37. Chadwick, "Theodore Presser," *The Etude* (January 1926), p. 10.

38. Information concerning Chadwick at Olivet was supplied by George Hanson and supplemented by catalogues, programs, and other material in the Olivet College Library.

39. Chadwick, "Theodore Presser," *The Etude* (January 1926), p. 10.

40. Chadwick, "The Popular Music—Wherein Reform is Necessary," *Proceedings of the Music Teachers' National Association 1877* (Delaware, Ohio: Geo. H. Thomson, Job Printer, 1877), pp. 34–39.

41. Ibid., p. 40.

42. William Dana Orcutt, *Christian Science Monitor* clipping, n.d. (1931?), Chadwick Collection, New England Conservatory of Music Library.

43. Engel, "Chadwick," p. 444.

44. Chadwick, "Musical Atmosphere and Student Life," *New England Conservatory Magazine* 9, no. 4 (May 1903):138–41; reprinted from *The Musical World* with additions.

45. Ethel Smyth, *Impressions That Remained* (London: Longman, Green, 1923), 1:173.

46. F. O. Jones, *A Handbook of American Music and Musicians* (Canaseraga, New York: F. O. Jones, 1886), p. 31.

47. Engel, "Chadwick," p. 445.

48. "Nr. 2781 Herr George Whitefield Chadwich [sic] aus Boston, geb. in Lowell am 13.11.1854. Aufgenommen am 3. . 1.1878. Sein Vater Herr Arlanso Chadwich [sic] ist Versicherungs-Agend in Lawrence unweit Boston. Herr Ch. hatte 3 Jahr, mit Unterbrechungen, Unterricht in der Theorie der Musik und Composition, sowie im Orgen-Spiel bei Herrn Thayer in Boston; im Pianoforte-Spiel Längere Zeit bei seinem Onkel [sic] und 3 Monate bei Herrn Petersilia, ausserdem auch noch 3 Monate in der Composition bei Herrn Musikdirektor Jadassohn. Wohnung: Nordstrasse Nr. 25, 4 Treppen Abegegangen zu Ostern 1879." Herr Fritz Saupe, Verwaltungsleiter, Hochschule für Musik, Leipzig, to author, April 17, 1956.

49. Chadwick, *Etude* (January 1926), p. 10.

50. Harry Newton Redman, interview with the author, October 29, 1955.

51. *Monthly Musical Record,* July 1, 1878, p. 104.

52. *Folio* (September 1878), p. 329.

53. "So springt doch der in seiner Arbeit sich kundgebende, klare Gedankengang immerhin zu deren Gunsten." *Neue Zeitschrift für Musik* (Leipzig, June 21, 1878), p. 273.

54. "Herr Chadwick besitzt ein ganz ungewöhnliches Compositionstalent, wie seine durchaus nicht schülerhaften Arbeiten, als zwei Streichquartette, Ouverturen für Orchester etc. zur Genüge darthun. Die Stunden mit ihm waren mir stets ein Vergnugen." See endnote 48. Elson adds: "The writer had Jadassohn's personal assurance that Chadwick, the young American, was the most brilliant student in his class" (*History,* p. 171).

55. "Herr Ch. besitzt leider nur sehr wenig Anlage zum Klavierspiel. Er gab sich viele Mühe, spielt auch—wie sich bei seinem ausgezeichneten allgemeinen Talent voraussetzen lässt—recht musikalisch, aber ohne eigentliche Klaviertechnik." Op. cit.

56. Engel, "Chadwick," p. 446.

57. *Neue Zeitschrift für Musik* (June 20, 1879), p. 269.

58. City of Lawrence, Vital Statistics, *Deaths,* 3:83.

59. Registry of Deeds, Essex County (Lawrence), 21:243–45, 53:393.

60. Ibid., 166:115.

61. Program pasted on the back of the original manuscript score of *Rip,* New England Conservatory of Music Library.

62. Josephine W. Duveneck, *Frank Duveneck* (San Francisco: John Howell Books, 1970), p. 75. For details of Chadwick's relationship with the Duveneck Boys, see Victor Fell Yellin, "Chadwick: American Musical Realist," *Musical Quarterly* 61, no. 1 (January 1975).

63. Adelline Adams, *Childe Hassam* (New York: American Academy of Arts and Letters, 1938), p. 26. See also Donelson F. Hoopes, *Childe Hassam* (New York: Watson-Gupthill, 1979), p. 58: "There [Appledore, Celia Thaxter's house on the Isle of Shoals] he [Hassam] met George Chadwick, the composer, who bought the first picture Hassam ever offered for sale." Hoopes also mentions Ross Turner, Chadwick's artist friend to whom he dedicated his overture *Thalia,* as having met Hassam at Appledore during the summer of 1890 (p. 38).

64. J. Weston Nicholl, "Recollections of Rheinberger," *Church Music Review* (February 1902), p. 37.

65. Elson, *European Reminiscences* (Philadelphia: Theodore Presser, 1891), pp. 264–65.

66. *Musical Record,* December 20, 1879.

67. *Musical Record* (May 8, 1880), p. 199.

68. William Dean Howells, *The Rise of Silas Lapham* (New York: Holt, Rinehart and Winston, 1949), p. 135.

69. *Dwight's Journal of Music* (October 23, 1880).

70. Isabel Parker Semler, *Horatio Parker, A Memoir for His Grandchildren* (New York: G. P. Putnam's Sons, 1942), pp. 39–40.

71. Steel-engraved card in the *Foote Scrap Book, no. 1.,* Music Department, Boston Public Library.

72. *Musical Record,* February 22, 1882.

73. *Musical Record* (April 15, 1882), p. 450.

74. Park Street Congregational Church, *Reports of the Prudential Committee,* 1866–83.

75. *Boston Evening Transcript,* June 23, 1923.

76. Warren Storey Smith, interview with the author, Boston, October 29, 1955.

77. Smith, interview with the author, Boston, October 25, 1955.

78. Massachusetts, Vital Statistics, *Marriages,* 363:89.

79. Massachusetts, Vital Statistics, *Marriages,* 291:24. Massachusetts, Supreme Judicial Court, April Term, 1885 (Suffolk SS).

80. Charles E. Mills, interview with the author, Dedham, Mass., July 5, 1956.

81. Semler, *Parker,* opp. p. 84.

82. Anna Ploessl Parker to Horatio W. Parker, Ma33 Z Cl., Yale University Music Library. Also noted in William C. Rorick, "Horatio Parker Letters and Papers in the Yale University Music Library: An Annotated Bibliography of the 1901–1919 Collection" (New York University, 1977), p. 10. Grace Whiting was the wife of Arthur Whiting (1861–1936), one of Chadwick's more memorable composition students who later made a reputation as an early proponent of playing baroque music on original instruments.

83. Chadwick, *Horatio Parker* (New Haven: Yale University Press, 1921), p. 23.

84. In this regard it is instructive to note that MacDowell shared similar views: "American writers [originally 'musicians'] claim Bach, Beethoven, and Wagner as their musical ancestors. They will and must *bravely* work for the beautiful in art according to each one's ideals, and not lose themselves in trying to discover in 'Dixy' [sic] a national flavour which must be infused in all their works. . . . To attempt to nationalize music is to narrow it. Wagner did not grow out of 'Du lieber Augustin' and a great American composer will not grow out of 'Dixy.'" See Margery Morgan Lowens, *The New York Years of Edward MacDowell* (Ann Arbor, Mich.: University Microfilms, 1971), p. 102.

85. *Boston Evening Transcript,* March 4, 1884.

86. Kathryn Corbin relates in her study of John Leslie Breck, a painter who was an intimate of Monet at Giverny, that "during the mid-1890s Breck . . . enjoyed the friendship of artists . . . many of who were fellow members of the St. Botolph Club. . . . he frequently participated in the events at his club, wrote songs with George W. Chadwick, a composer." See her "John Leslie Breck, American Impressionist," *The Magazine Antiques* (November 1988), 1142–49.

87. *Musical Record,* June 1884, p. 9.

88. B. J. Lang, the Boston pianist, conductor, and composer, was most persuasive in getting MacDowell to settle in Boston. Earlier he had arranged for Chadwick, on holiday in Europe, to visit MacDowell in Wiesbaden. Templeton Strong, MacDowell's fast friend and son of the musical diarist, recollected the encounter of the up-and-coming Chadwick with his younger compatriot: ". . . we spent a very pleasant evening together in the garden of the Kurhaus, conversing and listening to the excellent orchestra. Chadwick gave us the latest musical news of Boston, and was, as ever, exceedingly amusing. Some time after Summer, 1888, Arthur Foote, another well-known American composer, also came to Wiesbaden to see the MacDowells and we spent a few very agreeable hours together." From this account it is difficult to explain the reason for the

subsequent coolness between MacDowell and most of the young Bostonians, especially Foote. See Lowens, *MacDowell,* pp. 37–38 and footnotes 148 and 149.

89. Julien Tiersot, *Musiques pittoresques. Promenades musicales a l'Exposition de 1889* (Paris: Library Fischbacher, 1889), p. 55.

90. *Musical Herald* (August 1892), p. 162; reprinted from the *Boston Herald.*

91. Actually, Theodore Thomas had first asked Edward MacDowell to write the music to Monroe's *Ode.* But, according to Margery Morgan Lowens, "After considerable negotiations between MacDowell and the Bureau of Music, the composer declined the 300-dollar commission . . ." (Lowens, *MacDowell,* pp. 58–59).

92. Foote, *Scrap-Book,* May 1893, Department of Music, Boston Public Library.

93. Foote, *Scrap-Book* May 28, 1893, Department of Music, Boston Public Library.

94. *Musical Record* (December 1890), p. 7; quoted from the *Boston Home Journal.*

95. See Yellin, "George Chadwick and Populist Music" (Lecture, Department of Music, State University of New York at Buffalo, April 11, 1983).

96. Arlo Bates, *The Pagans* (Boston: Ticknor and Co., 1888) p. 209.

97. Ibid., pp. 277, 234.

98. "A Quiet Lodging: The First Prompters Book," New England Conservatory of Music Library. Of course, "Apthorp" refers to William Foster Apthorp, the critic of the *Boston Evening Transcript* from 1881 to 1903.

99. *Boston Daily Advertiser,* February 18, 1897, p. 1.

100. *Boston Herald,* February 18, 1897, p. 1.

101. Henry Morton Dunham, *The Life of a Musician* (New York: Richmond Borough Publishing Co., 1931), pp. 155–56.

102. Harry Newton Redman, interview with the author, October 29, 1955.

103. *Boston Home Journal,* February 20, 1897, p. 11.

104. *Musical Times* (London), April 1, 1897, p. 261.

105. A member of the conservatory board (taking over his father's position), Eben Dyer Jordan (1857–1916) had earlier secured Chadwick as the new director after Faelten's forced resignation. He was also responsible among others for placing the business affairs of the conservatory in the hands of a financial manager, Ralph L. Flanders. It is interesting to see that in contemporary conservatory advertising in the Boston Symphony Orchestra programs, Flanders's name, at the bottom of the page, was printed twice the size of Chadwick's name, given at the top as director.

106. Allen Lincoln Langley, "Chadwick and the New England Conservatory of Music," *Musical Quarterly* 21, no. 1 (January 1935):42–43.

107. Edward Burlingame Hill to author, December 5, 1955.

108. Raymond Morin, *The Worcester Musical Festival* (Worcester, Mass.: Worcester County Musical Association, 1946), pp. 80–81.

109. Frederick R. Burton, *New York Times,* September 29, 1901.

110. See Yellin, "The Conflict of Generations in American Music—(A Yankee View)," *Arts and Sciences* 1, no. 2 (Winter 1961–62).

111. *Boston Globe,* December 29, 1905.

112. *Boston Evening Transcript,* April 19, 1930.

113. *Boston Herald,* April 6, 1931.

114. *Christian Science Monitor,* April 8, 1931.

115. Olin Downes, "George Whitefield Chadwick," *New York Times,* April 12, 1931.

116. *Massachusetts Society of the Sons of the American Revolution, Roll of Membership with Ancestral Records* (The Society, 1920), p. 103.

117. Ibid., pp. 19, 23.

118. Smith, interview with the author, October 25, 1955.

119. Chase, *America's Music,* pp. 337, 372, 373.

120. J. H. Vail, ed., *Report of the Music Committee* (Litchfield County Choral Union, 1908); reprinted in *Litchfield County Choral Union* (Norfolk, Conn.: 1912), 1:191–93.

121. Irving Lowens, Chairman, American Recording Project Committee, "The American Recordings Project, Progress Report of the Committee," *Notes* 17, no. 2 (March 1960):213–20.

122. Chadwick, *Harmony: A Course of Study* (Boston: B. F. Wood Music Co., 1897).

123. Ibid., p. 259.

124. Jules Jordan (1850–1927), the musical arbiter of Providence, Rhode Island, for forty years, related an anecdote that seems to confirm either Chadwick's aversion to pedagogy or his wry way of expressing a negative answer: "For instance, while I was singing . . . with George W. Chadwick's choir in Boston I asked him to give me lessons in counterpoint. Said he, (in effect), 'You don't need them; all you need is to write, write, write. That's the best schooling!'" Jules Jordan, *The Happenings of a Musical Life* (Providence, R.I.: Palmer Press, 1922), p. 42.

PART TWO

1. John C. Schmidt, *The Life and Works of John Knowles Paine* (Ann Arbor, Mich.: UMI Research Press, 1980), pp. 48–61, 65, 83–97.

2. Margery Morgan Lowens, *The New York Years of Edward MacDowell* (Ann Arbor, Mich.: University Microfilms, 1971), pp. 250–54, 300–15.

3. *Boston Musical Year Book* (Boston: George H. Ellis, 1884), 1 (1883–84):14; 2 (1884–85):11.

4. *Boston Evening Transcript,* March 10, 1884, p. 1.

5. *Boston Evening Transcript,* December 13, 1886, p. 1.

6. G. H. Wilson, Boston Symphony Orchestra program, February 6–7, 1891.

7. *American Art Journal* (April 21, 1894), p. 25.

8. George W. Chadwick to Theodore Thomas, St. Botolph Club, December 15, 1894, Newberry Library, Chicago.

9. Paul Zschorlich, *Tageblatt* (Leipzig); quoted in the *Boston Globe,* December 29, 1905, on the occasion of a concert of Chadwick's works by the Concordia. Of course, Elgar's symphonies had yet to appear, the first in 1908, the second in 1911. Zschorlich may have heard Elgar's most widely played orchestral work, the *Enigma Variations* (1899), upon which he based his opinion.

10. The holograph, whose title page reads "To/ Mr. Arthur Foote/ Quartet in D major/ (No 3)/ for Stringed instruments/ by/ Geo. W. Chadwick," was discovered by and is now in the possession of David Kelleher, New York City.

11. *Boston Evening Transcript,* March 5, 1887. See also G. H. Wilson, *The Musical Year Book of the United States,* vol. 4, and *The Boston Record* (Boston: G. H. Wilson, 1887), pp. 8, 49.

12. H. E. Krehbiel, *Review of the New York Musical Season, 1887–1888* (New York: Novello, Ewer & Co., 1888), p. 36.

13. Ibid., p. 36.

14. Ibid. Krehbiel damned Chadwick with faint praise when he said: "Mr. Chadwick, in this quartet at least, stops talking when he has nothing more to say. It is not burdened with remplissage, but is straightforward. . . ."

15. William Foster Apthorp, *Boston Evening Transcript,* December 22, 1896.

16. ———, *By the Way* (Boston: Copeland and Day, 1898), 3:123.

17. It should be said here that the use of a hymn tune is not in itself either novel or indicative of an "American" musical idiosyncrasy, too many prior examples from the masters being available. What is novel is Chadwick's treatment.

18. *Boston Evening Transcript,* February 25, 1890, p. 1. As a matter of fact, the principal theme

of the overture *Thalia* (1883), which turns up again in the comic opera *The Peer and the Pauper* (1884) and even later in *Everywoman,* the Broadway show, seems to bear out the critic's (Apthorp's?) wish.

19. H. T. Parker, *Boston Evening Transcript,* April 4, 1932, p. 8.

20. R.R.G., *Boston Evening Transcript,* December 3, 1901, p. 13.

21. Gustav Dannreuther, younger brother of Edward George Dannreuther, the eminent Wagnerian and musicologist (*Musical Ornamentation*), had presented Chadwick's Third Quartet for strings in 1887 in New York. See page 16 supra.

22. Parker, *Boston Evening Transcript,* February 10, 1908, p. 13.

23. Stephen Crane, "Maggie: A Girl of the Streets," in *Great Short Works of Stephen Crane* (New York: Harper & Row, 1965), p. 171.

24. Parker, *Boston Evening Transcript,* February 10, 1908, p. 13.

25. Ibid.

26. Chadwick to Theodore Thomas, July 9, 1900, Newberry Library, Chicago.

27. R.R.G., *Boston Evening Transcript,* November 22, 1904, p. 15.

28. *New York Times,* February 3, 1912, p. 11.

29. Parker, *Boston Evening Transcript,* February 18, 1924, p. 11.

30. Washington Irving, *The Sketch Book of Geoffrey Crayon, Gent.,* ed. Haskell Springer (Boston: Twayne Publishers, 1978), pp. 28–42.

31. Joseph Jefferson, *Rip Van Winkle* (1895; reprint ed., New York: AMS Press, 1969).

32. See miscellaneous clippings pasted in the manuscript score of *Rip Van Winkle,* New England Conservatory of Music Library.

33. *Boston Daily Advertiser,* December 1879.

34. *Boston Traveller,* December 1879.

35. *Dwight's Journal of Music,* December 20, 1879, p. 205.

36. Gilbert Chase, *America's Music* (1955; rev. ed., New York: McGraw-Hill, 1966), pp. 369–71.

37. Rupert Hughes, *Contemporary American Composers* (Boston: L. C. Page, 1900). Actually, Chase must have consulted the edition revised by Arthur Elson in 1914 since *Aphrodite* was first sketched in 1910 and performed in 1913. In any case, Hughes, who severed his connection with the book, did not deal with *Aphrodite.*

38. Chase, *America's Music,* pp. 370–71.

39. *Boston Herald,* April 6, 1913. Hale's statement notwithstanding (he also misspoke by locating the head of Aphrodite donated by Francis Bartlett in the Boston Public Library rather than in the Museum of Fine Arts), a check of all references to Aphrodite in the so-called *Greek Anthology* fails to discover any direct relationship either in the epigraph in the printed score or in the composer's program notes for the first performance.

40. *Winsted* [Connecticut] *Evening Citizen,* June 5, 1912.

41. Parker, *Boston Evening Transcript,* April 5, 1913. Parker's characterization seems to echo for music the term used to describe one of the important trends in nineteenth-century American painting beginning with such painters as Fitz Hugh Lane, Martin Johnson Heade, and Winslow Homer.

42. Louis C. Elson, *Boston Daily Advertiser,* April 5, 1913. "His 'Aphrodite' is one of his largest scores. But everything that Mr. Chadwick composes is of importance in the history of American music. He is the foremost figure in native composition today and we hold him to be the greatest composer our country has yet produced."

43. Richard Aldrich, *New York Times,* January 9, 1912.

44. Chase, *America's Music,* 3rd rev. ed. (Champaign-Urbana: University of Illinois Press, 1987), pp. 388–89.

45. When the American architect H. H. Richardson's "Master Builder," Orlando Whitney

Norcross (1831–1920), died, his memorial read: "OF•STURDY•ANGLO-SAXON•STOCK." See James F. O'Gorman, "O. W. Norcross . . . A Preliminary Report," *Journal of the Society of Architectural Historians* 32, no. 2 (May 1973):105.

46. Mrs. H. H. A. Beach (1867–1944), although not a Chadwick student, was very much a part of the Boston school of which he was an influential member. Henry Hadley (1871–1937) was a Chadwick product who rivalled his mentor as a versatile man of music as a composer in all forms, conductor, and active member of professional musical organizations. Louis Adolphe Coerne (1870–1922) received the first Ph.D. in music granted by an American university for his "Evolution of Modern Orchestration" (Harvard University, 1905). A prolific composer, he is the author of more than fifty works.

47. Robert Burns, "Tam O'Shanter," in *The Norton Anthology of English Literature* (New York: W. W. Norton, 1968), pp. 32–37.

48. According to Chadwick's own program printed at the head of the score for *Tam O'Shanter,* his musical metaphor of the church, Kirk Alloway, was taken from "part of the old Scottish tune called 'Martyrs.'" But this attribution is somewhat misleading since Chadwick does not use the well-known so-called "Martyrs Tune," first printed here in the ninth edition of the Bay Psalm Book (1698), where it probably came from the Scottish Psalter (1615) via Thomas Ravenscroft's *Psalter* (1621). It was most popular during the nineteenth century and is found in many tune books such as Mason and Webb's *Cantica Laudis* (1850), where it is characterized as "this favorite old tune." Instead, what Chadwick employs is suspiciously similar to a melody quoted in his colleagues' competitive *Modern Harmony* (1905), by Arthur Foote and Walter Spalding, called a Gaelic tune "Martyrs" (p. 250). It is most likely that having perused the text out of both courtesy and curiosity, Chadwick was so struck by the tune that when he began the process of fabricating melodic materials for his ballad, this Foote and Spalding illustration of the "old modes" (Aeolian beginning on B) sprang to the articulate part of his imagination. A serendipity, the scalewise tune, with Chadwick's off-beat accompaniment, gives the music a certain majesty possessed neither by the common New England hymn tune, which he did not use, nor by the other folksy *Tam* themes that he invented.

49. Burns, Tam O'Shanter," p. 32n.

50. Chadwick, *Tam O'Shanter* (Boston: Boston Music Co., 1917), prefatory remarks by composer, p. 2.

51. Burns, "Tam O'Shanter," p. 35, ll. 143–46.

52. Ibid., p. 32, ll. 5–6.

53. Ibid., p. 33, ll. 41–44.

54. Ibid., p. 34, ll. 123–24.

55. Chase, *America's Music,* pp. 369–70. Chase's opinions are discussed more fully in this book on pages 137–43.

56. *Boston Evening Transcript,* January 15, 1883, p. 1.

57. Steven Ledbetter, "George W. Chadwick: A Sourcebook" (1983), 1:104.

58. Donald Moffat to author, April 19, 1956. Moffat quotes the painter Charles E. Mills, one of the Duveneck Boys, to the effect that Ross Sterling Turner (1847–1915) was a member of that informal group.

59. Chase, *America's Music,* p. 363.

60. Louis Moreau Gottschalk (1829–69) published "The Last Hope" for piano in 1854 in Paris, three years before Wagner began working on *Tristan und Isolde.* The impact of his music upon American composers of the Second New England School cannot be overestimated. See also Leon Plantinga, *Romantic Music* (New York: Norton, 1984), pp. 289–90.

61. Another example of the influence of Gottschalk on Chadwick's music. See also the discussion of "Jubilee" from the *Symphonic Sketches.*

62. Writing in his informal "Memories of Eighty Years," later published as *Fourscore,* Robert Grant, Chadwick's librettist for *The Peer,* remembered: "Society drew a breath of relief when a foil was provided by the *musicales* of Mr. and Mrs. Montgomery Sears given in their large house at the corner of Arlington and Commonwealth Avenue. . . . At these entertainments, one met besides one's fashionable acquaintances, young men of artistic talent, especially painters and musicians, many of whom were foreigners, and any actress of the first rank or operatic stars who happened to be in town. This semi-Bohemian atmosphere was highly beneficial to Boston, serving to enlarge its social outlook" (1:286, Houghton Library, Harvard University). Grant's popular "Boston" novel *The Chippendales* (New York: Charles Scribner's Sons, 1909) echoes this memory. Referring to the members of old society present at a musicale given by the nouveau-riche owners of a Commonwealth Avenue house, a young Harvard assistant professor comments: "The opportunity to hear Melba sing free during the supper hour was too much for the average New England conscience" (p. 215).

63. Henry Wadsworth Longfellow, *The Complete Poetical Works of Henry Wadsworth Longfellow* (Boston: Houghton, Mifflin Company, 1893), p. 618. Longfellow's poem is a translation of the original German lyric by Siegfried August Mahlmann.

64. Max Heinrich (1853–1916) gave an interview in which he said: "Do I do anything of Chadwick's Certainly. Everything that Mr. Chadwick has ever written I think I know. I think I was perhaps the man who first sang Mr. Chadwick's songs. Chadwick would come to my studio with a bunch of songs about so thick (measuring about four inches) and ask me to look them over and pick out the ones I wanted dedicated to me. I would say, 'dedicate them all to me.' And he would usually dedicate the fiery ones to me . . . though I don't see why, for I am not like that at all" (*Music* 20 [November 1901]:396–402).

65. Amy Woodforde-Finden, *Kashmiri Song,* in *Four Indian Love Lyrics* (New York: Boosey & Co., 1902), pp. 16–19.

66. Sidney Lanier, *Poems,* ed. Charles R. Anderson. (Baltimore: The Johns Hopkins University Press, 1945), pp. 144, 365–66.

67. *Song Edition, Musical Record and Review,* 1, no. 3 (1901).

68. *New York Times,* December 9, 1895, p. 4.

69. *Springfield Republican,* May 7, 1896, p. 7.

70. Ibid., p. 7.

71. For details concerning *Tabasco,* see Victor Fell Yellin, "The Life and Operatic Works of George Whitefield Chadwick" (Ph.D. diss., Harvard University, 1957), pp. 159–85.

72. *Boston Evening Transcript,* January 30, 1894.

73. *Boston Gazette,* February 4, 1894.

74. *Boston Journal,* February 7, 1895.

75. Three typewritten pages (in the author's possession) of a libretto by Barnet entitled "The Lovers of Provence" with pencil indications for music as well as specific rhythms, meter, and tempo in the composer's hand would seem to point towards another collaboration. Incidentally, the plot seems to be drawn from the same source as John Knowles Paine's opera *Azara: Aucassin et Nicolette;* see John C. Schmidt, *The Life and Works of John Knowles Paine* (Ann Arbor, Mich.: UMI Research Press, 1980), p. 195. Also see Yellin, "Life and Operatic Works of GWC," p. 185.

76. Two versions of the libretto, one for the Cadet Show and another for the Seabrooke production, exist in typescripts in the New England Conservatory Library.

77. According to Boston news reports, the orchestral score was actually made by Lucius Hosmer (1870–1935), who studied composition with Chadwick at the New England Conservatory. Whether or not he worked under Chadwick's direction or supervision is not known. In the case of Chadwick's last stage work, *Love's Sacrifice* (1917), Allen Lincoln Langley has written that

its orchestration was done as a project in an orchestration class given by the composer ("Chadwick and the New England Conservatory of Music," *Musical Quarterly* 21 [1935]: 49–50).

78. Langdon, who later became the historian of American Telephone and Telegraph, was a prime mover in the field of municipal pageants. An organizer, producer, and writer, he was almost solely responsible for the explosion of these civic historical entertainments in the early twentieth century. Ostensibly in celebration of some centenary of its founding, a city or town would use the Langdon pageants to indoctrinate both its native-born as well as its immigrant population in traditional "American" values and to create stereotypical views of local history that emphasized the sacrifices of its first families. While Langdon did not work with Chadwick on any of these projects, he was successful in gaining the cooperation of such composers as Daniel Gregory Mason and Arthur Farwell in writing and arranging music appropriate to these festivals. See the Langdon Collection, John Hay Whitney Library, Brown University.

79. Chadwick's concern for the dramatic and theatrical elements of opera is clearly demonstrated in a rather curt note, dated August 1, 1897, sent to an aspiring librettist, Harry Lyman Koopman, the librarian at Brown University, who had proposed a collaboration (most probably Koopman's *The Witch*): "I am returning your libretto by express as requested. It is not practical in its present shape and I advise you have it entirely remodeled by a practical stage man. Dramatic producers are inclined to fight shy of colonial subjects and I have yet to hear of one that has been a success. Yours Truly, GW Chadwick" (John Hay Whitney Library, Brown University).

80. Carl Zerrahn (1826–1909) had dominated New England music since his arrival from Germany after the 1848 revolution as a flutist and later director of the Germania orchestra. He became conductor of the Handel and Haydn Society in 1854, the leader of the Harvard Symphony concerts (until 1882) and the Worcester Festivals, and the choral director of the World Peace Jubilee of 1872.

81. See reviews in the *Boston Evening Transcript,* September 27, 1901, and the *New York Times,* September 29, 1901.

82. David Bispham, *A Quaker Singer's Recollections* (New York: Macmillan Company, 1920). In a letter dated September 6, 1901, from London, Bispham tells a Mr. Vert that he will "sail for America tomorrow to take part in the Festival at Worcester, Mass, where among other work I sing in Caesar Franc's 'Beatitudes,' and create the part of *Holofernes* in Chadwick's new Cantata, 'Judith;'. . ." (Irving and Margery Lowens Collection, Baltimore, Md.). Besides the unconventional spelling, it is interesting to note that Bispham thought he was participating in the performance of something less than opera.

83. Significantly, D. W. Griffith's first four-reeler was *Judith of Bethulia* (1913), starring Nance O'Neill, who created the role of the heroine for Thomas Bailey Aldrich's play. Its immediate success in both the United States and in Europe, in contrast to the succès d'estime of Chadwick's opera, foreshadowed the rise and simultaneous fall of each dramatic medium as the century progressed. I am indebted to Martin Williams for bringing Griffith's movie to my attention.

84. *New York Daily Tribune,* March 5, 1911.

85. See newspaper clippings, advertisements, programs, proof slips, and other ephemera regarding *Everywoman* in the Theatre Collection, New York Public Library.

86. Philip Hale, *Everywoman,* Theatre Collection, New York Public Library.

87. *Everywoman,* Theatre Collection, New York Public Library.

88. *Boston Evening Transcript,* November 14, 1911.

89. *Westminster Gazette,* September 13, 1912.

90. *London Globe,* September 13, 1912.

91. *Times* (London), September 13, 1912. A reading of "modal" for "moral" makes more sense. Doubtless a typographical error occurred in the first sentence, which should read "harmonically modal."

92. Daybook. Material copied by Theodore Chadwick, the composer's son and quoted in Yellin, "Life and Operatic Works of George Whitefield Chadwick," pp. 248–49.

93. M. S. Pike, "Home Again," in *Parlor Gems,* ed. C. M. Cady (New York: Wm. A. Pond & Co., 1875), pp. 118–19. See also M. S. Pike, "Home Again," in *The Star Collection of Instrumental Music,* no. 4 (Arranged for Wind and String Instruments by John W. Moore) (Boston: Oliver Ditson & Co., 1858), p. 20.

Index

Musical works are by Chadwick unless indicated otherwise.